READING
HEBREWS
IN CONTEXT

READING
HEBREWS
IN CONTEXT

THE SERMON AND SECOND TEMPLE JUDAISM

BEN C. BLACKWELL, JOHN K. GOODRICH,
AND JASON MASTON, EDITORS

ZONDERVAN ACADEMIC

Reading Hebrews in Context
Copyright © 2023 by Ben C. Blackwell, John K. Goodrich, and Jason Maston

Requests for information should be addressed to:
Zondervan, *3900 Sparks Dr. SE, Grand Rapids, Michigan 49546*

Zondervan titles may be purchased in bulk for educational, business, fundraising, or sales promotional use. For information, please email SpecialMarkets@Zondervan.com.

ISBN 978-0-310-11601-1 (softcover)
ISBN 978-0-310-11602-8 (ebook)

Cover design: LUCAS Art & Design
Cover photo: © Renata Sedmakova / Shutterstock
Interior design: Denise Froehlich
Typesetting: Sara Colley

Printed in the United States of America

22 23 24 25 26 27 28 29 30 31 32   /TRM/   15 14 13 12 11 10 9 8 7 6 5 4 3 2 1

For Elam, Silas, Andrew, Kathryn, Iain, and Justin.
We did our best (Heb 12:10).

Contents

Foreword

The Epistle to the Hebrews is one of the most intriguing documents in the New Testament, distinctive in its rhetorical style, its interpretation of Israel's Scriptures, and its presentation of the significance of Christ and his death. Although associated with Paul's letters, it is the work of a well-educated and insightful but anonymous Christian teacher. The unique qualities of the text, probably best understood as a homily, challenge contemporary readers who want to probe its message. This volume offers an insightful collection of readings of Hebrews that use a shared framework for approaching the text. Lay readers looking to gain insight into the message of Hebrews and into a major tool of critical scholarship will find these essays extremely valuable.

The framework shared by the essays, conveyed in the title *Reading Hebrews in Context*, is that the unique characteristics of Hebrews can be fruitfully examined by exploring the literary and conceptual world from which Hebrews emerged. That world could be broadly defined in various ways to include the literary, social, and conceptual complexities of the first century. This volume focuses on elements of that larger world obviously relevant to a work that uses biblical traditions and Jewish cultic practice to explain the significance of Christ. Each essay offers an introduction to a piece of Jewish literature that shares some concerns or motifs with Hebrews. Each scholar then explores the significance of those common elements. The points of comparison are arranged in the order in which they appear in Hebrews, so that the essays also offer a reading of Hebrews itself in light of the comparative material.

The compilation highlights two bodies of literature often cited by commentators on Hebrews. One is the work of the Jewish philosopher Philo of Alexandria, who lived from around 25 BCE to around 45 CE. His allegorical reading of the Torah, in which he attempted to reconcile Moses and Platonic philosophy, is used to illuminate the presentation of Jesus as the "image" of God (ch. 1), the exposition of God's swearing (ch. 8), the contrast between the "passing and the permanent" (ch. 12), the interpretation of righteous sacrifice (ch. 14), and the understanding of the significance of going "outside the camp," where not only sacrificed animals were burned but also

Moses pitched his tent (ch. 20). The use of passages from Philo to illuminate Hebrews recalls a strand of scholarship that saw in Philo a key to reading the Christian text. The essays here also note differences as well as similarities, a useful reminder that the author of Hebrews is not beholden to a single element of its context but creatively evokes many of its components.

A second body of comparative material comes from the Dead Sea Scrolls. The Community Rule, a central document of the sect behind the Qumran Scrolls, illuminates the chief warning passage in Hebrews (ch. 7). Interpreting the mysterious priest-king mentioned in Genesis 14 and Psalm 110, 11QMelchizedek illustrates the speculative world to which the homilist's treatment probably alluded (ch. 9). Sectarian self-definition in the Damascus Document, found originally in the nineteenth century in the genizah, or scroll depository, of the Cairo synagogue and then at Qumran, illuminates the reflections in Hebrews on messianism and priesthood (ch. 10) and also on the theme of a new covenant (ch. 11). Lesser known, but equally intriguing, is the Songs of the Sabbath Sacrifice, a text that offers a reading of Sabbath liturgical prayer anticipating later Jewish mystical traditions. This text is usefully compared with the images of a heavenly sanctuary in Hebrews (ch. 13). Once again, the essays appropriately note both similarities and differences between Hebrews and the comparanda.

Jewish "apocrypha and pseudepigrapha," terms helpfully explained, play their part. Fourth Ezra illuminates the treatment of suffering (ch. 2); the book of Jubilees, a retelling of the biblical story, provides background for the defeat of the devil in Hebrews 2 (ch. 3); the Wisdom of Solomon enshrines the image of Wisdom as a guide through the desert, a theme relevant to Hebrews' exposition of Psalm 95 (ch. 4). The Wisdom of Ben Sira assists with the priestly imagery and the figure of Aaron (ch. 6). Second Maccabees, with its famous scene of the mother and her seven martyred sons, provides background for resurrection hope, important in Hebrews 11 (ch. 16), also illuminated by the rewriting of biblical history in the Biblical Antiquities, aka Pseudo-Philo, (ch. 17). The Psalms of Solomon, with its notion of divine discipline, parallels the treatment of suffering experienced by the community in Hebrews 12 (ch. 18).

Philo and Qumran have long been regular parts of the Jewish world used to illuminate Hebrews. Less frequently encountered are Josephus, the first-century Jewish historian, here used to explore the theme of the promised rest in Hebrews 4 (ch. 5). Mishnah Yoma, the early rabbinic treatment of the Day of Atonement is an apt parallel for a central motif of Hebrews (ch. 15). The Samaritan Pentateuch combines texts from Exodus and Deuteronomy in a way that parallels the combined allusions to those texts in Hebrews (ch. 19).

The essays in this volume, written by scholars who have made important contributions to the understanding of Hebrews, offer an inviting introduction both to the biblical text itself, to the project of reading that text in its literary and cultural context, and, through its bibliographical aids, a guide to the contemporary scholarly conversation about Hebrews. Readers wanting to explore the Jewish context of this unique early Christian homily will find in this volume a very valuable guide.

HAROLD W. ATTRIDGE
Sterling Professor of Divinity, emeritus
Yale University Divinity School

Abbreviations

Old Testament, New Testament, Apocrypha

Gen	Genesis	Ezek	Ezekiel
Exod	Exodus	Hag	Haggai
Lev	Leviticus	Mal	Malachi
Num	Numbers	Matt	Matthew
Deut	Deuteronomy	1–2 Cor	1–2 Corinthians
Josh	Joshua	Eph	Ephesians
1–2 Sam	1–2 Samuel	Phil	Philippians
1–2 Kgs	1–2 Kings	Col	Colossians
1–2 Chr	1–2 Chronicles	Heb	Hebrews
Neh	Nehemiah	Jas	James
Ps	Psalms	Rev	Revelation
Prov	Proverbs	1–4 Macc	1–4 Maccabees
Isa	Isaiah	Sir	Sirach/Ecclesiasticus
Jer	Jeremiah	Wis	Wisdom of Solomon

Dead Sea Scrolls

1QapGen	Genesis Apocryphon
1QS	Serek Hayaḥad/Rule of the Community (also Community Rule)
1QpHab	Habakkuk Commentary
1QH^a	Hodayot/Thanksgiving Hymns
4Q22	4QPaleoExod^m
4Q41	4QDeut^n
4Q158	4QBibPar
4Q174 (4QFlor)	Florilegium
4Q175 (4QTest)	Testimonia
4Q252 (4QCommGen A)	Commentary on Genesis A
4Q285	Sefer Hamilḥamah
4Q400–401, 11Q17	Songs of the Sabbath Sacrifice
4Q543–549	Visions of Amram

11Q13 (11QMelchizedek)   Melchizedek Scroll
CD/DD (4Q266–73/4QD^{a-h}; 5Q12; 6Q15)   Damascus Document

Other Ancient Texts

1 En.	1 Enoch
Ag. Ap.	Josephus, *Against Apion*
Alleg. Interp.	Philo, *Allegorical Interpretation* (*Legum allegoriae*)
Ant.	Josephus, *Jewish Antiquities*
Dreams	Philo, *On Dreams*
Herm. Vis.	Shepherd of Hermas, Vision(s)
Jub.	Jubilees
J.W.	Josephus, *Jewish War*
LAB	Philo, *The Biblical Antiquities* (*Liber antiquitaum biblicarum*)
Mart. Isa.	*Martyrdom of Isaiah*
m. Yoma	Mishnah Yoma
Praep. ev.	Eusebius, *Preparation for the Gospel*
Prelim. Studies	Philo, *On the Preliminary Studies*
Pss. Sol.	Psalms of Solomon
Sacrifices	Philo, *On the Sacrifice of Cain and Abel*
SamP	Samaritan Pentateuch
Spec. Laws	Philo, *On the Special Laws* (*De specialibus legibus*)
T.Levi	Testament of Levi

Journals, Periodicals, Reference Works, Series

AB	Anchor Bible
ACCS	Ancient Christian Commentary on Scripture
AnBib	Analecta Biblica
BZAW	Beihefte zur Zeitschrift für die alttestamentliche Wissenschaft
BZNW	Beihefte zur Zeitschrift für die neutestamentliche Wissenschaft
CBQ	*Catholic Biblical Quarterly*
CBQMS	Catholic Biblical Quarterly Monograph Series
CQS	Companion to the Qumran Scrolls
CSCO	Corpus Scriptorum Christianorum Orientalium

DDD	*Dictionary of Deities and Demons in the Bible*
DJD	Discoveries in the Judaean Desert
EDSS	*Encyclopedia of the Dead Sea Scrolls.* Edited by Lawrence H. Schiffman and James C. VanderKam. 2 vols. Oxford: Oxford University Press, 2000.
FRLANT	Forschungen zur Religion und Literatur des Alten und Neuen Testaments
HDR	Harvard Dissertations in Religion
HSS	Harvard Semitic Studies
HTS	Harvard Theological Studies
JBL	*Journal of Biblical Literature*
JETS	*Journal of the Evangelical Theological Society*
JSJSup	Supplements to the Journal for the Study of Judaism
JSNT	*Journal for the Study of the New Testament*
JSPSup	Journal for the Study of the Pseudepigrapha Supplements Series
JTS	*Journal of Theological Studies*
KEK	Kritisch-exegetischer Kommentar über das Neue Testament (Meyer-Kommentar)
LCL	Loeb Classical Library
LNTS	Library of New Testament Studies
LQ	*Lutheran Quarterly*
NICNT	New International Commentary on the New Testament
NovTSup	Supplements to Novum Testamentum
NTL	New Testament Library
NTS	*New Testament Studies*
PACS	Philo of Alexandria Commentary Series
PTSDSSP	Princeton Theological Seminary Dead Sea Scrolls Project
RevQ	*Revue de Qumran*
SBLDS	Society of Biblical Literature Dissertation Series
SBLRBS	Society of Biblical Literature Sources for Biblical Study
SNTSMS	Society for New Testament Studies Monograph Series
STDJ	Studies on the Texts of the Desert of Judah
StPB	Studia Post-biblica
TBN	Themes in Biblical Narrative
TSAJ	Text and Studies in Ancient Judaism
VTSup	Supplements to Vetus Testamentum

| WBC | Word Biblical Commentary |
| WUNT | Wissenschaftliche Untersuchungen zum Neuen Testament |

OTHER ABBREVIATIONS

AD	*anno Domini* (in the year of our Lord)
BC	before Christ
ca.	circa (approximately)
DSS	Dead Sea Scrolls
LXX	Septuagint
MT	Masoretic Text
NT	New Testament
OT	Old Testament

Introduction

BEN C. BLACKWELL, JOHN K. GOODRICH, AND JASON MASTON

> The text lives only by coming into contact with another text
> (with context). Only at the point of this contact between texts
> does a light flash, illuminating both the posterior and anterior,
> joining a given text to a dialogue.
>
> —M. M. Bakhtin

The Epistle to the Hebrews is arguably the most beautifully written and theologically robust composition of the New Testament. Although obfuscated by the "riddles" of unknown authorship, audience, provenance, and purpose, Hebrews is now widely regarded as an ancient Christian homily ("word of exhortation," 13:22) by an anonymous Christ follower who was as well versed in the Jewish Scriptures as he was in Hellenistic rhetoric. Indeed, the sermon exhibits unparalleled hermeneutical ingenuity and homiletical skill as it relentlessly seeks to inspire struggling believers to hold firmly to the Lord Jesus Christ by way of faith and endurance.[1] Scholars continue to debate the precise structure of the sermon, yet what it lacks in clear arrangement it makes up for in literary elegance, pastoral counsel, and exceedingly high Christology. As John Calvin lauded, "Since the Epistle addressed to the Hebrews contains a full discussion of the eternal divinity of Christ, His supreme government, and only priesthood, and as these things are so explained in it, that the whole power and work of Christ are set forth in the most graphic way, it rightly deserves to have the place and honor of an invaluable treasure in the Church."[2]

The homily opens with a glimpse to the past, briefly reminding readers about God's illustrious history of prophetic revelation, before sharing that

---

1. Scott D. Mackie considers the author of Hebrews "the NT's preeminent 'Old Testament theologian.'" "Introduction," in *The Letter to the Hebrews: Critical Readings*, ed. S. D. Mackie (London: T&T Clark, 2018), 1–6, at 3.
2. John Calvin, *Hebrews and 1 & 2 Peter*, trans. W. B. Johnston (Grand Rapids: Eerdmans, 1994), ix.

1

God has now climactically spoken to "us" in a superior way—through his Son, Jesus Christ. The Son, we are told, is not simply God's heir. He is also the radiance of God's glory, the embodiment of his identity, the very creator and sustainer of the universe. This Son is attested throughout Scripture. What is more, he has lived up to his billing, having secured atonement and glorification for humanity before being exalted to God's right hand, thus demonstrating his solidarity with the human race, his authority over God's enemies, and his superiority to the angelic host.

This Jesus is also superior to Moses, much like a son is greater than his slave. Yet the Son's followers are just as susceptible to failure as those whom Moses led out of Egypt—they are just as vulnerable, that is, to perishing outside the promised rest as those who fell in the wilderness. And so every effort is required of Christ's followers to enter the eternal rest, lest God's very word pierce through their pious facades and lay bare all their hidden sins before the one who judges their innermost thoughts. Yet steadfast faith and obedience are indeed possible for God's people, as shown in Jesus when he himself endured tears and temptation—his sinlessness through suffering having qualified him for resurrection and thus appointment as perfect high priest in the order of Melchizedek.

As a Melchizedekian high priest, Jesus is likewise superior to the descendants of Levi. For Jesus is both inherently sinless and the recipient of a divine oath, which authorizes him to serve permanently as heavenly priest and to atone for sins once for all. Beyond that, Jesus serves in a superior sanctuary, mediates a superior covenant, and offers a superior sacrifice, so that those who are called to follow him might receive a superior inheritance and draw near to God with a superior heart. Such remarkable promises inspire readers to persevere as they exercise faith and follow in the footsteps of their scriptural heroes, of their church leaders, and of Jesus himself. By doing so, believers share in Christ's faith and show themselves to be members of his esteemed family.

This is a sermon that exhorts Jesus followers to endure in their existential wilderness as they journey from Egypt to Zion, from a place of potential apostasy to eschatological purity and perfection. But studying Hebrews can seem nearly as challenging as the very pilgrimage of faith it narrates. Indeed, this is hardly a text for the directionally impaired. The sermon constantly gazes backward through scriptural history, forward to the eschaton, upward to the heavenly tabernacle, and downward to the wayward feet of the reader. It is an epistle that calls its audience to pay close attention to the Son, to the Spirit, and to the saints. It is a warning against losing sight of salvation history, against losing confidence in Jesus's earthly and celestial ministries, and ultimately against forfeiting one's participation in the coming kingdom.

In short, meditating on this epistle demands much of our imaginative and intertextual sensibilities. But it is certainly a worthwhile exercise. As one commentator wrote about Hebrews, "To read it is to breathe the atmosphere of heaven itself. To study it is to partake of strong spiritual meat. To abide in its teachings is to be led from immaturity to maturity in the knowledge of Christian truth and of Christ Himself. It is to 'go on unto perfection.'"[3]

Not all readings of Hebrews, however, are equally instructive. This sermon, like the rest of the Bible, was written at a time and in a culture quite different from our own. Accordingly, reading Hebrews "for all its worth," as most second-year biblical studies students will know, requires careful consideration of a passage's historical-cultural context.[4] This is particularly so for a work like Hebrews, whose creative exegesis of the Old Testament and whose critical engagement with first-century Jewish faith and practice require special hermeneutical attention. Although it is true that some contextual awareness is better than none, it is also true that failure to immerse oneself within the cultic and philosophical traditions circulating in the ancient Mediterranean world will likely result in not only unconscious imposition of alien meaning onto the biblical text, but also a poorer understanding of how Hebrews uniquely portrays the significance of Christ's death, resurrection, and exaltation, as well as urges Christ followers to stay the course of discipleship.

The history of interpretation demonstrates just this sort of contextual neglect—or in most cases involving this epistle, contextual misappropriation. For instance, when Hebrews was largely assumed to have been written by the apostle Paul for the first millennium and a half of the church, a host of assumptions were imported into the interpretive process that significantly colored how Hebrews was understood. To give just one example, patristic theologian Theodore of Mopsuestia (ca. AD 350–428) erroneously appealed to Pauline authorship to defend a variant reading of the Greek text of Hebrews 2:9. In fact, he rejected what is now regarded as the preferred manuscript tradition, which supports the translation *"by the grace* of God he might taste death for everyone" (emphasis added) in favor of a textual tradition that instead rendered the clause *"without* God he might taste death

---

3. E. Schuyler English, *Studies in the Epistle to the Hebrews* (Neptune, NJ: Loizeaux, 1976), 11.

4. Gordon D. Fee and Douglas Stuart, *How to Read the Bible for All Its Worth*, 4th ed. (Grand Rapids: Zondervan Academic, 2014), esp. 27–31.

for everyone." The justification Theodore offered for his decision—and for his overstated criticism of those who supported the majority reading[5]—was based largely on a pattern he perceived Paul to have maintained elsewhere in the New Testament with respect to his discourse of grace:

> It is not his custom to append "by the grace of God" capriciously, but always there is some logical train of thought involved. For example, he talks about grace when . . . talking about his experience [1 Cor 15:10] . . . [o]r when it is his task to speak concerning God's love for humankind [Eph 2:8–9]. . . . But in Hebrews Paul is discussing what is being set forth by him concerning Christ, what sort of person he is and how he differs from the angels (the starting point of his discussion), and in what respect he seems to be lower than them because of his death. What need was there then for him to say, "by the grace of God"? It is out of place for him to speak concerning his goodness concerning us.[6]

The external evidence in the manuscript tradition now weighs decidedly against Theodore's judgment about the original reading of the Greek text.[7] But even apart from text-critical considerations, Theodore's logic was misdirected by an inadequate understanding of who had even authored the words he was seeking to untangle. Writing as he did in the fourth and fifth centuries, Theodore could not avail himself of the best tools of historical criticism. And although not even post-Enlightenment methodologies can guarantee accurate results, modern linguistic and rhetorical analysis have shown conclusively that Paul was not responsible for the sermon.[8]

Once the assumption of Pauline authorship was abandoned, scholars began to propose alternative theories about the origin and theological pedigree of Hebrews.[9] For instance, many exegetes have since observed

---

5. Theodore of Mopsuestia, cited in E. M. Heen and P. D. W. Krey, eds., *Hebrews*, ACCS (Downers Grove, IL: InterVarsity, 2005), 38: "Some suffer something very laughable here."

6. Trans. from Heen and Krey, 38–39. For the original Greek, see K. Staab, ed., *Pauluskommentare aus der griechischen Kirche: Aus Katenenhandschriften gesammelt und herausgegeben*, Abhandlungen 15 (Münster: Aschendorff, 1933), 204.

7. William L. Lane, *Hebrews 1–8*, WBC 47A (Dallas: Word, 1991), 43: "The textual support for the reading χάριτι θεοῦ ('by the grace of God') is very strong (P[46] ℵ A B C D 33 81 330 614 it vg co al) and seems decisive." Ironically, several of the best manuscripts listed here position Hebrews among the Pauline letters.

8. See the highly accessible discussion in Patrick Gray and Amy Peeler, *Hebrews: An Introduction and Study Guide*, T&T Clark Study Guides to the New Testament (London: T&T Clark, 2020), 1–5.

9. Note, however, that some scholars have continued to observe the influence of Pauline

4

that our author has an affinity to **Platonic philosophy** (e.g., Heb 8:5)—a worldview that distinguishes the *phenomenal* world (that which is visible, changeable, and corruptible) from the *noumenal* world (that which is invisible, unchangeable, and thereby superior).[10] Given the confluence of Middle Platonism and scriptural exegesis in the works of the first-century Jewish philosopher **Philo** of Alexandria, proposals have routinely surfaced, linking the worldview of Hebrews to that of Philo. The first known contribution along these lines was made by Hugo Grotius in 1644, followed by Johann Gottlob Carpzov a century later.[11] The position was defended further in the late nineteenth century in the works of Joseph McCaul and Eugène Ménégoz.[12] However, the most celebrated statement to this effect came in the middle of the last century from Ceslas Spicq through a series of journal articles that climaxed in a monumental two-volume commentary, *L'Épître aux Hébreux*.[13]

Spicq argued his point by identifying a host of similarities in vocabulary, puns and metaphors, arguments and exegesis, and themes and schemes of thought shared by Philo and Hebrews. Based on these parallels, Spicq argued not merely that Hebrews was influenced by the Philonic tradition but that the sermon's author had been trained in the tradition itself: "Certainly, the doctrine of Hebrews is first of all and totally evangelical; but the man [Philo] remains under the Christian; the structure of the mind, the approaches of thought are not modified by the light of faith."[14] In fact, Spicq concluded that

theology and the Pauline school in Hebrews even after rejecting that Paul himself produced the sermon.

10. For fine summaries of Platonism and how it relates to Hebrews, see Luke Timothy Johnson, *Hebrews: A Commentary*, NTL (Louisville: Westminster John Knox, 2006), 17–21; and James W. Thompson, "What Has Middle Platonism to Do with Hebrews?," in *Reading the Epistle to the Hebrews: A Resource for Students*, ed. E. F. Mason and K. B. McCruden (Atlanta: Society of Biblical Literature, 2011), 31–52.

11. Hugo Grotius, *Annotationum in Novum Testamentum: Annotationes in Acta Apostolorum et Epistolas Apostolicas* (Paris: Gulielmi Pele, 1644), 810, at Heb 4:10; Johann Gottlob Carpzov, *Sacrae Exercitationes in S. Pauli Epistolam ad Hebraeos ex Philone Alexandrino* (Helmstedt, Germany: Weygand, 1750). See also J. J. Wettstein, *Novum Testamentum Graecum*, vol. 2 (Amsterdam: Dommer, 1752). Cf. James Burtness, "Plato, Philo, and the Author of Hebrews," *LQ* 10 (1958), 54–64, at 54.

12. Joseph B. McCaul, *The Epistle to the Hebrews, in a Paraphrastic Commentary, with Illustrations from Philo, the Targums, the Mishna and Gemara, the Later Rabbinical Writers, and Christian Annotators, etc., etc.* (London: Longmans, Green, and Co., 1871); Eugène Ménégoz, *La Théologie de L'Épître aux Hébreux* (Paris: Fischbacher, 1894), 197–219.

13. Ceslas Spicq, *L'Épître aux Hébreux*, 2 vols. (Paris: Lecoffre, 1952–53), 1:39–91.

14. Spicq, 1:91: "Certes, la doctrine de *Hebr.* est avant tout et totalement évangélique; mais l'homme demeure sous le chrétien; la structure de l'esprit, les démarches propres de la pensée ne sont pas modifiées par la lumière de foi."

the author of Hebrews was, in the words of Ménégoz, "a Philonian converted to Christianity."[15]

Spicq's thesis enjoyed an initial period of acceptance,[16] though in time scholars would challenge both the details of his analysis and the boldness of his conclusions. Brief critical engagements with Spicq appeared not long after the release of his commentary,[17] yet it was Ronald Williamson's *Philo and the Epistle of the Hebrews* that exposed the shortcomings of Spicq's work.[18] Williamson examined both Philo and Hebrews to show hermeneutical and theological distance between the two authors.

> We can only insist that in the realm of vocabulary there is no proof that the choice of words displayed in the Epistle to the Hebrews has been influenced by Philo's lexicographical thesaurus. In the case of the O.T. made by the two writers striking fundamental differences of outlook and exegetical method appear (including a readiness on the part of the Writer of Hebrews to turn to areas of the O.T. more or less shunned by Philo), which suggest that they belonged, in the days when both of them were Jews, to entirely different schools of O.T. exegesis. . . . But it is in the realm of ideas, of the thoughts which words and O.T. texts were used to express and support, that the most significant differences between Philo and the Writer of

---

15. Spicq, 1:91: "un philonien converti au christianisme"; cf. Ménégoz, *La Théologie de L'Épître aux Hébreux*, 198.

16. Cf. Sidney G. Sowers, *The Hermeneutics of Philo and Hebrews: A Comparison of the Interpretation of the Old Testament in Philo Judaeus and the Epistle to the Hebrews* (Louisville: John Knox, 1965).

17. R. P. C. Hanson, *Allegory and Event: A Study of the Sources and Significance of Origen's Interpretation of Scripture* (London: SCM, 1965), 83–86; Friedrich Schröger, *Der Verfasser des Hebräerbriefes als Schriftausleger* (Regensburg, Germany: Pustet, 1968), 301–7.

18. It is noteworthy that challenges to the Philo-Hebrews linkage began to appear decades prior to the appearance of Spicq's commentary. Ernst Käsemann wrote, "With his store of concepts and ideas, Philo often moves within range of our letter. Yet sober observation cannot miss the material discrepancy between the two. The difference between a cosmological, psychological philosophy and the soteriology of Hebrews is all the more evident the deeper we penetrate details that at first seem analogous. . . . It must be conceded without qualification that Philo and Hebrews have different orientations and that for this reason any direct dependence of the latter on the former is out of the question." Ernst Käsemann, *The Wandering People of God: An Investigation of the Letter to the Hebrews*, trans. R. A. Harrisville and I. R. Sandberg (1937; repr., Minneapolis: Augsburg, 1984), 67.

Otto Michel assessed the situation of Hebrews similarly: "The form of its utterances is Hellenistic, but not the content. . . . It is [its] apocalyptic conceptuality that sets Hebrews in decisive contrast to the Hellenism of the Wisdom literature and of Philo. No worse error can be made than to interpret Hebrews by way of Philo." *Der Brief an die Hebräer*, KEK 13, Auslage 7 (Göttingen: Vandenhoeck and Ruprecht, 1936), 175, cited in Käsemann, 67.

Hebrews emerge. On such fundamental subjects as time, history, eschatology, the nature of the physical world, etc., the thoughts of Philo and the Writer of Hebrews are poles apart.[19]

Although scholars continue to identify similarities between Hebrews and Philo (and Platonism generally),[20] Williamson's comparative analysis opened the door for new contexts to emerge in which to interpret the message of Hebrews, notably, Jewish **apocalypticism**—a worldview that emphasizes God's revelation of a celestial world consisting of angelic beings and of a predetermined history bound for future **eschatological** judgment.[21]

The similarities between Hebrews and Jewish eschatological traditions were periodically observed in the early twentieth century, but it was C. K. Barrett who propelled this dimension of the author's thinking into the mainstream. In fact, even prior to Williamson, Barrett was instrumental in beginning to show the ideological distance between Philo and Hebrews.

> Certain features of Hebrews which have often been held to have been derived from Alexandrian Platonism were in fact derived from apocalyptic symbolism. This is in itself an important conclusion, but it is not the whole truth. The author of Hebrews, whose Greek style is so different from that of most of the N.T., may well have read Plato and other philosophers, and must have known that his images and terminology were akin to theirs. He had seized upon the idealist element in apocalyptic, and he developed it in terms that Plato—or, better, Philo—could have understood. But his parables are parables for the present time—eschatological parables. The shadows in his

---

19. Ronald Williamson, *Philo and the Epistle to the Hebrews*, NovTSup (Leiden: Brill, 1970), 576–77.

20. Johnson, *Hebrews*, 21: "The Platonism of Hebrews is real—and critical to understanding its argument—but it is a Platonism that is stretched and reshaped by engagement with Scripture, and above all, by the experience of a historical human savior whose death and resurrection affected all human bodies and earthly existence as a whole"; "despite the intriguing ways in which Hebrews shares elements with Qumran, the sort of Hellenistic Judaism represented by Philo remains the best overall symbolic world within which to read Hebrews" (28). Cf. James W. Thompson, *The Beginnings of Christian Philosophy: The Epistle to the Hebrews* (Washington, DC: Catholic Biblical Association of America, 1982); James W. Thompson, *Strangers on the Earth: Philosophy and Rhetoric in Hebrews* (Eugene, OR: Cascade, 2020); Kenneth L. Schenck, "Philo and the Epistle to the Hebrews: Ronald Williamson's Study after Thirty Years," *Studia Philonica Annual* 14 (2002): 112–35.

21. John J. Collins, *The Apocalyptic Imagination: An Introduction to Jewish Apocalyptic Literature*, 3rd ed. (Grand Rapids: Eerdmans, 2016).

cave[22] are all shadows of an event that happened once for all, the death of Jesus; and the death of Jesus affected the cleansing of men's consciences from guilt, the inauguration of a new covenant and the dawn of the new age. In all this the eschatological imagery is primary, as it must always be in any Christian approach to philosophical discourse. If the eschatology, rough, crude and intractable as it may appear, is abandoned, there can be no guarantee that the unique act of God in the weakness, humility and agony of his Son will remain central, or that the conviction will be maintained that through this act all things were made new and the powers of the age to come were released.[23]

Barrett's study on the eschatology of Hebrews was a genuine breakthrough—and its timing rather fortuitous. Barrett's essay coincided with the earliest publications of the **Dead Sea Scrolls**, so it was not long before scholars were linking Hebrews to the **Qumran** community.

The first wave of attempts to bring Hebrews into conversation with the Dead Sea Scrolls came separately from Yigael Yadin and Hans Kosmala. Based on the shared interest among Hebrews and the scrolls in such Old Testament figures as angels, Moses, prophets, and priests, Yadin and Kosmala argued that the "addressees" of the epistle had direct connections to Qumran, being either "a group of Jews originally belonging to the [Dead Sea Scroll] Sect who were converted to Christianity" (Yadin), or perhaps a group of Jews still active in the Essene community (Kosmala).[24] This new Qumran theory even influenced Spicq, who revised his original thesis by claiming that while the sermon's author was influenced by Philo, the original readers were "Esseno-Christians."[25] These proposals were topped off by the 1965 publication of a newly discovered Qumran manuscript centered on a Melchizedekian messiah figure (11QMelchizedek), which provided a striking parallel to the high priestly role of Jesus Christ in Hebrews 7.[26]

---

22. Here Barrett is alluding to Plato's "allegory of the cave" (*Republic* 514a–520a).

23. C. K. Barrett, "The Eschatology of the Epistle to the Hebrews," in *The Background of the New Testament and Its Eschatology: Studies in Honour of C. H. Dodd*, ed. W. D. Davies and D. Daube (Cambridge: Cambridge University Press, 1956), 362–93, at 393.

24. Yigael Yadin, "The Dead Sea Scrolls and the Epistle to the Hebrews," *Scripta Hierosolymitana* 4 (1958): 36–55, at 38. Cf. Hans Kosmala, *Hebräer-Essener-Christen* (Leiden: Brill, 1959).

25. Ceslas Spicq, "L'Épître aux Hébreux: Apollos, Jean-Baptiste, les Hellénistes et Qumrán," *RevQ* 1 (1958–59): 365–91.

26. Marinus de Jonge and Adam s. van der Woude, "11QMelchizedek and the New Testament," *NTS* 12 (1965–66): 301–26. Cf. Eric F. Mason, "Hebrews and the Dead Sea Scrolls:

Much like the position advocated by Spicq and others, however, the Qumran-only hypothesis was overstated. If Hebrews is not likely to be the product of a Jesus follower who had been directly influenced by Philo, then neither is it likely to have been written for an audience with personal contact with the scroll community. Whatever impact one or the other of these contextual arenas had on Hebrews, it was probably indirect.[27] What is more, it was probably not alone. As Lincoln Hurst assessed the situation in 1990, "The numerous backgrounds proposed this century for Hebrews cannot all be correct. What is probable is that they are all *partially* correct."[28] Indeed, as scholars became more cognizant of the fact that none of these traditions fit the textual data seamlessly, and that many beliefs and practices were shared across early Jewish traditions, the either-or approach that dominated scholarship for well over a century largely evaporated. Accordingly, historical studies on Hebrews began more consistently to draw upon a wider and deeper reservoir of historical sources.[29] As Kenneth Schenck explains,

> Many studies from the past assumed that the epistle's conceptual framework largely derived from some monolithic system of thought. We now see that categories like "Greek thought," "Hebrew thought," "Platonic," and "apocalyptic" were overly simplistic in the way scholars referred to them as mutually exclusive and self-contained ideologies. In reality these categories could interpenetrate and intermingle extensively with one another.[30]

Some Points of Comparison," *Perspectives in Religious Studies* 37 (2010): 457–79. Thus, David A. deSilva asserts, "The author's presentation of the reality in which he and his audience live is very much the cosmos of apocalypticism." *Perseverance in Gratitude: A Socio-Rhetorical Commentary on the Epistle "to the Hebrews"* (Grand Rapids: Eerdmans, 2000), 27.

27. The legacy of Spicq is in part carried on by Stefan Nordgaard Svendsen, who argues that Hebrews had firsthand knowledge of Philo's allegorical methods. Stefan Nordgaard Svendsen, *Allegory Transformed: The Appropriation of Philonic Hermeneutics in the Letter to the Hebrews*, WUNT 2/269 (Tübingen: Mohr Siebeck, 2009). Yet Attridge is correct to assert, "The extreme and simplistic positions positing a direct and exclusive dependence of Hebrews on Philo or the Essenes have been easily refuted." Harold W. Attridge, *Hebrews: A Commentary on the Epistle to the Hebrews*, Hermeneia (Minneapolis: Fortress, 1989), 29.

28. L. D. Hurst, *The Epistle to the Hebrews: Its Background of Thought*, SNTSMS 65 (Cambridge: Cambridge University Press, 1990), 132 (emphasis in original). It bears noting, however, that Hurst strongly preferred the Jewish apocalyptic tradition to the Philonic parallels (131, 133).

29. For a brief survey of recent approaches, see David M. Moffitt, "The Epistle to the Hebrews," in *The State of New Testament Studies: A Survey of Recent Research*, ed. S. McKnight and N. K. Gupta (Grand Rapids: Baker Academic, 2019), 389–406, at 394–98.

30. Kenneth L. Schenck, *Cosmology and Eschatology in Hebrews: The Settings of the Sacrifice*, SNTSMS 143 (Cambridge: Cambridge University Press, 2007), 2.

According to Schenck, the consequence is that "scholars now more often than not take seriously the possibility that Hebrews reflects a creative mixture of ideologies."[31]

Thus, rather than allowing the debate to move along a polarity between Philo (Platonic philosophy) and the Dead Sea Scrolls (Jewish apocalypticism) wherein the only correct way to read the author's rhetoric and worldview are in the light of a single contextual consideration, it is more promising to go the path of those like Schenck, Gabriella Gelardini, and others who are content to identify the "home" of Hebrews generally as the quite diverse thought world of Second Temple Judaism.[32] When the contextual horizon of Hebrews is so widened, "Not only the Septuagint could be of interest," Gelardini explains, "but also Targumic texts; not only Qumran texts but also intertestamental literature; not only Philo but also Josephus; and finally not only patristic but also midrashic texts."[33] Such an approach, as Gelardini maintains, "suits Hebrews well, for it not only opens up numerous new points of reference for the writing, whether on themes, texts or contexts, but also points to an exciting new future."[34]

As promising as this may be, it is unfortunately the case that many readers of the Bible today, especially in the evangelical tradition, give little, if any, attention to early Jewish texts. For some, this is simply a matter of *familiarity*. Being generally unaware of the literature produced during the Second Temple period, many assume that the so-called "silent years" between the Testaments witnessed little to no development beyond the inherited traditions of the Hebrew Scriptures. Such readers therefore overlook early Jewish literature because they assume that the New Testament was written in a literary-theological vacuum.

For others, this avoidance is a matter of *canonicity*. Although aware of the existence of extrabiblical Jewish literature, these readers often consider

---

31. Schenck, 2. Cf. Attridge, *Hebrews*, 29–30: "One contribution of the scrolls is to have made historians of Judaism and Christianity more acutely aware of a variety of Jewish traditions that were already attested in Jewish apocrypha and pseudepigrapha and frequently, in a modified form, and Philo. This rich Jewish heritage—which includes speculation on the divine world and its inhabitants, the world to come, and the eschatological agent or agents of God's intervention into human affairs—is an important part of the general background of Hebrews, but there is no single strand of Judaism that provides a clear and simple matrix within which to understand the thoughts of our author or his texts."

32. See here, esp., Gabriella Gelardini, *Deciphering the Worlds of Hebrews: Collected Essays*, NovTSup 184 (Leiden: Brill, 2021), 5.

33. Gelardini, 5n19.

34. Gelardini, 5. See the various contexts explored in Gabriella Gelardini and Harold W. Attridge, eds., *Hebrews in Context*, Ancient Judaism and Early Christianity 91 (Leiden: Brill, 2016).

ancient religious books lying outside of Scripture to be theologically irrelevant or even dangerous. Accordingly, they bar these works from hermeneutical consideration, basing such avoidance on their commitment to *sola Scriptura* or related post-Reformation doctrines on the clarity and sufficiency of Scripture.

For still other readers, the neglect of Second Temple literature is simply a matter of *utility*. Despite realizing that the Jewish people authored important religious works between the Testaments, many remain unsure how these noncanonical texts can be studied profitably alongside the Bible. They therefore disregard early Jewish literature, being either regretful they do not have the training to apply extrabiblical insights or anxious they might distort the New Testament message if they tried.

While we understand the above concerns, the rewards for even nonspecialists studying Second Temple texts far outweigh the challenges and supposed risks of doing so. Indeed, there are many advantages to becoming familiar with early Judaism and the relevant literature. Bruce Metzger helpfully assessed the importance of these works (especially the **Apocrypha**) for biblical studies over a half century ago:

> Though it would be altogether extravagant to call the Apocrypha the keystone of the two Testaments, it is not too much to regard these intertestamental books as an historical hyphen that serves a useful function in bridging what to most readers of the Bible is a blank of several hundred years. To neglect what the Apocrypha have to tell us about the development of Jewish life and thought during those critical times is as foolish as to imagine that one can understand the civilization and culture of America today by passing from colonial days to the twentieth century without taking into account the industrial and social revolution of the intervening centuries.[35]

Concerns about canonicity are also difficult to justify. We, too, embrace the evangelical and wider Protestant belief in the authority of inspired Scripture. Refusing to engage early Jewish literature on theological grounds, however, goes well beyond this commitment. Even Martin Luther famously insisted that the books of the Apocrypha "are not held as equal to the sacred Scriptures, and nevertheless are useful and good to read."[36] In fact, the

---

35. Bruce M. Metzger, *An Introduction to the Apocrypha* (Oxford: Oxford University Press, 1957), 151–52.

36. Cited in *The Apocrypha: The Lutheran Edition with Notes* (St. Louis: Concordia, 2012),

Apocrypha were included in most early Protestant printings of the Bible (e.g., Luther's Bible and the King James Version), even if separated into their own section. It was only in the early nineteenth century that Bibles began to be printed without them. Obviously the mishandling of these texts remains a real concern to those in the church, just as it does to many within critical scholarship; over half a century ago Samuel Sandmel warned the academy of illegitimate uses of background material, calling it "parallelomania."[37] Yet the appropriate solution to the misuse of comparative literature is not its outright dismissal but its responsible handling by students of Scripture. As Schenck maintains, "We cannot avoid the matter of Hebrews' 'background of thought' in interpretation. Words do not have meaning independent of their use in some socio-conceptual framework. One cannot make a judgement on any text's meaning without either intentionally or accidentally investing its words with meanings from some cultural dictionary."[38]

Many readers seem particularly anxious about the illegitimate imposition of external meaning onto the biblical text. That is a fair concern. What some fail to realize, however, is that comparative studies are (or should be) just as interested in exposing the theological differences between texts as observing their similarities. As John Barclay explains, "Recognizing both similarity and difference, and giving due weight to each, seems now an essential component of any worthwhile comparative enterprise."[39] Thus, while one should avoid utilizing early Jewish literature merely as a foil for the New Testament documents, their differences must be highlighted if their individual meanings are to be appreciated and a dialogue between them is to take place. To interpret Hebrews well, then, students must not ignore Second Temple Jewish literature, but engage it with frequency, precision, and a willingness to acknowledge theological continuity *and* discontinuity.

While scholarly studies that seek to situate Hebrews within Judaism are plenty, there exist virtually no nontechnical resources for beginning and intermediate students to assist them in seeing firsthand how Hebrews is

---

xviii. See also how Matthew Barrett defends the sufficiency of Scripture while also urging Protestants to recognize the value of extrabiblical data for the task of hermeneutics: "Such factors demonstrate the high importance of general revelation, even guarding us against certain biblicist caricatures of *sola Scriptura*." *God's Word Alone—The Authority of Scripture: What the Reformers Taught . . . and Why It Still Matters* (Grand Rapids: Zondervan, 2016), 338–39.

37. Samuel Sandmel, "Parallelomania," *JBL* 81 (1962): 1–13.

38. Schenck, *Cosmology and Eschatology in Hebrews*, 2.

39. John M. G. Barclay, "'O wad some Pow'r the giftie gie us, To see oursels as others see us!' Method and Purpose in Comparing the New Testament," in *The New Testament in Comparison: Validity, Method, and Purpose in Comparing Traditions*, LNTS 600, ed. J. M. G. Barclay and B. G. White (London: T&T Clark, 2020), 9–22, at 13.

similar to and yet different from early Jewish literature. This volume seeks to fill this void. In this book we investigate the relation between the sermon and Second Temple Judaism by bringing together a series of accessible essays that compare and contrast the perspectives and hermeneutical practices of the author of Hebrews and his various kinsmen. Going beyond an introduction that merely surveys historical events and theological themes, this book examines select passages in Second Temple Jewish literature to illuminate the context of Hebrews' theology and the nuances of its message.

Following, then, the progression of Hebrews, each chapter in the volume (1) pairs a major unit of the sermon with one or more sections of a thematically related Jewish text, (2) introduces and explores the theological nuances of the comparator text, and (3) shows how the ideas in the comparator text illuminate those expressed in Hebrews. The end of each chapter also contains a short list of other thematically relevant Second Temple Jewish texts recommended for additional study and a focused bibliography pointing students to critical editions and higher-level discussions in scholarly literature. Finally, at the end of the book is a glossary where readers will find definitions of important terms. Whether one reads the entire book or only a few essays, it is our hope that the reader will gain a new appreciation for extrabiblical Jewish texts, begin to see the many benefits of studying the New Testament alongside of its contemporary literature, and acquire a better understanding of the theology of Hebrews and a more radiant view of the great high priest to whom it bears witness.

Before proceeding to our comparisons, however, it is necessary briefly to survey the events of the **Second Temple period** and the literature that it produced.

Introducing the Second Temple Period and Early Jewish Literature

FROM THE FIRST TEMPLE PERIOD TO THE SECOND

In the exodus, a pivotal event in the history of national Israel, Abraham's descendants were liberated from Pharaoh after nearly four centuries of forced labor. The Israelites were led by God into the desert and given the Mosaic law at Sinai to regulate Hebrew life and religion, with the sacrificial system at the center of their community (Exod 19:1–8). Separated from the nations by their distinctive way of life (Lev 20:22–26), the Israelites were to keep the commandments God had given them lest they profane the holy **covenant** and be exiled from the land of promise (Lev 26:14–39; Deut 28:15–68; 30:15–20).

From the conquest of Canaan to the end of the united monarchy, the nation inhabited the land for almost five hundred years. During that era, King Solomon built the first temple in the mid-tenth century, fulfilling David's original aspiration for the project (1 Kgs 6:1–8:66). After Solomon's death, the kingdom divided. Following a series of evil rulers, Israel's northern ten tribes (the kingdom of Israel/Samaria) were captured and exiled by Assyria in 722 BC (2 Kgs 17:1–23; 18:9–12). The southern two tribes (the kingdom of Judah) remained faithful for a while but ultimately fared no better. By the beginning of the sixth century the Babylonians had waged war on Jerusalem, and in 586 BC King Nebuchadnezzar destroyed the city, including the first temple, and exiled many of its inhabitants (2 Kgs 24:10–25:21; 2 Chr 36:17–21).

The Babylonian captivity marked a low point in Israel's history. The nation had faced the full brunt of the Deuteronomic curses as a result of their covenant disobedience. Consequently, the Israelites were without a homeland, just as Yahweh had promised would happen through Moses and the prophets.

Yet even before their captivity, God had also promised that he would return his scattered people to the land and fully restore the nation (Lev 26:40–45; Deut 30:1–10; 32:34–43; Isa 40:1–66:24; Jer 30:1–31:40; Ezek 36:8–37:28). Israel was to experience the glory of its former days, and as it would turn out, they did not remain under Babylonian rule for long. In 539 BC Cyrus of Persia conquered Babylon and famously decreed that all exiles could return to their ancestral homelands (2 Chr 36:22–23; Ezra 1:1–4). Many Israelites therefore gradually returned to and rebuilt Jerusalem. Zerubbabel was instrumental in the rebuilding of the temple, while Nehemiah oversaw the construction of the city walls (Ezra 3:8–6:15; Neh 2:9–6:15). The building of this second temple in 516 BC marked the beginning of the Second Temple period.

The newly renovated city, however, was not what was promised. When Israel's returnees gazed at the new temple's foundation, some celebrated while others cried over its unimpressive stature (Ezra 3:10–13; Hag 2:3). Israel's promised restoration had not fully arrived at the hands of Ezra and Nehemiah. As the centuries to follow would demonstrate, the peace and prosperity God swore to his people had yet to be realized in the period immediately following the Babylonian exile. Instead, generation after generation witnessed subjugation and suffering at the hands of still other foreign powers—namely, Medo-Persia, Greece, and Rome—and these experiences significantly colored the texts these Jews produced.

Israel survived under the rule of the Medo-Persian Empire from 539 to about 332 BC, when the Greek Empire led by Alexander the Great conquered the known world. Alexander's rule would not last long. Following his death in 323 BC, Alexander's territories were partitioned among his military generals, who established their own kingdoms (e.g., the Ptolemaic kingdom in Egypt, the **Seleucid Kingdom** in Syria) and continued the former ruler's systematic spread of **Hellenism**, or Greek culture (1 Macc 1:1–9; 2 Macc 4:7–17). These kingdoms, which were often embroiled in war with one another, also created challenges for the Jews who were positioned geographically between them. The Seleucid Kingdom in particular, under the rule of **Antiochus IV Epiphanes** in 167 BC, raided Jerusalem (1 Macc 1:20–40), desecrated the temple (1:47, 54, 59), outlawed observance of the covenant (1:41–53), and prohibited possession of the Torah (1:56–57). In his pursuit of **Hellenization**, Antiochus banned the Jews' customs (1:41–44) and violently forced their assimilation (1:50, 57–58, 60–64). But Antiochus's persecution was not passively tolerated. The Jewish resistance that arose in response (the **Maccabean Revolt**, 167–160 BC) resulted in the Jews' repossession of the land, rededication of the temple, and institution of the festival of Hanukkah (1 Macc 4:36–59; Josephus, *Ant.* 12.316–325).

With the renewed national sovereignty of the **Hasmonean Kingdom**, various groups held differing opinions about how to manage the political and temple leadership of Israel. This infighting eventually led to the weakening of the Jewish national leadership, and Pompey, a Roman general contemporaneous with Julius Caesar, seized control of Israel in 63 BC, making it a territory of the Roman Republic. Although Rome largely tolerated Jewish religious practices, pressures leading toward political, cultural, and religious assimilation were ever present. Eventually the **Zealots** (a Jewish resistance group) fomented the hopes of another successful revolt. But the Romans, under the soon-to-be emperor Titus, defeated the Jews and destroyed the Second Temple in AD 70 (Josephus, *J.W.* 6.220–270), thus bringing an end to the Second Temple period.

The Second Temple period (516 BC–AD 70) began with the Jews under the control of the Persians and ended under the control of the Romans. This was without question a time of crisis for the Jewish people, and devout men and women reflected on their experiences in a variety of ways. With the continuous pressures of consecutive foreign nations pushing the Jews toward

READING HEBREWS IN CONTEXT

assimilation, numerous Second Temple Jewish literary works preserve their thoughts and hopes about God and life in the covenant. These reflections survive in the numerous literary works produced during this period. We turn now to survey these texts.

OVERVIEW OF SECOND TEMPLE JEWISH LITERATURE

The Second Temple Jewish writings were composed by numerous authors in multiple languages over several hundred years. Moreover, they derive from geographical provenances extending over much of the **ancient Near East**. Thus, there is no easy way to characterize or categorize these texts. Still, scholarly surveys of ancient Judaism normally assign individual Second Temple Jewish texts to one of three main literary bodies—the Septuagint, the Apocrypha, or the Pseudepigrapha—collections that were unrecognized by the original authors, having been determined by later editors and scholars. Accordingly, these corpuses overlap in different places.

The **Septuagint** (abbreviated **LXX**) is a collection of Jewish texts in Greek that includes the Greek translation of the Old Testament as well as other Jewish writings. It was the most widely used Greek version in antiquity, though other Greek versions also existed. The Old Testament **Apocrypha** (also called the **deuterocanonical** books) are a subset of the texts found in the Septuagint (though not in the Hebrew Bible) that were accepted as authoritative by patristic (and medieval) Christians and included in the Vulgate (a Latin translation that became the authoritative version for the medieval church).[40] Different Christian groups have variations in their **canonical** lists related to the Apocrypha, but the primary collection includes the books of Tobit, Judith, Additions to Esther, the Wisdom of Solomon, Sirach (Ecclesiasticus), Baruch, the Epistle of Jeremiah, Additions to Daniel (the Prayer of Azariah, Song of the Three Young Men, Susanna, and Bel and the Dragon), and 1 and 2 Maccabees. Certain churches also afford special status to works such as 1 and 2 Esdras (= "Ezra" in Greek), the Prayer of Manasseh, and Psalm 151. In addition to the Greek translation of the Hebrew Bible and what later became known as the Apocrypha, the LXX also includes, in certain copies, the books of 3 Maccabees, 4 Maccabees, 1 Esdras, the Psalms of Solomon, and Odes of Solomon (including the Prayer of Manasseh).

---

40. The canonical status of these texts for patristic Christians is unclear, but they did treat them as authoritative. These texts were later included in the Old Testament by Roman Catholic and Orthodox Christians because of their reception by the church in the patristic period.

The Old Testament **Pseudepigrapha** (meaning "falsely attributed writings") is a diverse body of ancient Jewish works, many of which claim to be authored by famous Old Testament persons, although they did not write them. Some Septuagint works mentioned above are also falsely attributed. For example, neither the Wisdom of Solomon nor Psalms of Solomon were authored by Israel's third king, though they bear his name. In distinction to the Septuagint and the Apocrypha as fixed bodies of texts, all early Jewish religious writings not considered to be (deutero)canonical are commonly placed in the open category of pseudepigrapha—aside from **Philo**, **Josephus**, and the **Dead Sea Scrolls**.[41]

While these classifications (especially Apocrypha) are widely used and indeed useful for classifying texts that may be considered authoritative in certain religious traditions, an alternative and more descriptive way to group these writings is according to genre. We survey the main early Jewish literary genres below.[42]

The first early Jewish literary genre to be familiar with is *history*. Several works fall into this category, including 1–2 Esdras and 1–2 Maccabees. The books of 1–2 Esdras (Vulgate) refer to the books of Ezra and Nehemiah and thus report Israel's immediate postexilic history.[43] The books of 1–2 Maccabees chronicle important events between the biblical testaments, including the **Maccabean Revolt**. Together the early Jewish histories are essential for understanding the events, influences, challenges, and commitments of the Second Temple Jewish people.

A second early Jewish literary genre is *tales*. According to James VanderKam, these are "stories with no serious claim to historicity but [which] aim to inculcate wise teachings through the stories and the speeches they narrate."[44] To this category belong such books as Tobit, Judith, Susanna, 3 Maccabees, and the Letter of Aristeas. These works normally cast important, sometimes heroic, men and women at the center of their narratives in order to model Jewish piety and inspire trust in God's promises.

Our third genre is *rewritten Scripture*. Often books belonging to this

---

41. Loren T. Stuckenbruck, "Apocrypha and Pseudepigrapha," in *Early Judaism: A Comprehensive Overview*, ed. J. J. Collins and D. C. Harlow (Grand Rapids: Eerdmans, 2012), 173–203, at 191–92.

42. Our overview generally follows the categories of James C. VanderKam, *An Introduction to Early Judaism* (Grand Rapids: Eerdmans, 2001), 53–173.

43. The contents of 1–2 Esdras differ in the ancient Greek (LXX) and Latin (Vulgate) corpuses in which they were transmitted. The title 2 Esdras, for instance, can refer to the apocalyptic work also known as 4 Ezra; in other cases it refers to the book of Nehemiah (Vulgate) or to the books of Ezra and Nehemiah combined (LXX).

44. VanderKam, *Introduction to Early Judaism*, 69.

group also take a narrative form, since these works typically reproduce, paraphrase, and elaborate on the accounts of specific Old Testament events and characters. To this category belong such books as Jubilees (a retelling of the biblical events from creation to Mount Sinai) and Pseudo-Philo's Biblical Antiquities (a selective narration from creation to the death of Saul). Also considered by some scholars as rewritten Scripture are the Life of Adam and Eve (an account of the advent of death and restoration of life) and the Testaments of the Twelve Patriarchs (an elaboration on Jacob's final words to his twelve sons in Genesis 49), the Samaritan Pentateuch (a version of the Torah with certain biblical passages transported to new locations), and Joseph and Aseneth (a romance based on the patriarch's presumed marriage to a gentile in Genesis 41:45, 50; 46:20). Works such as these are important for demonstrating how biblical literature was interpreted during the Second Temple period, when exegetical commentaries were quite rare.[45]

Fourth among the early Jewish literary genres is *apocalypse*, which normally consists of otherworldly visions given to a human recipient (seer) through the mediation of a supernatural, sometimes angelic, being. Many Jewish apocalypses were written during times of great distress. They therefore seek to bring comfort to suffering Jewish communities by providing a heavenly perspective on past, present, and future events. Often coded in elaborate symbolism, these visions typically anticipate the eventual cessation of evil and political oppression. Early Jewish apocalypses include 4 Ezra, the Sibylline Oracles, the Testament of Moses, the Apocalypse of Zephaniah, and several portions of 1 Enoch: The Book of Watchers (1 En. 1–36); the Similitudes/Parables of Enoch (1 En. 37–71); the Astronomical Book (1 En. 72–82); the Book of Dreams (1 En. 83–90); and the Apocalypse of Weeks (1 En. 91.11–17; 93.1–10).

The fifth and sixth genres, *poetry* and *wisdom literature*, are similar in both content and style to their antecedent biblical literature (Job, Psalms, Proverbs, Ecclesiastes). Hebrew poems are normally songs of praise and lament utilizing meter and structural parallelism. The songs written during this period of Jewish history commonly entreat the Lord for deliverance from pain and oppression. Examples include the Psalms of Solomon, the Prayer of Manasseh, and the Prayer of Azariah and Song of the Three Young Men. Wisdom literature appeals to common experience to instruct people how

---

45. Cf. Molly M. Zahn, "Rewritten Scripture," in *The Oxford Handbook of the Dead Sea Scrolls*, ed. T. H. Lim and J. J. Collins (Oxford: Oxford University Press, 2010), 323–36.

to live virtuously. Examples include Sirach (Ecclesiasticus), the Wisdom of Solomon, and perhaps Baruch and the Epistle of Enoch (1 En. 91–108).[46]

Four additional collections deserve special mention, the origins of which we know far more about than the various works previously surveyed. First are the works of Philo (ca. 20 BC–AD 50), introduced above. As a diaspora Jew influenced by Platonism from Alexandria, Egypt, Philo authored numerous philosophical treatises and exegetical studies on the Pentateuch. Second are the books of the historian Josephus (AD 37–ca. 100). Once a Jewish Pharisee and military leader, Josephus was taken captive during the war against Rome and eventually made a Roman citizen and dependent of Emperor Vespasian. Josephus's four extant works include a history of the Jewish people (*Jewish Antiquities*), an account of the Jewish war (*Jewish War*), a work in defense of Judaism and the Jewish way of life (*Against Apion*), and an autobiography (*The Life*).

Third are the **Dead Sea Scrolls (DSS)**. Although the majority of the scrolls discovered near **Qumran** are ancient copies of the Old Testament or versions of apocryphal and pseudepigraphal texts (e.g., Tobit, 1 Enoch, Jubilees), many are **sectarian** documents—works that describe how the Dead Sea community originated and was organized and how members of the community should live and worship. These works are labeled by the Qumran cave number in which they were found (1Q, 4Q, etc.) and a cataloging number, though many have other shortened names describing their content (e.g., 1QS = Rule of the Community; 4Q400 = Songs of the Sabbath Sacrifice; 11Q13 = 11QMelchizedek).[47] Citing the Damascus Document is more complex. Although two medieval manuscripts (abbreviated CD) were originally found in the Cairo Geniza in Egypt, ten ancient manuscripts were discovered in the Qumran caves (4Q266–73; 5Q12; 6Q15). Altogether the textual tradition is abbreviated DD.

The fourth collection is the rabbinic literature. This literature is extensive and consists of the Mishnah, the Jerusalem Talmud, the Babylonian Talmud, the Targumim, and a variety of other writings. The Mishnah and Talmuds (or Talmudim) come from after the New Testament period, while some of the Targumim and other writings may stem from the New Testament period. While one must be careful about imposing later traditions on the earlier period, when used properly the rabbinic writings can shed much light on the practices and beliefs of Judaism in the first century.

---

46. VanderKam, *Introduction to Early Judaism*, 115–24.
47. A copy of Songs of the Sabbath Sacrifice was discovered at Masada, so it may not have originated among the Dead Sea Scroll community.

Our goal here has been only to provide a concise overview of certain foundational elements for understanding early Jewish history and literature. For a full account, the reader should consult the resources listed below. Having oriented ourselves to the first-century Jewish context, we now turn to read Hebrews in conversation with some of these Second Temple Jewish texts.

For Further Reading

For the most comprehensive overview of early Jewish literature, see Craig A. Evans, *Ancient Texts for New Testament Studies: A Guide to the Background Literature* (Peabody, MA: Hendrickson, 2005), which summarizes the literature and provides the bibliographic details for critical texts, research tools, and key scholarly works. The volume's appendixes also show how Jewish literature can illuminate the New Testament. See also David W. Chapman and Andreas J. Köstenberger, "Jewish Intertestamental and Early Rabbinic Literature: An Annotated Bibliographic Resource Updated (Part 1)," *JETS* 55 (2012): 235–72; and David W. Chapman and Andreas J. Köstenberger, "Jewish Intertestamental and Early Rabbinic Literature: An Annotated Bibliographic Resource Updated (Part 2)," *JETS* 55 (2012): 457–88.

Standard Translations of Early Jewish Literature

Bauckham, Richard, James R. Davila, and Alexander Panayotov, eds. *Old Testament Pseudepigrapha: More Noncanonical Scriptures.* Grand Rapids: Eerdmans, 2013.

Charlesworth, James H., ed. *The Old Testament Pseudepigrapha.* 2 vols. New York: Doubleday, 1983–85.

Coogan, Michael D., Marc Z. Brettler, Carol Ann Newsom, and Pheme Perkins, eds. *The New Oxford Annotated Apocrypha: New Revised Standard Version.* Rev. 4th ed. Oxford: Oxford University Press, 2010.

García Martínez, Florentino, and Eibert J. C. Tigchelaar, eds. *The Dead Sea Scrolls Study Edition.* 2 vols. Leiden: Brill, 1997–98.

Pietersma, Albert, and Benjamin G. Wright, eds. *A New English Translation of the Septuagint.* Oxford: Oxford University Press, 2007.

Introductions to Early Jewish Literature

Chapman, Honora Howell, and Zuleika Rodgers, eds. *A Companion to Josephus.* Blackwell Companions to the Ancient World. Chichester: Wiley-Blackwell, 2016.

Collins, John J. *The Apocalyptic Imagination: An Introduction to Jewish Apocalyptic Literature*. 3rd ed. Grand Rapids: Eerdmans, 2016.

Collins, John J., and Daniel C. Harlow, eds. *Early Judaism: A Comprehensive Overview*. Grand Rapids: Eerdmans, 2012.

deSilva, David A. *Introducing the Apocrypha: Message, Context, and Significance*. 2nd ed. Grand Rapids: Baker Academic, 2018.

Gurtner, Daniel M. *Introducing the Pseudepigrapha of Second Temple Judaism: Message, Context, and Significance*. Grand Rapids: Baker Academic, 2020.

Helyer, Larry R. *Exploring Jewish Literature of the Second Temple Period: A Guide for New Testament Students*. Downers Grove, IL: InterVarsity Press, 2002.

Kamesar, Adam, ed. *The Cambridge Companion to Philo*. Cambridge: Cambridge University Press, 2009.

Mason, Steve. *Josephus and the New Testament*. 2nd ed. Peabody, MA: Hendrickson, 2002.

Murphy, Frederick J. *Apocalypticism in the Bible and Its World: A Comprehensive Introduction*. Grand Rapids: Baker, 2012.

Nickelsburg, George W. E. *Jewish Literature between the Bible and the Mishnah: A Historical and Literary Introduction*. 2nd ed. Minneapolis: Fortress, 2011.

Strack, H. L., and G. Stemberger. *Introduction to the Talmud and Midrash*. Edinburgh: T&T Clark, 1991.

VanderKam, James C. *An Introduction to Early Judaism*. Grand Rapids: Eerdmans, 2001.

VanderKam, James C., and Peter Flint. *The Meaning of the Dead Sea Scrolls: Their Significance for Understanding the Bible, Judaism, Jesus, and Christianity*. San Francisco: HarperCollins, 2002.

CHAPTER 1

Philo of Alexandria and Hebrews 1:1–14: The Firstborn and Image of God

ANGELA COSTLEY

In the opening chapter of Hebrews, we read that, whereas God spoke multifariously through the prophets, he is now speaking through his Son (1:1–2). That Son is the one through whom he made the universe; he is nothing other than the radiance of God's glory and the exact representation of his being (1:2–3). Having made purification for sins, he now sits at God's right hand in heaven, exalted above the angels (1:3–4). The contrast between the Son and the angels continues for the rest of the chapter (1:5–14). The description is very striking, highlighting the Son's intimate involvement with God's creative activity and superior celestial status. However, the author's description of the Son's being closely associated with God in creation and having a status above that of the angels bears striking similarities to the work of another first-century writer. When we look at the writings of Philo of Alexandria, we find a contemporary author who reflected on a celestial being closely united to God in his creative activity. In this chapter we will compare Hebrews' cosmic description of Christ and his exalted position among the heavenly beings with Philo's theology of the *logos* ("word") in *On the Confusion of Tongues* (142–46).

Philo of Alexandria

"BE EAGER TO TAKE HIS PLACE UNDER GOD'S FIRSTBORN *LOGOS*, THE ELDER ANGEL"

Philo was a Jewish philosopher who lived in Alexandria, Egypt, at the turn of the eras. Although the dates of his writings are disputed, he is famed for his allegorical interpretations of Scripture, among which is *De confusione linguarum* (*On the Confusion of Tongues*). This is an exposition of the Tower of Babel story (Gen 11:6–9). Whereas this tale is commonly thought to explain the many languages we now have, Philo saw the tale as signifying a "fall," as Joshua Reeves puts it, from the "divinity of perfect communication and our rebirth as fractious, rhetorical beings."[1] By confusing their language, God conquered their initial evil.

While solving one problem, however, the confusion of tongues set people further against each other once their linguistic unity had been broken. This is because the confusion of tongues bred distrust and fear of "the others" (*Confusion* 11–12). Thus, by the first century, Philo observed that though they had long lived apart, the various sections of argumentative and fragmented humanity still filled the land and sea with horrors (*Confusion* 10). The problem, in fact, had not really been that they all used one language. Rather, the problem was the orientation of their hearts. This is what caused them to rival each other in wrongdoing (*Confusion* 10) and to behave with impiety toward God (*Confusion* 15).

The Tower of Babel incident and its consequences form the background to the section under consideration. As part of his exposition in *On the Confusion of Tongues* 142, Philo zoomed in on the fact that the biblical text inserts the phrase "[the tower] which the sons of men built" (Gen 11:5). This phrase seems to state the obvious, but for Philo it signified an underlying truth about human pride by which people behave impetuously and in rejection of the creator: "Those who ascribe a multitude of fathers to things that exist, as it were, and who by introducing their many deities, have simultaneously poured ignorance and confusion about things over everything, and those who have handed down pleasure as the final goal of the soul have truly become the builders of said city [i.e., Babel] and of its acropolis" (*Confusion* 144).

Philo's statement was likely directed against the Stoics and Epicureans, two of the leading groups of philosophers, for fueling the fractious nature of humanity.[2] For the Stoics, the god Zeus was identified with eternal reason (*logos*) and was the originating principle who permeated the whole world. However, the Stoics also incorporated polytheism into their philosophy ("multitude of fathers . . . many deities"). Epicurus, on the other hand, taught

---

1. Joshua Reeves, "The State of Babel after the Fall: Philo Judaeus and the Possibility of Rhetoric," *Advances in the History of Rhetoric* 17 (2014): 34–42, at 34.
2. Ronald Williamson, *Philo and the Epistle to the Hebrews*, ALGHJ 4 (Leiden: Brill, 1970), 125.

that the cosmos was made up of atoms that operated according to a natural law, and there was no purpose in nature (rather, "ignorance and confusion"). The gods were also made of atoms and worthy of no praise or worship. All that mattered was human "pleasure."

As the discourse continues, we see that, for Philo, these philosophers were "like bowmen . . . who do not take skillful aim," trying variously to account for the origin of the world without knowledge of the God of Israel, the true "maker and father of all" (*Confusion* 144). The goal of life, Philo insisted, is really to live by knowledge of this one creator God (*Confusion* 145). Those who thereby acknowledge God are designated his "sons" (probably a reference to Deut 14:1) and are begotten by God. Indeed, "is not he himself your father?" (*Confusion* 145, referencing Deut 32:6).[3]

As Philo continues, we read that if one is not yet ready to become a son of God, he should "be eager to take his place under God's firstborn *logos*, the elder angel, who is as an archangel" (*Confusion* 146). Particularly interesting is the connection of becoming a *son of God* to the role of the *logos*. The Greek term *logos* usually means "word" or "reason" but is here characterized as a unique personal entity. In this passage, relationship with God is in some way facilitated by the *logos*, who is also designated "God's firstborn." Elsewhere Philo describes the *logos* as both the source of virtue (*Confusion* 81; cf. *Posterity* 102) and as the attainable image of God. In *On the Confusion of Tongues* 97, he says it is fitting for those who desire to see God at least to see his *logos*. Thus, according to Philo, placing oneself under the *logos* by acquiring reason and virtue is how one draws nearer to God and eventually enters his family. As Ronald Williamson puts it, "Ascent to the *visio Dei* [vision of God] is only possible because God has expressed his inward Thought . . . in his *Logos*."[4]

Logos as Firstborn, Elder Angel, and Intermediary of Creation. The designations "God's firstborn" and "elder angel" in *On the Confusion of Tongues* 146 were also significant for Philo. Both designations lend the *logos* an added superiority over and above that of an ordinary angel. However, the use of

---

3. By alluding to these two verses in Deuteronomy, Philo was probably seeking to stress the uniqueness of God's people in relation to the rest of humanity. In its original context, Deuteronomy 14:1 refers to the Israelite nation as distinct from pagans who inexplicably "cut" themselves and "shave" their heads." Because the Israelites are children of the Lord, they are not permitted to do such things. And in Deuteronomy 32:6, the reference is to Israelites who have acted unjustly (Deut 32:5–7), committed idolatry, and thus denied their creator (Deut 32:17). In a caution against apostasy to the above philosophies, Philo picks up on the call to separateness and repentance in both verses, respectively. The implication is that belief in God the creator, the true God, and faithfulness to him are the criteria for divine sonship.

4. Williamson, *Philo*, 126.

a term from the semantic field of sonship is perhaps the most significant since it highlights the intensely intimate connection between the *logos* and God in Philo's thought. In the ancient world, it was the firstborn who most often inherited, who carried on the father's work and duties as his own when the father died. The term "firstborn" is therefore a superlative—this is the closest, most prized, kindred relationship possible to the divine. These titles also commence a chain of additional heavenly designations for the *logos*. The *logos* is subsequently described in the Greek as *arche*, which can mean "leader" but also "beginning" (*Confusion* 146). Elsewhere in Philo, we read that the "divine *logos*" was also God's intermediary in creation (e.g., *Creation* 20). This theology likely underpins the use of this latter term, "beginning," in *On the Confusion of Tongues* 146. It is also possibly a reference to the Greek of Genesis 1:1, where we also find *arche*, and to the rest of that chapter, where God created by speaking, that is, through his word (*logos*).[5]

Logos as God's Image. Philo continues in *On the Confusion of Tongues* 146 by saying the *logos* merits additional attributions. These include "Name of God"—a term used in the Bible to designate God's concentrated presence (e.g., 1 Kgs 5:3; 2 Chr 2:4)—and the description "the one who sees Israel" (*Confusion* 147), which might be a reference to God himself who "looks down" on Israel in Deuteronomy 26:13. Significantly, the *logos* is also called "humanity according to the image [of God]." Philo's thought is here rooted in Middle Platonism's conceptions of forms and reality. Here, it seems that God is the ultimate "form," the *logos* is a kind of copy or image of God, and then humanity has been made in the image of the *logos*, the latter therefore forming a link between the human and the divine. I said above that the *logos* is the intermediary in creation. As Kenneth Schenck points out, at times Philo keeps the Stoic idea of a pervading *logos* in that the *logos* was involved not only in creation but also in directing the affairs of the world (cf. *Cherubim* 35–36).[6] The *logos* is a kind of cosmic glue holding creation together, as Schenck puts it, and because the *logos* is both intimately related to God and connected to humanity, it provides a pathway to lead souls to God in *On the Confusion of Tongues* 145–47.[7]

---

5. L. K. K. Dey, *The Intermediary World and Patterns of Perfection in Philo and Hebrews*, SBLDS 25 (Missoula, MT: Scholars, 1975), 10–11. Cf. Kenneth Schenck, *A Brief Guide to Philo* (Louisville: Westminster John Knox, 2005), 60.

6. Schenck, *Brief Guide*, 58. Although sometimes the *logos* was seen as a kind of instrumental cause; for instance, God is described as a pilot in *On the Migration of Abraham* 6, and the *logos* as a rudder by which God steered the universe. Schenck (*Brief Guide*, 59) argues that the corporeal world is also said to be a copy of the *logos* in *Allegorical Interpretation* 3.96.

7. Schenck, 60–61.

In sum, our analysis of *On the Confusion of Tongues* shows us that, according to Philo's theology, people are united to God through an intermediary, the *logos*, who is a heavenly being superior to the angels. The *logos* is also a personal being who reflects God's image. Below, we will see that Hebrews emphasizes the same qualities with respect to the Son.

Hebrews 1:1–14

"The Son is the radiance of God's glory and the exact representation of his being"

The Son as Creator and Divine Image. Although the term *logos* is not used explicitly in Hebrews 1, the Son is described in similar terms; he is even designated as the one through whom God speaks (Heb 1:1–2), and thus, one might say, as God's "Word." The possibility of a *logos* background for Hebrews 1 becomes more apparent when we consider 1:3, where we have the phrase "sustaining all things by his powerful word," though the Greek term used for "word" is *rhema* and not *logos*. The question is whether this phrase might refer to God's sustaining the world through the Son, though another possibility is that the Son himself is doing the sustaining. If a Philonic-style *logos* is in the background, the former might make more sense, especially since the Son is, similarly, also a distinct personality involved in the God of Israel's creative activity. This is first mentioned in 1:2 and made even clearer in 1:10, where, in words taken from Psalm 102:25, we hear that the Son laid the foundations of the earth and made the heavens. Furthermore, according to Philo, it is by humankind's spirit that humanity is likened to the divine *logos* (*Confusion* 147). This comparison in Philo between the soul of a human being and the divine *logos* is itself only possible because the *logos* is an *image of the divine*.[8] In Hebrews 1:3, the Son is similarly introduced as "the radiance of God's glory and the *exact representation* [*charactēr*] of his being" (emphasis added).[9] The Son, then, is described in a distinct way, but he somehow emanates from God, has his source in the divine, and reflects God's image in a way reminiscent of the *logos* in Philo.

Moreover, as the Hebrews narrative continues, this Son is seen to take a human form, Jesus the mediator who offers the ultimate sacrifice (2:9; 3:1; 4:14; 12:24; et al.), precisely as a model for humanity so that they can

---

8. Ceslas Spicq, *L'Épître aux Hébreux* (Paris: Lecoffre, 1952–53), 1:49.
9. Cf. *On the Creation of the World* 146, where we have the Greek term *charactēr*, meaning "stamp" or "exact likeness."

become holy, even sharing in God's own holiness (12:10; 13:12). One might say that Hebrews' Son is in some way a mediator of deification in virtue of his intimate connection to God. And while this is distinct from Philo's own conception of the *logos*, which does not become human, nevertheless, both Son and *logos* serve as a kind of bridge between humanity and the divine by virtue of their sharing characteristics with both. Indeed, the descriptions in Hebrews 1:13 mingle the Son's divinity and humanity seamlessly. This leads us to another point, that the latter descriptions in Hebrews 1 should be understood against the incarnational context of the epistle as a whole, which is what permits the shifting between earthly and heavenly descriptions of Christ as the chapter continues.

The Son as Firstborn and Superior to Angels. Both Philo and Hebrews also define their respective characters (*logos* and the Son) in terms of their position or status above angels. For Hebrews, this begins in the introduction, often known as the *exordium* (1:1–4). The contrast between the Son and the angels in the first chapter highlights that the Son's descent was temporary, to redeem humanity (cf. 2:9–16). He became far superior even to the angelic beings, having inherited his name once he had offered sacrifice for sin (1:3–4). That said, he is by nature greater: angels function as servants (1:7, 14) and have a changeable character (1:7), whereas the Son is unchangeable and will now govern creation forever (1:8–10).

Significantly, another term from the semantic field of kinship appears in 1:6, alongside a quotation placing the Son above the angels. He is the "firstborn," a term attributed by Philo to the *logos*. The quotation in Hebrews 1:6 is possibly from Psalm 97:7 (LXX Ps 96:7), but it might in fact be from Deuteronomy 32:43 (whereas Philo references Deut 32:6; see note 3):

> And again, when God brings his firstborn into the world, he says,
> "Let all God's angels worship him." (Heb 1:6)

> "Rejoice, Heavens, with him and worship him all sons of God!"
> (LXX Deut 32:43, my translation)

In the Deuteronomy passage, the "sons of god" could indeed be interpreted as angels, given the heavenly setting. A similar thought to Philo's might then account for Hebrews 1:6, where Jesus is depicted as superior to angels. Whatever the source of the quotation, the Son in Hebrews is indeed designated as God's superior "firstborn," just like Philo's *logos*. This title, "firstborn," designates the status of the *logos* above the angels and humanity in Philo, and also the Son's exalted status above the same in Hebrews by depicting a superlative expression of sonship to communicate intimacy with the divine.

The Son as Leader of Companions. The Son is further depicted as a leader above humanity in Hebrews 1:8–9: "But about the Son he says, . . . 'You have loved righteousness and hated wickedness; therefore God, your God, has set you above your companions.'" This is clearly a post-resurrection, even post-ascension, depiction. The mention of "your companions" is also Hebrews' first mention of the faithful. Ceslas Spicq claims that in depicting the Son as exalted after the resurrection, God vests humanity with all his glory, "crowning" it for his "eternal and active reign" (cf. 1:8).[10] When we look at our passage in the overall context of the epistle, we see that this passage points forward to 2:9–18, where we find a further reference to the Son's having been "made lower than the angels" (a distant hook to 1:4). In 2:9 the Son is also "crowned with glory and honor" (a reference back to 1:8–9), which enables him to lead his siblings to "glory" (2:10). Thus, the term "companions" in 1:9 becomes significant as Hebrews' first suggestion of human conformity unto Christ.

To return to what was said earlier about the Son and *logos* as bridges between God and humanity, it is also significant that in Philo, to become a son of God, a person can first be ordered in accordance with the *logos*: "If he be not yet ready to be called a 'son of God,' let him be eager to take his place under God's firstborn *logos*" (*Confusion* 146). Indeed, the other name of the *logos* is "he who sees Israel" (*Confusion* 146), which suggests an incorporation of God's people into the *logos*'s protection. In fact, the Greek might also be translated "the one who sees, namely, Israel." Thus, the *logos* is arguably a kind of leader unto which humans are conformed—or, if we favor the latter interpretation, of which humans can become a part. It might be possible that conformity to the *logos-Son* underpins this citation in Hebrews. This leader-Son is both superlatively related to God as his firstborn, reflection, and express image (Heb 1:3, 6), as well as to humanity, having assumed it. Because of this, the Son shares in divinity and humanity, as does Philo's *logos*, enabling him to bridge heaven and earth, and providing a path for humans to cross over into the realm of the divine.

A Few Words of Caution. As we have seen, Philo offers many instructive parallels to Hebrews 1:1–14. It is, however, important to exercise some caution in drawing parallels between Philo's depiction of the *logos* and

---

10. Spicq, *L'Épître*, 2:16. Spicq says the name in 1:4 refers to "Son" in *L'Épître*, 2:14–15, but it might also refer to the divine name, much in the same way Philo calls the *logos* the name of God in *On the Confusion of Tongues* 146.

Hebrews' description of Christ. In *Confusion* 145 it is not the *logos* who is the Son of God, as Jesus is depicted in Hebrews, but rather those who belong to its company.[11] We should also beware of personifying the *logos*.[12] In the description of the *logos* as "humanity according to God's image," we possibly see a hint of theology found elsewhere in Philo, whereby the *logos* is "God's image and the ideal form which he stamped upon the world" (cf. *Creation* 25).[13] Philo arguably took impetus for his own *logos* concept from the Stoics and "translated it into Jewish monotheism," so that it became a way of referring to God's very mind.[14] This concept of *logos* acted as a mediator in that it denoted the thought of God as expressed in a form that was accessible to humans, but it was not a "person" in either the proto-Trinitarian or incarnated sense that can be argued for in Hebrews' theology of the embodied Son who offers sacrifice in our passage.[15] If it be a separate entity in our passage in Philo, it is another type of angel, being called an "archangel" in *Confusion* 146, something Hebrews stresses the Son is absolutely not.

Indeed, if Hebrews were adopting Philonic *logos* theology, we might ask why the term *rhema* (also meaning "word") instead of *logos* is used in 1:3 in "the Son is the radiance of God's glory and the exact representation of his being, sustaining all things by his powerful *word*" (Heb 1:3, emphasis added).[16] What we might conclude is that the concept of a divine *logos* might have influenced, either directly or indirectly, the descriptions of the Son in Hebrews, either because our author knew Philo or because such concepts were circulating at that time and could form a point of contact with his audience.

FOR FURTHER READING

Additional Ancient Texts

Philo's conception of the *logos* is found throughout his writings. For instance, see *On the Cherubim* 106 and *On Dreams* 1:149. On the participation of

---

11. Though, in Hebrews 2:7–12, the Son leads his siblings heavenward, and so humanity might still be seen to become sons of God through the actions of the Son. Cf. Hebrews 12:5–7.

12. Williamson, *Philo*, 104.

13. Williamson, 127.

14. Williamson, 127.

15. Williamson, 105.

16. Grammatically, this could be either the Son's or God's word. It might be possible to argue that this refers to the word of the Son rather than the Father, and possibly the term is used to avoid confusion. Were the term *logos* to be used, with the similarity of the description of Christ in such *logos*-like terms, the use of *logos* at this point would have made the text refer rather to the "word" of the Father.

humanity in kinship with God, see also *On the Creation of the World* 8, 20, 142–46. See also *Who Is the Heir?* 236 on God's oneness. On the role of the *logos* in creation, see *On the Cherubim* 35–36; *On the Migration of Abraham* 6; *Allegorical Interpretation* 3.96 and *Who Is the Heir?* 205.

English Translations and Critical Editions

Philo. Translated by Francis Henry Colson et al. 12 vols. LCL. Cambridge, MA: Harvard University Press, 1929–62.

Brill is currently publishing a new Philo of Alexandria Commentary Series. There is not currently one for *On the Confusion of Tongues*, but those interested in Philo's *logos* creation theology might consult David T. Runia, *Philo of Alexandria, On the Creation of the Cosmos according to Moses: Introduction, Translation and Commentary*, vol. 1 (Leiden: Brill, 2001).

Secondary Literature

Burtness, James. "Plato, Philo, and the Author of Hebrews." *LQ* 10 (1958): 197–219.

Costley, Angela. *Creation and Christ: An Exploration of the Topic of Creation in the Epistle to the Hebrews.* WUNT 2/527. Tübingen: Mohr Siebeck, 2020.

Runia, David T. *Philo in Early Christian Literature.* CRINT 3/3. Minneapolis: Fortress, 1993.

Sowers, Sidney. *The Hermeneutics of Philo and Hebrews: A Comparison of the Interpretation of the Old Testament in Philo Judaeus and the Epistle to the Hebrews.* Richmond, VA: John Knox, 1965.

Svendsen, Stefan Nordgaard. *Allegory Transformed: The Appropriation of Philonic Hermeneutics in the Letter to the Hebrews.* WUNT 2/269. Tübingen: Mohr Siebeck, 2009.

Tobin, Thomas H. "Interpretations of Creation in the World of Philo of Alexandria." Pages 108–28 in *Creation in the Biblical Traditions.* Edited by Richard J. Clifford and John J. Collins. CBQMS 24. Washington, DC: Catholic Biblical Association of America, 1992.

CHAPTER 2

4 Ezra and Hebrews 2:1–9:
Suffering and God's Faithfulness
to His Promises

FÉLIX H. CORTEZ

T he Letter to the Hebrews was written as a "word of exhortation,"
involving both encouragement and warning, to a discouraged congregation (13:22). The congregation had begun their Christian life
with enthusiasm. They had experienced God's care and blessing in the
form of "signs, wonders and various miracles," and the reception of gifts
of the Holy Spirit (2:3–4). They had also remained firm when tested with
suffering, persecution, insult, and even prison and loss of property (10:32–
34). But then they became disheartened. They were probably drained both
psychologically and financially, and the memory of their first experience
as believers was receding into the past. They were tired and in danger
of losing heart and had begun to "drift away" from the gospel (2:1; 12:3,
12–13). Some had also stopped attending church meetings and were in
danger of a "bitter root" of unbelief growing among them (10:25; 12:15;
3:12). What had happened? It seems part of their problem was that their
hopes and expectations had not been fulfilled as soon as they had expected
them to be.

Their hope was expressed in Hebrews 2:6–8:

> "What is mankind that you are mindful of them,
> a son of man that you care for him?
> You made them a little lower than the angels;
> you crowned them with glory and honor
> and put everything under their feet."

32

In putting everything under them, God left nothing that is not subject to them. Yet at present we do not see everything subject to them.

The congregation understood that Christian believers were to be the inheritors of God's original purpose for humanity. Their hope was for the world to be subjected to them, but that hope had not been fulfilled.[1] Instead of being crowned with "glory and honor" (2:7b), they were suffering abuse at the hands of those to whom the world had not been promised. Their precarious situation raised questions of **theodicy**, that is, questions about the trustworthiness and righteousness of God. If God promised to put "everything under them," then why "at present" did they not see "everything subjected to them" (2:8b–c)?

The question of suffering and theodicy was not limited to the congregation addressed in Hebrews. Many Second Temple texts addressed this same issue, but in various ways. One among them is 4 Ezra. The purpose of this chapter is to compare the responses of the author of Hebrews and the author of 4 Ezra to the theodicy questions of their audiences. Both share a similar understanding of the people of God as the inheritors of God's purposes for humanity at creation and a similar disillusionment with their lack of fulfillment. Their particular solutions to the theodicy problem, however, are different in important respects. Those differences identify the unique character of early Christianity in the context of Judaism of the first and early second century AD.

4 Ezra 6.55–59

"WHY DO WE NOT POSSESS OUR WORLD?"

Fourth Ezra is an early Jewish **apocalypse** written probably around AD 100, thirty years after the fall of Jerusalem.[2] Ezra, the purported author,

---

1. Some scholars understand Hebrews 2:6–8 to refer to Jesus as a human being and not to humanity or the church (e.g., Gareth Lee Cockerill, *The Epistle to the Hebrews*, NICNT [Grand Rapids: Eerdmans, 2012], 130). This chapter understands 2:6–8 as referring to God's purpose for humanity. Then, in 2:9–18, the author identifies Jesus as the representative of humanity in whom God's purpose for them is fulfilled (e.g., William L. Lane, *Hebrews 1–8*, WBC 47A [Dallas: Word, 1991], 47).

2. The setting of the book is fictional. It purports to have been written by Ezra thirty years after the fall of Jerusalem in the sixth century BC (4 Ezra 3.1). Most scholars read this assertion as a figurative reference to the fall of Jerusalem at the hands of the Romans in AD 70. The first unquestionable reference to 4 Ezra is found in Clement of Alexandria's *Stromateis* 3:16 (quoting 4 Ezra 5.35), which was written toward the end of the second century AD.

was troubled by the destruction of the temple and the prosperity of the oppressors, and he found himself questioning the righteousness of God. Ezra, however, received seven visions in which Uriel, an angel, answered his questions. For some, 4 Ezra is perhaps the best work on theodicy ever written, due to its answers to deep, incisive questions.[3]

Our focus is on 4 Ezra 6.55–59, a section of the third vision. Here Ezra referred to God's original purpose for humanity when he created them and asked God why it was that his purpose had not been fulfilled for Israel. This section is significant for us because it contains the same reference to creation and the same concern for the lack of fulfillment that we find in Hebrews 2:5–9. The passage reads,

> I have spoken all these things before you, Lord, because you said that you created this world for us. As for the other nations, which have descended from Adam, you have said that they are nothing, that they are like spittle, and you have compared the abundance of them to a drop on a bucket. And now, O Lord, these nations that are reckoned as nothing lord it over us and devour us. But we, your people whom you have called your firstborn, your only begotten, your dearly beloved, have been delivered into their hands. So, if the world was in fact created for us, why do we not possess our world as an inheritance? How long will this continue? (4 Ezra 6.55–59)[4]

God's Plan for Israel. Ezra believed that the world was created for Israel. In other words, it was God's plan that Israel would stand in Adam's place as the earthly viceroy of God. Israel, as the firstborn of the nations, would inherit dominion over them.[5] This view was not unique but seems to have been particularly prominent in first-century Judaism.[6] The problem was that the fall of Jerusalem completely denied the purpose of God. Instead of inheriting the nations and exerting dominion over them, Israel was being devoured by them. Thus, Ezra asked, "Why?" and "How long?"

Ezra posed these questions because the Lord "said" that he had created

---

3. E.g., James H. Charlesworth, "The Interpretation of the Tanak in the Jewish Apocrypha and Pseudepigrapha," in *The Ancient Period*, ed. A. J. Hauser and D. F. Watson, vol. 1 of *A History of Biblical Interpretation* (Grand Rapids: Eerdmans, 2003), 253–82, at 271. See also Bruce W. Longenecker, *2 Esdras* (Sheffield: Sheffield Academic, 1995), 38.

4. Based on the translation by R. H. Charles, ed., *The Apocrypha and Pseudepigrapha of the Old Testament in English* (Oxford: Clarendon, 1913), 2:579.

5. Jub. 2.20; Pss. Sol. 18.4. Also Exod 4:22–23.

6. See below, "Additional Ancient Texts"; also Deut 10:15–16; 14:2; Jer 31:7.

the world for Israel (6.55). The author, however, does not explain where God said that. But the reference to God's word calls attention to its role in the magnificent work of creation described in the previous paragraph (6.38–54). The word of God was the agent that had brought about creation (6.38, 43). Since God commanded into existence all the material aspects of creation, how is it possible that God's main word—that the world was created for Israel—had failed? Is God's word impotent to accomplish what he promised regarding Israel?[7]

Bound by Covenant. The wider context suggests that the failure of God's purpose for Israel also has covenantal implications. Israel is the descendant of Abraham with whom God made an eternal **covenant** in which he promised that he would never forsake them (3.15). Ezra recognized that Israelites had sinned, despite having received God's law (3.17–19).[8] That, however, does not explain God's lack of mercy. First, God did not take away the evil heart from them (3.20–27). Second, Israel had kept the commandments better than Babylon or the other nations (3.28–36). More importantly, however, Ezra suggested that God was bound by covenant to be merciful to Israel.[9]

Uriel's response to Ezra's question can only be understood in the context of the whole work. In the first two visions, Uriel insists that a mortal creature such as Ezra should not hope to understand God's ways. Uriel does not deny the covenant promises, however. In the following visions, Uriel reveals to Ezra that there are two ages. The present age is dominated by sin and suffering for the righteous, but in the new age God will intervene for them and remove their evil heart (6.26–28). It is not clear whether God alone will bring salvation (10.53–54) or salvation will come through the agency of his **messiah**. It is clear, however, that the messiah will not use military means.[10] Uriel also explains that only a righteous remnant will be saved. Thus, the role of the righteous is to keep the law and leave salvation to God alone.

The solution to the theodicy problem that 4 Ezra proposes is similar to the solution that the Letter to the Hebrews suggests. There are, however, significant differences.

---

7. Longenecker, *2 Esdras*, 38.

8. See also 4 Ezra 8.34–36, where the author alludes to Psalm 8:4 to refer to humankind's general sinfulness.

9. Richard Bauckham, "Apocalypses," in *Justification and Variegated Nomism: Volume One—The Complexities of Second Temple Judaism*, ed. D. A. Carson, Peter T. O'Brien, and Mark A. Seifrid (Grand Rapids: Baker, 2001), 135–87, at 163.

10. 4 Ezra 12.31–34; 13.8–11, 37–38.

Hebrews 2:1–9

"We do not see everything subject to them"

We have already noted that the author of Hebrews 2:5–9 also conceived of believers as the inheritors of the world and that the lack of fulfillment of God's purpose raised important theodicy questions for them. An analysis of the passage will show elements of similarity and difference.

God's Plan for Believers. Like 4 Ezra, the author of Hebrews understood that the promises of God would be fulfilled in the "world to come" (2:5). Therefore, "at present we do not see everything subject to them [believers in Jesus]" (2:8). There is a very significant difference in the argument of Hebrews, however. The purposes of God had begun to be fulfilled in Jesus, the Messiah. The author explained, "But we do see Jesus . . . now crowned with glory and honor" (2:9).

God has begun to act in Jesus on behalf of believers. Jesus has ascended and is seated at the right hand of God as the viceroy over creation (1:3, 5–14). God has begun to distribute his gift and inheritance to believers in the present through the Holy Spirit (2:4; 6:4). Thus, believers have been enlightened and "tasted the goodness of the word of God and the powers of the coming age" (6:5). In other words, the "world to come" is not only a promise but also a reality. It has burst into the present, though it remains a heavenly or spiritual reality.

Bound by Covenant. The covenant is also an important concern of the passage. The author described God's purpose for humanity as a "testimony," which in the original language refers to a solemn declaration (2:6). Therefore, God is bound by those words. But the passage implies that sin is an impediment for the fulfillment of those promises.[11] The impediment, however, has been overcome by the death of the Messiah for everyone. His death is for the transgressions committed against the covenant (9:15–22). More significantly, he died "to do away with sin" (9:26). The new covenant has provided in the present what in 4 Ezra would be accomplished in the coming age. It has taken away the "evil heart" by writing the law on the hearts of believers (8:6–10). Believers in Jesus now have a clean conscience (9:14; 10:1–4).

The Letter to the Hebrews and 4 Ezra share a similar worldview. The most significant difference between them is the role of the Messiah. While

---

11. The author suggests this by explaining that Jesus died "so that by the grace of God he might taste death for everyone" (2:9; and 2:14–18; 9:15–22).

the role of the Messiah is not completely clear in 4 Ezra, the figure of Jesus is central to the argument of Hebrews. Jesus is both an agent and mediator. As God's agent, he is the one who brings believers into glory. He is the captain of their salvation (2:10). As mediator he represents believers and his death propitiates for their sins (2:9, 17–18; 9:15–22). He also guarantees the new covenant (7:22).

The enthronement of Jesus is extremely significant for Hebrews (8:1). By crowning their representative with glory and honor, God proved that he is faithful to the promises he made to believers. More importantly, Jesus is the forerunner of believers, the pioneer of their salvation (2:10). Thus, believers are invited to look to Jesus, who is the "pioneer and perfecter" of their faith (12:2). They should see their future in Jesus's present. The source of hope in 4 Ezra is the trustworthiness of the word of God. In Hebrews the source of hope is the reality of Jesus's exaltation. God's word has become reality in Jesus (1:2).

For Further Reading

Additional Ancient Texts

Other early Jewish works that express the idea that the world was made for Israel are 2 Baruch (14.19; 15.7; 21.24), which is also an apocalypse written after the destruction of the temple, and the Testament of Moses (1.12), probably written in the first century AD before the destruction of Jerusalem. Among rabbinic writings, the view that the world was created for Israel is found in Sifre on Deuteronomy 11:21; b. Berakot 32b; Genesis Rabbah 12:2; Tanḥuma Ber. 3, 10. The Shepherd of Hermas, a Christian work, says that the world was created for the church (Vis. 1.1.6 and 2.4.1).[12]

English Translations and Critical Editions

Longenecker, Bruce W. *2 Esdras*. Guides to the Apocrypha and Pseudepigrapha. Sheffield: Sheffield Academic, 1995.

Metzger, Bruce M. "The Fourth Book of Ezra: A New Translation and Introduction." Pages 517–59 in vol. 1 of *The Old Testament Pseudepigrapha*. Edited by James H. Charlesworth. Garden City, NY: Doubleday, 1983.

New English Translation of the Septuagint (2 Esdras)

---

12. For further references, see Michael E. Stone, *Fourth Ezra*, Hermeneia (Minneapolis: Fortress, 1990), 188–89.

New Revised Standard Version (2 Esdras)

Stone, Michael E. *Fourth Ezra*. Hermeneia. Minneapolis: Fortress, 1990.

Wong, Andy, with Ken M. Penner and David M. Miller, eds. "4 Ezra." In *The Online Critical Pseudepigrapha*. Edited by Ken M. Penner and Ian W. Scott. Atlanta: Society of Biblical Literature, 2010. https://pseudepigrapha.org/docs/intro/4Ezra.

Secondary Literature

Bauckham, Richard. "Apocalypses." Pages 135–87 in *Justification and Variegated Nomism: Volume One—The Complexities of Second Temple Judaism*. Edited by D. A. Carson, Peter T. O'Brien, and Mark A. Seifrid. Grand Rapids: Baker, 2001.

Coggins, R. J., and M. A. Knibb. *The First and Second Books of Esdras*. Cambridge: Cambridge University Press, 1979.

Henze, Matthias, and Gabriele Boccaccini, eds. *Fourth Ezra and Second Baruch: Reconstruction after the Fall*. Supplements to the Journal for the Studies of Judaism 164. Leiden: Brill, 2013.

Moo, Jonathan. *Creation, Nature, and Hope in 4 Ezra*. FRLANT 237. Göttingen: Vandenhoeck and Ruprecht, 2011.

Myers, Jacob M. *I and II Esdras: Introduction, Translation and Commentary*. AB. Garden City, NY: Doubleday, 1974.

Najman, Hindy. *Losing the Temple and Recovering the Future: An Analysis of 4 Ezra*. Cambridge: Cambridge University Press, 2014.

CHAPTER 3

Jubilees and Hebrews 2:10–18: Passover and the Defeat of the Devil

DAVID M. MOFFITT

In Hebrews 2:10–18 the author continues to explain his puzzling claims in 1:4–14 and 2:5–9 about the elevation of the divine Son of God above the angels. There are real tensions in Hebrews 1 regarding the Son. On the one hand, the Son is the agent and sustainer of all of creation (esp. 1:2–3, 10–12). On the other hand, the Son has also been elevated above the angels. How can the Son, who existed before creation and through whom God created all things, have been elevated above the angels whom he created? When was the Son ever below the angels such that his status and position would change? These tensions find resolution in 2:5–18 where the author states that the heavenly Son of God became the incarnate human being, Jesus. As a human being, the preexistent, divine Son died, was perfected, and was elevated to the throne at his Father's right hand.

The author's argument in Hebrews 2 partly relies on his reading of Psalm 8 (Heb 2:5–9). This psalm indicates that while human beings presently stand a little lower than the angels, God always intended to place the angels under human authority. Thus, the divine Son was "made a little lower" than the angels by becoming a human being. This happened so that he could then be the "son of man" who would ultimately be exalted above all creation, including the angels. Jesus is the preexistent Son of God who, as a human being, was made lower than the angels for a time but has now been elevated above them to the royal throne in the heavens. Thus, the incarnation of the divine Son resolves the tension of Hebrews 1. As a human being, God's Son has been crowned with glory and exalted to the place of rule over all that he himself created.

Hebrews only further underlines the importance of the heavenly Son's incarnation in 2:10–18. The divine Son's humanity not only means that he is the "son of man" elevated to God's heavenly throne, it also means that he is able to make his fellow human beings holy (2:10–11). He does this by representing them before his Father as their incarnate high priest (2:12–13; 16–18), a theme the author develops much more robustly in 4:14–10:25.

Yet the Son's ongoing high-priestly work of intercession for his siblings (see esp. 7:25) is only one aspect of how he saves them. An additional part of his salvific work is highlighted in 2:14–15. Jesus has liberated his siblings from the power of one of the very angelic beings over whom he has now been exalted—the malevolent angel known as "the devil."

Our author does not give any clear indication that he knows or is drawing from the Second Temple Jewish text known as Jubilees. Nevertheless, the Jubilees account of Moses's deliverance of Israel from Egypt in terms of the people's liberation from the malevolent angelic being known as Mastema, who is identified with Satan, offers some highly illuminating parallels to aspects of Hebrews' argument that help make sense of the author's claims about Jesus's defeat of the devil in 2:14–15.

Jubilees

"ALL THE POWERS OF MASTEMA HAD BEEN LET LOOSE TO SLAY ALL THE FIRSTBORN IN THE LAND OF EGYPT"

The book of Jubilees was likely composed sometime in the early to mid-second century BC.[1] Jubilees consists of a rewriting of Genesis and the first part of Exodus. The book begins with Moses on Mount Sinai, where an angel reveals to him the history of the world up to that point as it is written down on tablets in heaven. Jubilees then retells many of the stories found in Genesis from creation up to the events of Exodus 19–24. The name of the book comes from the fact that it divides the history it relates into forty-nine-year periods or "jubilees" (a unit of time defined in Leviticus 25).

Mastema as Satan. In Jubilees the main enemy of God and his people

---

1. For an excellent introduction to and survey of Jubilees, see especially James C. VanderKam, *The Book of Jubilees*, Guides to the Apocrypha and Pseudepigrapha (Sheffield: Sheffield Academic, 2001). More detailed discussion can be found in James C. VanderKam, *Jubilees: A Commentary*, 2 vols., Hermeneia (Minneapolis: Fortress, 2018).

is Mastema, "the chief of the spirits" (10.8).[2] He is a malevolent angelic being explicitly identified as "the Satan" in Jubilees 10.11.[3] These very verses also make it clear that God allows Mastema to command a host of other evil spirits. Mastema, in other words, is the powerful evil angel known in biblical texts as Satan. He is the accusing spirit who seeks to lead humanity to destruction and to test and tempt God's people. He also holds sway over a host of demons, other malevolent angels who have rebelled against God. There are even clear parallels between Mastema in Jubilees and Satan in Job (see esp. Job 1:6–12; 2:1–6). Jubilees says that Mastema sought to test Abraham by having him offer Isaac. Mastema, like Satan in Job, went before God in heaven and said, "Behold, Abraham loves Isaac his son, and he delights in him above everything else; ask him to offer Isaac as a burnt-offering on the altar, and you will see if he will do this command, and you will know if he is faithful in everything in which you test him" (Jub. 17.16).

Moses's Defeat of Mastema. Jubilees 48–49 retells the story of Israel's exodus from Egypt at the first Passover. These chapters focus on aspects of Exodus 2, 4, and 7–14. Mastema initially attempted to thwart Israel's liberation from Egypt by trying to kill Moses when he returned to Egypt from Midian. The angel speaking with Moses on Mount Sinai reminds him that Mastema sought "with all his power . . . to slay you and deliver the Egyptians out of your hand when he saw that you were sent to execute judgment and vengeance on the Egyptians" (Jub. 48.3). When Mastema's first attempt to prevent the exodus failed, he and his minions sought other means to keep Israel enslaved. Jubilees explains that these evil spirits were at work in the actions of Pharaoh and the Egyptians. It was Mastema who "helped the Egyptian sorcerers" perform signs and wonders like Moses performed (48.9). After Moses led the people out of Egypt, it was Mastema who "hardened the Egyptians' hearts and made them stubborn" so that they pursued the fleeing Israelites (48.17). Jubilees also states that as the people of Israel "were eating the Passover in Egypt . . . all the powers of Mastema had been let loose to slay all the firstborn in the land of Egypt, from the firstborn of Pharaoh to

---

2. All citations of Jubilees are taken and/or modified from the translation of R. H. Charles, ed., *The Apocrypha and Pseudepigrapha of the Old Testament in English: With Introductions and Critical and Explanatory Notes to the Several Books* (Oxford: Clarendon, 1913).

3. This malevolent being shows up in the Qumran Scrolls sometimes called Belial and is likely to be identified with the angel of darkness (see, e.g., 1QS 3–4). For further information, see Michael Mach, "Demons," *EDSS* 1:189–92; and, J. W. van Henten, "Mastemah," *DDD* 1033–35.

the firstborn of the captive maidservant in the mill, and to the cattle" (49.2). Mastema's forces were, however, prevented from entering any "house on the doorframes of which they saw the blood of a lamb," having to "pass by (it), so that all those that were in the house should be saved because the sign of the blood was on its doorframes" (49.3).

The identification in Jubilees both of Mastema as the evil power at work within Pharaoh and the Egyptians and of Mastema's demonic minions as the agents who struck down the firstborn during the night of the first Passover are remarkable when compared with the account in Exodus itself. In Exodus the Lord is the one who both hardens Pharaoh's heart (e.g., Exod 14:4) and strikes down the firstborn when Pharaoh refuses to let the people go (e.g., Exod 12:12, 29). There is, however, one important exception to this last point. Exodus 12:23 explains that the Lord did not permit "the destroyer" to enter houses with blood on their doorframes. This verse suggests not the Lord but some other agent, the destroyer, struck down the firstborn at Passover. Jubilees has seized upon this verse and, together with a number of other interpretive moves and traditions, identified "the destroyer" with Mastema and his demonic hosts. This means that in Jubilees the exodus is far more than a showdown between Pharaoh and Moses, who is backed by Israel's God. By identifying Mastema, whom Jubilees also refers to as an "evil destroyer" (cf. Jub. 23.29), in play behind the scenes, Jubilees has recast the story of Israel's exodus in terms of a larger battle between Israel's God and Moses on one side, and Satan who seeks to accuse and destroy Israel itself and Pharaoh on the other. Moses's liberation of Israel was, in other words, as much a kind of defeat of Mastema, the destroyer, as it was a freeing of the people from Egyptian enslavement.

Jubilees does not imagine Mastema as a fully independent agent of evil doing whatever he pleases to foil and hinder God's purposes. Clearly Mastema seeks to keep Israel in slavery. Clearly, too, he hardens Pharaoh's heart and impels the Egyptians to pursue Israel after they are liberated. As in Exodus, however, this was all part of the Lord's plan. Thus, Jubilees says, Mastema's actions were "the device . . . devised by the Lord our God that he might smite the Egyptians and cast them into the sea" (Jub. 48.17). Nevertheless, and this is significant for reading Hebrews 2:14–15, Jubilees demonstrates the existence of a Jewish interpretive tradition that understood the exodus to be as much about the liberation of God's people from the power of Mastema, the satanic "destroyer," as it was about being freed from Pharaoh and the Egyptians.

Hebrews 2:10–18

"BY HIS DEATH HE MIGHT BREAK THE POWER OF HIM WHO HOLDS THE POWER OF DEATH"

The Destroyer as the Devil. Hebrews only explicitly refers to the first Passover once. In Hebrews 11:28 the author speaks of Moses faithfully keeping "the Passover and the application of blood, so that the destroyer of the firstborn would not touch the firstborn of Israel." Yet Hebrews' reference to "the destroyer" of Exodus 12:23 as the agent who struck down the firstborn at the first Passover is telling. In the light of Jubilees (together with a number of other texts and Jewish traditions about Satan and the angel of death), it appears that Hebrews envisions the first Passover in terms of Moses's liberation of Israel from the malevolent angel who killed the firstborn. This evil spirit who seeks to enslave and destroy humanity is, moreover, the evil angel whom Jesus fully defeated—the devil.

Jesus's Defeat of the Devil. Hebrews 2:14–15 reads, "Since the children have flesh and blood, he too shared in their humanity so that by his death he might break the power of him who holds the power of death—that is, the devil—and free those who all their lives were held in slavery by their fear of death." That Jesus's defeat of the devil here recalls Moses's liberation of God's people at the first Passover from "the destroyer," the malevolent angelic figure Jubilees calls Mastema, can be seen from the fact that Hebrews' opening chapters draw heavily on the larger Exodus narrative. Hebrews connects Jesus's defeat of the devil with liberation from enslavement to the fear of death (2:15). The themes of liberation from enslavement are redolent of Passover and exodus. Moreover, the author's allusion to the giving of the law at Sinai through angels (2:2) and reference to God performing signs and wonders (2:4) among them has already pointed readers to the larger Exodus narrative. The fact that the writer moves on in Hebrews 3–4 to speak about Moses (3:2–6), the one who led God's people out of Egypt, and to compare readers to Israel in the wilderness (3:7–4:11), the very place Israel was after being freed from Egypt, all support the conclusion that the author of Hebrews was intentionally working with the story of the exodus and the liberation of God's people from enslavement when he spoke about Jesus's defeat of the devil and liberation of his siblings from the enslaving fear of the power of death.

Moses faced off against "the destroyer" when he performed the first Passover and led God's people safely out of bondage in Egypt (Heb 11:28). Jubilees offers a vivid account of this liberation in terms of a spiritual battle, clearly indicating that some Jews understood "the destroyer" of Exodus 12:23 to be the devil and his demons. Hebrews plays on this tradition of the devil as the true enslaver to show that when Jesus, the incarnate Son of God, died and rose again, the ultimate Passover and liberation of God's people occurred. God's Son, who took upon himself the blood and flesh of Abraham's seed (2:16), performed the Passover and exodus *par excellence* when, by means of his death and resurrection, he finally and fully liberated his siblings from the power of their age-old enemy. By his death and resurrection, he has defeated the devil himself. Now, as the exalted human being "crowned with glory and honor" (2:9), Jesus rules even over the angels who must worship him. Satan, the great tempter and accuser of God's people, has been defeated and put in his proper place.

FOR FURTHER READING

Additional Ancient Texts

The story of the exodus in Exodus 7–14 forms part of the foundational narrative Hebrews uses. For other texts that speak about "the destroyer" in the broad context of the exodus and wilderness period, see Wisdom of Solomon 17–18 (esp. 18:25) and 1 Corinthians 10:10. For good information on this figure in rabbinic literature, see Louis Ginzberg, *The Legends of the Jews*, 1:537–38, esp. n. 216.

English Translations and Critical Editions

Charles, R. H., ed. *The Apocrypha and Pseudepigrapha of the Old Testament in English: With Introductions and Critical and Explanatory Notes to the Several Books.* 2 vols. Oxford: Clarendon, 1913.

VanderKam, James C. *The Book of Jubilees: A Critical Text.* 2 vols. CSCO 510. Leuven: Peeters, 1989.

_____. *Jubilees.* The Hermeneia Translation. Minneapolis: Fortress, 2020.

Wintermute, O. S. "Jubilees." Pages 35–142 in vol. 2 of *The Old Testament Pseudepigrapha.* Edited by James H. Charlesworth. Garden City, NY: Doubleday, 1985.

Secondary Literature

Dunnill, John. *Covenant and Sacrifice in the Letter to the Hebrews.* SNTSMS 75. Cambridge: Cambridge, 1992.

Ginzberg, Louis. *The Legends of the Jews.* 2nd ed. 2 vols. JPS Classic Reissues. Philadelphia: Jewish Publication Society, 2003.

Mach, Michael. "Demons." Pages 189–92 in vol. 1 of *Encyclopedia of the Dead Sea Scrolls*. Edited by Lawrence H. Schiffman and James C. VanderKam. 2 vols. New York: Oxford University Press, 2000.

Moffitt, David M. "Exodus in Hebrews." Pages 146–63 in *Exodus in the New Testament*. Edited by Seth M. Ehorn. LNTS 663. London: T&T Clark, 2022.

———. "Modelled on Moses: Jesus' Death, Passover, and the Defeat of the Devil in the Epistle to the Hebrews." Pages 279–97 in *Mosebilder: Gedanken zur Rezeption einer literarischen Figur im Frühjudentum, frühen Christentum und der römisch-hellenistischen Literatur*. Edited by Michael Sommer et al. WUNT 1/390. Tübingen: Mohr Siebeck, 2017.

Segal, Michael. *The Book of Jubilees: Rewritten Bible, Redaction, Ideology and Theology*. JSJSup 117. Leiden: Brill, 2007.

VanderKam, James C. *The Book of Jubilees*. Guides to the Apocrypha and Pseudepigrapha. Sheffield: Sheffield Academic, 2001.

———. *Jubilees: A Commentary*. 2 vols. Hermeneia. Minneapolis: Fortress, 2018.

van Henten, J. W. "Mastemah." Pages 1033–35 in *Dictionary of Deities and Demons in the Bible*. Edited by Karel van der Toorn, Bob Becking, and Pieter W. van der Horst. Leiden: Brill, 1995. 2nd rev. ed. Grand Rapids: Eerdmans, 1999.

CHAPTER 4

Wisdom of Solomon and Hebrews 3:1–19: The Spirit of Wisdom as a Guide through the Desert

MADISON N. PIERCE

Two threads running throughout Hebrews—divine speech and the wilderness experience of the ancestors—meet in Hebrews 3:1–19. The author begins with a comparison between Moses and Jesus (3:1–6). The two are prophets and priests, and both are faithful in the roles they have been assigned. These typical points of comparison are important for the author's appeal to Moses as an exemplar, but generally the connection between this section and the next section, where the Holy Spirit speaks the words of Psalm 95:7–11, is more difficult to discern. There the Spirit encourages the audience to listen to God's voice and to avoid the failure of their wandering ancestors in order that they might enter the promised "rest." But there is a connection between Hebrews 3:1–6 and 3:7–19. Rather than the roles of Moses listed above, the author of Hebrews draws upon the role of Moses as a leader. Like Jesus who is the "pioneer" of their faith (12:2) and leads many "sons and daughters to glory" (2:10), Moses is the one who led the people out of Egypt (3:16). Yet his leadership ultimately was ineffective in bringing God's people to the promised rest (3:19; 4:1, 11).

Neither Jesus nor Moses led the people alone. When the ancestors left Egypt, the pillar of cloud and fire guided them on their way. Hebrews imagines the current readers on that same journey toward rest, but do they have the same guide as their ancestors? This question regarding God's leadership of the people in the wilderness is not just something Hebrews addresses; other Second Temple texts also consider the contemporary Jewish experience in light of that defining journey. The Wisdom of Solomon is one such

46

text that employs wilderness imagery. A comparison between Hebrews and Wisdom will show that the answer about God's leadership is both yes and no. In some early Jewish literature, the pillar sometimes was identified as Sophia and sometimes as the Spirit of God. The association of these figures in Jewish literature helps us to understand the use of Psalm 95:7–11 by the author of Hebrews and why he would make the Holy Spirit its speaker.

Wisdom of Solomon

"WHO WOULD KNOW YOUR WILL IF YOU DID NOT GIVE SOPHIA, AND SEND YOUR SPIRIT FROM THE HIGH PLACES?"

As its name suggests, Wisdom of Solomon (sometimes called the Book of Wisdom or simply Wisdom) is written as though it is the wise reflections of King Solomon. Solomon is the implied author—the "voice" of this text—but he is not the actual author. Instead, this text was likely written by a Jewish person (hereafter "the Sage") in Alexandria. Though some scholars think the composition reflects more specific social and/or historical realities (e.g., Caligula's reign from AD 37–41),[1] a broader date between 200 BC and AD 50 is often put forward. As for the genre, Wisdom has affinities with the Writings (e.g., Proverbs, Ecclesiastes) and "wisdom literature," as well as with other "didactic exhortations" from its time.[2] Some try to discern whether Wisdom is more "Jewish" or more "Greek." But choosing between these two backgrounds is not necessary. The author interprets events in the history of the Jewish people, as well as Jewish teachings, but as one who is steeped in contemporary philosophies. Wisdom, like many texts in the New Testament, offers a glimpse into the integration of Jewish religion and culture within the broader **Hellenized** world.

As for Wisdom's structure, David Winston proposes the following:

1. Wisdom's Gift of Immortality (1:1–6:21)
2. The Nature and Power of Wisdom and Solomon's Quest for Her (6:22–10:21)
3. Divine Wisdom of Justice in the Exodus (11:1–19:22)[3]

---

1. David Winston, *The Wisdom of Solomon*, Anchor Yale Bible Commentary 43 (Garden City, NY: Doubleday, 1979), 23.
2. James M. Reese, *Hellenistic Influence on the Book of Wisdom and Its Consequences*, AnBib 41 (Rome: Biblical Institute Press, 1970), 118–21.
3. Winston, *Wisdom of Solomon*, 10–11.

This proposal divides the text into a third section at Wisdom of Solomon 11:1, which is likely the best place to break; however, many recognize how Wisdom of Solomon 10 sets up the discussion of the exodus in Wisdom of Solomon 11.

The Personification of Sophia. In Wisdom of Solomon 10, the Sage offers an account of how Sophia (or "Woman Wisdom") was at work at key points in the lives of God's people. In **canonical** literature (e.g., Prov 9), Sophia is a personification of pure wisdom—an extension of YHWH. In early Jewish literature, she is appropriately referred to as an "intermediary" (we will return to this below). The people whom Sophia serves are anonymous in Wisdom 10, though the figures and events in view are clear. Here are a few excerpts from the narrative (with the names added):

> She guarded the first-formed father of the world [Adam], though he was created alone. (10:1)

> She did not desert the righteous one [Joseph] when he was sold, but rescued him from sins. (10:13)

> She entered into the soul of the servant of the Lord [Moses] and stood against frightening kings with signs and wonders. (10:16)

In the final verses of this chapter, the Sage recounts the work of Sophia in the exodus as well as the wilderness. For example,

> She led them on a marvelous way
> and became a shelter for them by day,
> and by night a flame of stars. (10:17)

In Wisdom 11 the Sage shifts to a presentation of YHWH in their midst, who in many ways coordinates with Sophia. "She prospered their works by the hand of the holy prophet [Moses]" (11:1), but it is YHWH who gives them water from the rock (11:4; cf. Exod 17:1–7).

Sophia and the Spirit. In Wisdom of Solomon, Sophia appears to be interchangeable with the Word (or "Logos"; see, e.g., 9:1–2) as well as the Spirit of the Lord.[4] Her connection to or identification with the Spirit is not explicit,

---

4. Joseph R. Dodson, *The "Powers" of Personification: Rhetorical Purpose in the Book of Wisdom and the Letter to the Romans*, BZNW 161 (Berlin: de Gruyter, 2008), 54.

but the Sage appears to use parallelism to this end. For example, in Wisdom 1:5–6, as the Sage begins:

> For wisdom does not enter into a treacherous soul,
> nor does she dwell in a body involved in sins.
> For the holy spirit of discipline will flee deceit
> and will depart from foolish reasoning.

Also, in Wisdom 9:17:

> But who would know your will if you did not give Sophia,
> and send your Spirit from the high places?

In both instances the two lines of poetry express the same general idea but with different terminology. This implies that Sophia and the Spirit are parallel entities. Again, this *could* suggest an identification of the two figures, but more conservatively, it at least suggests a strong correlation. Elsewhere Sophia is described as a "benevolent spirit" (1:5) who has a "spirit" of her own (7:7, 22). The identification with the s/Spirit, in combination with the development of the character throughout this text, suggests that while Sophia is a personification, she cannot be limited to that. She is portrayed as an *intermediary*—one who acts on behalf of YHWH with his people.[5] One such act is that she offers rest:

> When I enter my house,
> I shall find rest with her;
> for companionship with her has no bitterness,
> and life with her has no pain, but gladness and joy.
> (Wis 8:16; cf. Sir 6:28)

In a similar way, "rest" is offered by the Holy Spirit in Isaiah 63:14. He offers rest, that is, relief from burden, to those who are in the midst of the wilderness experience.

Summary. The Sage uses a number of personifications in the Wisdom of Solomon. The most prominent is, of course, Sophia who acts on YHWH's behalf. Throughout Wisdom the Sage associates her with many

---

5. For more nuance, see Dodson, esp. 38–39. He identifies Sophia as a *hypostasis*—part personification and part being.

other figures as well. For example, at times she is brought into parallel with the Word or even the Spirit of the Lord, which likely implies that for the Sage, they are the same figure. Further, the roles, actions, and descriptions of this character fit well with other Jewish literature, including the Old Testament.

Hebrews 3:1–19

"AS THE HOLY SPIRIT SAYS . . ."

Though there are several places in Hebrews that exhibit verbal parallels with the Wisdom of Solomon (e.g., Heb 1:3 with Wis 7:25), one cannot say with absolute certainty that the relationship is one of literary dependence (i.e., that the writer of Hebrews was familiar with Wisdom), but it does seem likely. Nevertheless, conceptual dependence—or shared traditions and conceptual frameworks—is certain.[6] Though the shared traditions and frameworks are broader, many interesting parallels are found between Wisdom of Solomon and Hebrews. They both depict an intermediary figure playing a significant role in the wilderness experience and offering rest to those who are deserving (or withholding it from those who are not).

Turning to Hebrews, after his comparison between Jesus and Moses, the author connects what he is saying to the contemporary audience:

> And we are [God's] house, if indeed we hold firmly to our confidence and the hope in which we glory. (Heb 3:6)

After this conditional statement, the author offers the implications, and to do this, he does something surprising that is found nowhere else in the New Testament (except Heb 10:15–17).[7] When he quotes Scripture (here from Ps 95), he presents the Holy Spirit as the speaker:

> So, as the Holy Spirit says:

---

6. This language is indebted to Jonathan A. Linebaugh, *God, Grace, and Righteousness in Wisdom of Solomon and Paul's Letter to the Romans: Texts in Conversation*, NovTSup 152 (Leiden: Brill, 2013), esp. 36.

7. Others point to Acts 1:16 and 28:25, although there the Holy Spirit speaks *through* the human author of Scripture. In Hebrews the Spirit speaks directly to the contemporary audience. From my perspective, this comprises two separate categories of speech by the Spirit in the New Testament, and others could be named.

"Today, if you hear his voice,
> do not harden your hearts
as you did in the rebellion,
> during the time of testing in the wilderness,
where your ancestors tested and tried me,
> though for forty years they saw what I did.
That is why I was angry with that generation;
> I said, 'Their hearts are always going astray,
> and they have not known my ways.'
So I declared on oath in my anger,
> 'They shall never enter my rest.'" (Heb 3:7–11)

Of course, at this stage in Hebrews, the author has established a pattern for presenting Scripture as God's speech. The Father speaks in 1:5–13, and the Son speaks in 2:12–13. Now it is the Spirit's turn. But why does the Spirit speak this quotation at this stage in the argument?

The author uses the quotation from Psalm 95, spoken by the Spirit, to offer the audience the promised rest the ancestors failed to obtain (4:1). What many commentators do not recognize is how the presentation of this as the Spirit's speech affects the idea of rest. It is, after all, the *Spirit* who says: "They shall never enter *my* rest." Though this is striking, it is possible that the author (and his audience) understood a connection between the Spirit and the offer of rest. As we have seen, Sophia offers rest also (Wis 8:16; cf. Sir 6:28), and in Hebrew versions of Isaiah 63:14, the Spirit of the Lord offers rest to the faithful among the wilderness generation.[8] He also fights (!) those who rebel against him and grieve him (63:10), which is similar to the punitive response we see from the Spirit in Hebrews 3:7–11. These conceptual connections, in addition to several others between the role of the Spirit in Hebrews 3:7–19 and other Jewish literature,[9] offer some possible reasons that the author of Hebrews presents the Spirit as the speaker of this psalm.

With these connections in place, we can return to the author's argument in Hebrews 3:7–19. It is clear from Hebrews as a whole that Jesus is their leader. He is one who has entered rest already (4:10),[10] and he will

---

8. Of course, the author of Hebrews draws more often on Greek versions of Scripture. Nevertheless, the reading in the Hebrew versions is evidence of an extant tradition at the time.

9. Madison N. Pierce, *Divine Discourse in the Epistle to the Hebrews: The Recontextualization of Spoken Quotations of Scripture*, SNTSMS 178 (Cambridge: Cambridge University Press, 2020), ch. 4.

10. Nicholas J. Moore, "Jesus as 'the One Who Entered His Rest': The Christological Reading of Hebrews 4.10," *JSNT* 36, no. 4 (2014): 383–400.

lead the people to glory (2:10). Nevertheless, in the Jewish literature that I highlighted in this essay, another thread we see is Sophia (Wis 10:17) and the Spirit (Isa 63:14) serving as guides for the people of God through the desert. Hebrews 4 will present the people of God on this *same* journey in the desert like their ancestors, and for as long as it is called "today," the Spirit will guide them on their journey as they strive to enter the promised rest (4:11). The author of Hebrews draws upon these familiar traditions, but he also presses them. In Hebrews the Holy Spirit is not a mere intermediary. He has his own voice (3:7–11; 10:15–17), but he also works alongside the Father and the Son (see esp. 9:13–14). Though for us, the contemporary readers, the attribution of the Psalm 95 quotation to the Spirit is surprising, this would not be the case for the early recipients of Hebrews. Additionally, in Wisdom of Solomon (and perhaps even in Isaiah 63), "rest" appears to be respite—relief from burden or difficulty. The author of Hebrews likely uses this language to refer to their destination—Mount Zion, the heavenly Jerusalem (12:22–24), where they will join together with all God's people in celebration.

FOR FURTHER READING

Additional Ancient Texts

Many texts within the canon reflect on the wilderness journey taken by God's people. Among the most important for this passage are Isaiah 63:7–14 and Nehemiah 9:9–21. See also Sirach 6:18–37; Psalms 78, 105, 106.

English Translations and Critical Editions

New English Translation of the Septuagint
New Revised Standard Version
Ziegler, Joseph. *Sapientia Salomonis.* 2nd ed. Septuaginta 13. Göttingen: Vandenhoeck and Ruprecht, 1980.

Secondary Literature

Dodson, Joseph R. *The "Powers" of Personification: Rhetorical Purpose in the Book of Wisdom and the Letter to the Romans.* BZNW 161. Berlin: de Gruyter, 2008.
McGlynn, Moyna. *Divine Judgement and Divine Benevolence in the Book of Wisdom.* WUNT 2/139. Tübingen: Mohr Siebeck, 2001.
Moore, Nicholas J. "'In' or 'Near'? Heavenly Access and Christian Identity in Hebrews." Pages 185–98 in *Muted Voices of the New Testament:*

Readings in the Catholic Epistles and Hebrews. Edited by Katherine M. Hockey, Madison N. Pierce, and Francis Watson. LNTS 565. London: T&T Clark, 2017.

Pierce, Madison N. *Divine Discourse in the Epistle to the Hebrews: The Recontextualization of Spoken Quotations of Scripture*. SNTSMS 178. Cambridge: Cambridge University Press, 2020.

_____. "Hebrews 3:7–4:11 and the Spirit's Speech to the Community." Pages 173–84 in *Muted Voices of the New Testament: Readings in the Catholic Epistles and Hebrews*. Edited by Katherine M. Hockey, Madison N. Pierce, and Francis Watson. LNTS 565. London: T&T Clark, 2017.

Watson, Francis. *Paul and the Hermeneutics of Faith*. 2nd ed. London: T&T Clark, 2015.

CHAPTER 5

Josephus and Hebrews 4:1–13: The Promise of Entering God's Rest

BRYAN J. WHITFIELD

ebrews is full of comparisons. From the beginning, the author argues for the supremacy of the Son through whom God has spoken in these last days (1:1). Hebrews then develops that superiority in a series of comparisons: the Son is superior to the angels (1:5–2:18), to Moses (3:1–6), and to the Levitical priesthood (7:1–28). He is the mediator of a better covenant (8:1–13), entering the "greater and more perfect tabernacle" (9:11) with "his own blood" (9:12).

The exhortations of Hebrews also stress comparison. The author distinguished "what we have heard" (2:1) from "the message spoken through angels" (2:2) and from the message that came to the Israelites who left Egypt (3:16). These contrasts set up his warnings to "pay the most careful attention" (2:1) to the message and to see that no one who listens "has a sinful, unbelieving heart that turns away from the living God" (3:12).

As the writer of Hebrews begins this warning against unbelief (3:7–19), he quotes and interprets Psalm 95:7–11, but he also relies on the related narrative in Numbers 13–14 throughout Hebrews 3:7–4:13.[1] As a result, careful readers will examine the Torah as well as the Psalter to understand the comparison. But like all readers of Scripture, the author of Hebrews lived within a particular context that shaped his practice of reading. Reflection on the context of Second Temple Judaism thus provides insight into the way the author of Hebrews read Scripture. Examining how other authors interpreted the narrative of Israel's rebellion in the wilderness can help us to see more

---

1. Albert Vanhoye, "Long Journey or Imminent Access? The Biblical Context of Hebrews 3.7–4.11," in *A Perfect Priest*, ed. and trans. N. J. Moore and R. J. Ounsworth, WUNT 477 (Tübingen: Mohr Siebeck, 2018), 240–55.

clearly how the author of Hebrews interpreted this event, just as studying a series of paintings of the same scene by different artists helps us to see the style of each. Several Second Temple authors, including Pseudo-Philo, **Philo**, and **Josephus**, provided interpretations of Numbers 13–14. Here we focus on the account of Josephus.[2]

Josephus

"THEY BELIEVED THEIR WORDS WERE MORE TRUE THAN GOD'S PROMISE"

Josephus, the general who led part of the defense of Galilee during the First Jewish War with Rome, surrendered to the Romans and prophesied that Vespasian would become emperor. Under imperial sponsorship, Josephus moved to Rome and became a historian of the war and an apologist for Judaism. In his twenty-volume *Jewish Antiquities*, he recounted Jewish history from its beginnings until the time of the First Jewish War. In telling that story, he provided paraphrases of biblical history, including a retelling of Numbers 13–14 in *Antiquities* 3.300–315, the account of Moses sending the scouts into Canaan, their report, and the subsequent rebellion.

Struck with Terror. Josephus's account begins, not with God's command to send "some men to explore the land" (Num 13:1), but with Moses's speech once the people had reached the border. Moses emphasized God's decision "to offer two blessings" to the Israelites: "freedom and the acquisition of a prosperous land" (*Ant.* 3.300). Freedom was theirs, and God's promise of the land would be as well. No king, city, or nation would stand before their advance, but Canaan would not fall without struggle (*Ant.* 3.300–301). Moses ordered the scouts to assess the land's fertility and military strength. He encouraged the people to be of one mind and to honor God, their "helper in battle and ally in all things" (*Ant.* 3.302). After surveying Canaan for forty days, the scouts returned, "carrying fruits that the land bore" (*Ant.* 3.304). The beauty of the produce and the scouts' report at first stirred up "the multitude to do battle" (*Ant.* 3.304). But their description of the challenges ahead sent the people into a panic as they multiplied the difficulties found in the biblical accounts (*Ant.* 3.304). Most of the scouts were "struck with terror," and they spread that fear among the people (*Ant.* 3.305).

Be Courageous. As a result, the people concluded that conquest was

---

2. All translations of Josephus are my own.

impossible. They spent the night lamenting "as if God were not coming to their aid with deeds but only making promises with words" (*Ant.* 3.306). They gathered the next morning, intent on stoning Moses and Aaron and returning to Egypt (*Ant.* 3.307). But Joshua and Caleb, two of the scouts, waded into the middle of the crowd to restrain them. They begged the people "to be courageous and neither to accuse God of falsehood nor to trust those who had terrified them by having spoken lies about the Canaanites" (*Ant.* 3.308). Instead, the people were to trust those who urged them to move toward happiness and prosperity, especially since God was "sharing in their desire and fighting on their behalf" (*Ant.* 3.309). They concluded, "Let us go, therefore, against our enemies, having no apprehension, having faith in our leader, God, and following those of us who will show you the way!" (*Ant.* 3.309). These two scouts linked trust in God with moving forward into the land.

Seduced by the Scouts. Moses and Aaron prayed that God would calm the people's spirits, and the cloud that signaled God's presence came to rest on the tabernacle. Moses reported God's words when he emerged from the tent (*Ant.* 3.311). Despite the benefits God had provided, the people proved ungrateful. Moses concluded that the people, "seduced by the scouts' cowardice, believed their words were more true than God's promise" (*Ant.* 3.312). As a result, the people would not take possession of the land but would wander in the wilderness without city or home (*Ant.* 3.314). God would later give the land to the children of those whose lack of self-control led them to rebel.

Josephus's account highlights Moses's leadership, portraying him as a skilled general preparing his troops for battle. He stressed Moses's insight, strength of character, courage, and faith, a portrait that fits with his portrait in *Jewish Antiquities* as a whole. Similarly, Joshua and Caleb displayed courage and urged the people to choose faith in God and to follow them into the land. By contrast, the remaining scouts proved to be cowards who spread their lack of trust in God to the people. Sadly, the people, deceived by the scouts' report, trusted the scouts rather than God. Josephus regarded that choice as disobedience and unbelief, a rejection of God's truthfulness and faithfulness to his promise.

Hebrews 4:1–13

"WE WHO HAVE BELIEVED ENTER THAT REST"

In his discussion of the wilderness generation, the author of Hebrews also contrasts unbelief to confident faith (3:12–19) while stressing the significance of God's promise. But he also focuses on the theme of rest, an emphasis not found in Numbers 13–14 or in Josephus's account, but present in Deuteronomy (3:20; 12:9; 25:19) and in Psalm 95:11. As Hebrews 4 begins, the author introduces the theme of rest, shifting from warning to promise. Two exhortations ("let us be careful," 4:1, and "let us, therefore, make every effort to enter that rest," 4:11) frame 4:1–11, and both the noun and the verb for "rest" occur repeatedly (4:1, 3[2x], 4, 5, 6, 8, 10, 11). Within this larger unit, the writer interprets different parts of Psalm 95 in two smaller sections (4:1–5 and 4:6–11).

The Promise Still Stands. The first of these sections, framed by the repetition of the verb "enter" and the noun "rest" in 4:1 and 4:5, focuses on·Psalm 95:11. The opening "therefore" (4:1) points readers backward to the consequences of unbelief, but the shift to the first person ("let us," 4:1) reorients attention to the present. The wilderness generation did not enter God's rest. But the promise "still stands" (4:1) for those reading and hearing the author's message. The writer sets out two reasons the promise remains open.

First, like the generation at Kadesh, those who hear the message of Hebrews have received good news: "We also have had the good news proclaimed to us, just as they did" (4:2). Yet the wilderness generation proved faithless, so "the message they heard was of no value to them" (4:2). Although Joshua and Caleb reaffirmed and trusted God's promise, the majority of the people "did not share the faith of those who obeyed" (4:2).

Second, even now, those who hear the author's good news are entering the land: "Now we who have believed enter that rest" (4:3). That movement is not yet complete, as 4:11 reveals, but rest is more than a promise for the future. The readers were already experiencing God's faithfulness in their forward movement into rest that had begun. To make that clear, the writer distinguishes the geographic location of the rest of Canaan from the rest believers are now entering. Switching from exhortation to explanation, he clarifies the meaning of rest in Psalm 95:11 in light of Genesis 2:2. Although he quotes Genesis in 4:4, he begins the reference to it in 4:3, noting that God's "works have been finished since the creation of the world." Using the ancient exegetical technique of **gezerah shewa**, the writer uses the shared word "rest" to interpret its meaning in Psalm 95:11 on the basis of Genesis 2:2. The writer places the citation of Genesis 2:2 at the center of 4:3b–5 as well as at the center of his five scriptural citations in 3:15–4:7. All the other citations of Scripture are from Psalm 95. This concentric (or chiastic) structure focuses the reader's attention on the singular quotation of Genesis 2:2, which provides the key to understanding the phrase "my rest" in Psalm

95:11 (see table 5.1). Given this focus on Genesis, the phrase "my rest" is no longer the rest that God provides in the land of Canaan but the rest in which God participates, the primordial rest of the creation story, a rest *better* than the one promised the wilderness generation.

Table 5.1. Scripture Quotations in Hebrews 3:15–4:7

Ps 95:7–8 (Heb 3:15)
Ps 95:11 (Heb 4:3)
Gen 2:2 (Heb 4:4)
Ps 95:7 (Heb 4:7)
Ps 95:8 (Heb 4:7)

Who Will Enter the Rest? The second smaller section (4:6–11) focuses on a new question: If the wilderness generation did not enter rest, but the promise of rest remains (4:6), then who will enter that rest? To argue that his audience, those to whom the good news had been preached, could enter that rest, the writer develops an additional argument from Psalm 95:7b–8a focused on the word "today": "Today, if you hear his voice, do not harden your hearts" (Heb 4:7b). The present of "today" holds out a promise of another time in which people may respond to God's offer of rest. Physical entry does not constitute the rest described by the psalm: "For if Joshua had given them rest, God would not have spoken later about another day" (4:8). Another kind of rest remains for God's people, a "rest" defined in light of Genesis 2:2. The writer first calls it a "Sabbath-rest" (4:9), stressing the celebration and joy of eternal rest in God's presence. The writer then designates this rest as "God's rest" (4:10), making it even clearer that the rest people experience is God's own, the rest that follows the work of creation. Those who enter that rest, whether Christ or those he leads to glory as his brothers and sisters (2:10), also rest "from their works" (4:10).

The Power of the Divine Word. With 4:11 the writer closes the second section (4:6–11) as well as the larger unit (4:1–11) as he repeats key words and phrases from 4:1 and 4:6. He returns to exhortation, urging his audience to strive to enter God's rest and to avoid the fate of the Israelites in the wilderness.

This closing note of judgment provides an apt transition into 4:12–13, a finely crafted hymn. Opening with the "word of God" (4:12) and closing with the word of human response ("account," 4:13), the writer reflects on the power of the divine word by which the words of the psalm become a word for "today." This word, like God, is living (3:12; 9:14; 10:31; 12:22) and active, a sword that cuts to the innermost, judging even the heart. The writer once more echoes the language of the psalmist who warns against hard hearts (3:8, 15; 4:7) that "are always going astray" (3:10). The condition of the heart marks individuals as faithful or faithless. Given this interior focus of judgment, nothing escapes the creator's scrutiny. All stand accountable before God, unmasked and vulnerable (4:13). That exposure before God makes the high priestly ministry of Jesus all the more necessary and all the more remarkable.

Conclusion. In contrast to Josephus's account of the wilderness generation's rebellion, the writer of Hebrews stresses the themes of promise and rest, broadening the theological significance of his discussion. Introducing the theme of God's faithfulness to his promises, which he develops throughout the sermon (6:13, 15, 17; 9:15; 10:36; 11:9, 39), the writer inverts the psalmist's words of judgment to create a new prospect for his audience, assuring them that the promise of rest stands open for them. Unlike Josephus, he focuses on the application of the text for his audience. He wants his readers to act in the present, not simply to know something about the past.

In addition, the author of Hebrews connects the rest that stands open for his readers to the rest God experienced after creating the world. Centering his quotations from Psalm 95 around a single quotation from Genesis 2, he reframes rest so that it becomes not only the rest of the land of Canaan but also God's Sabbath rest. The **eschatological** rest of God's people echoes the primordial rest following creation, binding God's first interaction with human beings to their final journey into God's presence.

Comparing these two accounts underscores both the complexity of the argument of Hebrews and the sophistication of its use of Scripture. The unique blending of these themes reveals the skill and artistry of this unknown author who weaves together a rich scriptural tapestry that calls his readers to enter God's Sabbath rest.

For Further Reading

Additional Ancient Texts

For additional Second Temple accounts of the wilderness rebellion, see Sirach 16:9–11; 1 Maccabees 2:55–56; Damascus Document 3.7–9; Pseudo-Philo's Biblical Antiquities 15; and Philo, *On the Life of Moses* 1.220–36.

English Translations and Critical Editions

Josephus. Translated by H. St. J. Thackeray et. al. 10 vols. LCL. Cambridge, MA: Harvard University Press, 1926–65.

Judean Antiquities 1–4. Vol. 3 of *Flavius Josephus: Translation and Commentary*. Edited by Steve Mason. Translated by Louis H. Feldman. Leiden: Brill, 2000.

Secondary Literature

Attridge, Harold W. *The Interpretation of Biblical History in the* Antiquitates Judaicae *of Flavius Josephus*. HDR 7. Missoula, MT: Scholars Press, 1976.

Feldman, Louis H. "Josephus on the Spies." Pages 22–41 in *Internationales Josephus-Kolloquium Paris 2001: Studies on the Antiquities of Josephus*. Edited by Folker Siegert and Jürgen U. Kalms. Münsteraner Judaistische Studien 12. Paris: Münster, 2002.

Mason, Steve. *Josephus and the New Testament*. Peabody, MA: Hendrickson, 2003.

Vanhoye, Albert. *A Perfect Priest*. Edited and translated by Nicholas J. Moore and Richard J. Ounsworth. WUNT 477. Tübingen: Mohr Siebeck, 2018.

Whitfield, Bryan J. *Joshua Traditions and the Argument of Hebrews 3 and 4*. BZNW 194. Berlin: de Gruyter, 2013.

CHAPTER 6

Sirach and Hebrews 4:14–5:10: Called to Be High Priest, Just Like Aaron

BRYAN R. DYER

Jesus is our great high priest! This is a major theme in the Epistle to the Hebrews and a unique contribution to the New Testament canon. While this is hinted at earlier in the epistle (2:17; 3:1), the author begins to unpack this theme in 4:14–5:10. In these verses it is established that Jesus fulfills two of the major requirements for the high priesthood: humanity and a divine call. Regarding the qualification of a divine call, the author writes, "And no one takes this honor on himself, but he receives it when called by God, just as Aaron was" (5:4). This brief statement may seem insignificant, but the author is making an important claim. Aaron, the first high priest, is the model of a divine calling to the high priesthood. When the author goes on to establish Jesus's own calling in 5:5–6, he is connecting Jesus to Aaron—even though he will later argue that Jesus's high priesthood in the order of Melchizedek is superior to the Levitical priesthood (7:1–28).

Yet the connection to Aaron is important. Within **Second Temple Judaism**, when the line of high priests was often fraught with violence and questions of legitimacy, Aaron stood out as the ideal priest. After the temple was rebuilt, the role of high priest was sometimes obtained by corruption, bribery, and foreign influence. The high priesthood was contested especially from the time of Greek occupation, through the **Maccabean Revolt** and dynasty, and up to the time of the Roman Empire. Some literature from the period demonstrates disgust at the perceived corruption of the high priesthood (2 Macc 4; 1QpHab 8.10–13), while other sources uphold a continued reverence for the position and the priesthood. Sirach is an excellent example of a text that highly regards the priesthood while reflecting on Aaron as the ideal high priest. Originally written during some disruption within the high priesthood (after the death of Simon II) yet before the more egregious examples of high priestly corruption (cf. Jason [175 BC] and Menelaus [172 BC]), the text portrays Aaron as the idyllic high priest, directly called by God to the position.

Sirach
"HE CHOSE HIM OUT OF THE LIVING"

The comparative text under consideration goes by three different names: (1) Wisdom of Ben Sira, likely the more common name, especially for the original Hebrew version; (2) Sirach, the name given to the Greek translation of the text; and (3) Ecclesiasticus, the Latin version of the text. It was originally written in Hebrew in the early second century BC by an author identified as "Jesus son of Eleazar son of Sira" (Heb. *ben sira*; 50:27). The eulogy for Simon II in chapter 50 makes clear that Ben Sira wrote after 196 BC but likely before the difficult transitions among Simon's children (175 BC) and the Maccabean uprising (168 BC). The text was translated into Greek by the author's grandson around 117 BC. The details of this translation are described in a prologue added to the text by the translator. Since the author of Hebrews demonstrates familiarity with the Septuagint—within which the Greek translation of Sirach was preserved—we will refer to the Greek translation of Ben Sira's text (Sirach) for our analysis.[1]

Reverence for the Priesthood. Like other wisdom texts of Jewish literature, Sirach consists of collections of smaller passages on a variety of topics. It also demonstrates an array of literary forms, including proverbs, prohibitions, beatitudes, hymns, and refrains. The text includes several poems on finding wisdom (1:1–10; 4:11–19; 6:18–37; 14:20–15:10; 24:1–34; 38:24–39:11; 42:15–43:33), which may help point toward an overall structure. Of the many themes in Sirach—including wisdom, creation, and proper behavior—important for our purposes is the book's reverence for the priesthood. Throughout the book Ben Sira stresses proper worship (35:10–13; 43:30), sacrifices (34:21–24), and admiration for the priests (7:29, 31).

This emphasis on the priesthood is evident in 44:1–49:16 where Ben Sira offers a "hymn in honor of our ancestors."[2] Moving through Israel's history,

---

1. The Greek translation circulated within the LXX and is included in the sacred Scriptures of Roman Catholic and Orthodox traditions. Most English translations are derived from Greek translations of the text. Little manuscript evidence for the Hebrew version of the text was available until discoveries in the mid-nineteenth century AD led to the reconstruction of about two-thirds of Ben Sira's original Hebrew composition.
2. A title given to the section in the Greek translation.

the author praises the nation's ancestors, including Abraham, Moses, Joshua, Solomon, and others.[3] Retellings of Israel's history appear in the Hebrew Bible (Josh 24:2–14; Neh 9:6–38; Pss 78, 105, 106; Ezek 20:5–44) where the emphasis is on God's salvific activity. This passage in Sirach focuses more prevalently on human action.[4] Ben Sira's "hymn" is longer than those retellings and covers more historical ground. It also highlights the priesthood, including Aaron and Phinehas (who are described as second and third in glory behind Moses [45:2, 20, 23]), and Simon II, the most recent high priest. Sirach 50:1–21 is devoted to Simon, and it is likely that the entire hymn builds so that Israel's history reaches its climax with his priesthood.

Aaron as Ideal High Priest. Aaron is a significant figure in this hymn, especially in how he anticipates the high priesthood of Simon. Aaron is also given more attention than just about anyone else in the hymn (45:6–22). After praising Moses (44:23b–45:5), Ben Sira writes,

> He exalted Aaron, a holy man like Moses
> > who was his brother, of the tribe of Levi.
> He made an everlasting covenant with him,
> > and gave him the priesthood of the people.
> He blessed him with stateliness,
> > and put a glorious robe on him. (45:6–7)[5]

The next several verses describe Aaron's garments and priestly vestments (45:8–13). The author then states,

> Moses ordained him,
> > and anointed him with holy oil;
> it was an everlasting covenant for him
> > and for his descendants as long as the heavens endure,
> to minister to the Lord and serve as a priest
> > and bless his people in his name.
> He chose him out of the living
> > to offer sacrifice to the Lord,

---

3. There is an obvious parallel here with Hebrews 11, where a similar list of Israel's heroes is presented. For an examination of this and other similar texts, see Pamela M. Eisenbaum, *The Jewish Heroes of Christian History: Hebrews 11 in Literary Contexts*, SBLDS 156 (Atlanta: Scholars, 1997), 20–35.

4. Richard J. Coggins, *Sirach*, Guides to Apocrypha and Pseudepigrapha (Sheffield: Sheffield Academic, 1998), 78.

5. Translations from Sirach are from the NRSV.

> incense and a pleasing odor as a memorial portion,
>> to make atonement for the people. (45:15–16)

Ben Sira then describes the opposition to Aaron's high priesthood by Dathan, Abiram, and Korah (45:18–19; cf. Num 16). In response, the Lord destroyed the opposers and performed wonders against them (45:19). These wonders validated Aaron's position and cemented his heritage (45:20).

While describing the vestments Aaron wore (45:8–13) and the sacrifices he offered (45:14–22), this passage tells us a great deal about Ben Sira's understanding of Aaron and his place in Israel's history. Aaron was exalted and blessed by God (45:6–7), who also gave him glory (45:20) and authority (45:17). God chose Aaron from among all the living (45:16) and made a covenant with him (45:7, 15). To him was given the priesthood (45:7), of which he was the first (45:13), and this was to be passed down among his descendants (45:13, 15, 21). Aaron and his descendants' role as priests included ministering to God, blessing God's people, and making atonement for them (45:15–16).

Legitimacy through the Priestly Line. God's covenant with Aaron and his descendants is recalled a few times as the hymn to Israel's ancestors continues. As Ben Sira shifts focus to Aaron's grandson Phinehas, Aaron's covenant is confirmed as God establishes a covenant with Phinehas "that he and his descendants should have the dignity of the priesthood forever" (45:24). God's covenant with Aaron is likened to the covenant with David to confirm that "the heritage of Aaron is for his descendants alone" (45:25). In chapter 50 Simon's priestly activity in 50:11–21 is meant to parallel Aaron's (45:8–12). As he performs his priestly duties, Simon is surrounded by the sons of Aaron who support him (50:13, 16).

In this passage Aaron serves as the ideal high priest to whom all later priests are compared. He was the first high priest, exalted by God and uniquely chosen for this role. Ben Sira stresses the importance of the priestly line and assumes that a legitimate high priest must be a descendant of Aaron. Importantly, Ben Sira also connects Simon to Aaron to legitimize and uphold the later high priest.

Hebrews 4:14–5:10

"YOU ARE A PRIEST FOREVER"

The transitional verses in Hebrews 4:14–16 serve to introduce the topic that chapter 5 will address: Jesus the high priest. "Therefore, since we have a great high priest who has ascended into heaven, Jesus the Son of God, let us hold firmly to the faith we profess" (4:14). Jesus's high priesthood was likely a new or advanced concept for the audience of Hebrews (5:11). It was necessary, then, to present an argument for how Jesus is qualified for the role. In the beginning of chapter 5, the author describes two qualifications for "every high priest" (5:1). The first criterion is that a high priest must be human. He "is selected from among the people" (5:1), "is able to deal gently with those who are ignorant and are going astray," and "he himself is subject to weakness" (5:2). The second is that the high priest must be called by God: "And no one takes this honor on himself, but he receives it when called by God, just as Aaron was" (5:4). The remaining verses (5:5–10) detail how Jesus fulfills both of these criteria: God called him to the role (5:5–6) and Jesus was fully human (5:7–10).

Criterion of Calling. The author demonstrates how Jesus satisfies these two requirements for the high priesthood in reverse order. "In the same way," referring back to Aaron's divine calling, "Christ did not take on himself the glory of becoming a high priest" (5:5a). To demonstrate Jesus's own divine calling, the author quotes from Psalms 2:7 and 110:4, having God speak the words directly to Jesus:

But God said to him,

"You are my Son;
today I have become your Father."

And he says in another place,

"You are a priest forever,
in the order of Melchizedek." (Heb 5:5b–6)

In this way, the author confirms that Jesus was called directly by God to the high priesthood. Like Ben Sira, the author of Hebrews points to Aaron as the ideal high priest who was divinely called to the position. In his praise for Simon II, Ben Sira draws connections to Aaron to further legitimize his high priesthood (Sir 50:11–21). Similarly, the author of Hebrews draws upon Aaron in his own praise of Jesus's high priesthood. Just as Aaron was called by God to be a high priest, so, too, Jesus was divinely called.

Hebrews 5:6 is the first mention of Melchizedek, but the figure is taken up in detail later in the epistle (6:20; 7:1–15). The mention of Aaron in Hebrews 5:4 may have raised the obvious objection to Jesus's validity to be high priest: he was not a Levite. While this exact point is addressed later (7:13–14), the author teases his response here. Jesus is a high priest in the order of Melchizedek, a high priesthood outside of, and prior to, the Levitical line. However, at this point in the epistle, the author is simply establishing Jesus's divine calling to demonstrate how he met the basic requirements to be a high priest. Just like Aaron, the first and ideal high priest, Jesus was called to the position directly by God.

Criterion of Humanity. Concerning the criterion that a high priest be human, the author earlier teased how Jesus fulfilled this requirement in 4:15: "For we do not have a high priest who is unable to empathize with our weaknesses, but we have one who has been tempted in every way, just as we are—yet he did not sin." In Hebrews 5:7–10 he offers further evidence by presenting a portrait of Jesus during his days on earth—although a better translation would be "in the days of his flesh," as the Greek here is the term often used for one's body or flesh.[6] Jesus is presented as crying out to God, fearing death, and experiencing suffering. The author uses a popular wordplay, "to suffer, to learn," in 5:8 to further emphasize Jesus's humanity. The point is that Jesus was fully human and experienced human "weakness" in its fullness.

Even though Aaron is not mentioned explicitly here in Hebrews 5:7–10, Sirach offers an interesting parallel to the author's discussion of the importance of the high priest's humanity. Hebrews states that "every high priest is selected from among the people and is appointed to represent the people" (5:1). This is corroborated in Ben Sira's declaration that God chose Aaron "out of all the living" (Sir 45:16). Both Hebrews and Sirach demonstrate an understanding that the high priest is necessarily a human—not a spiritual or divine being. This is because the high priest serves as a representative of those whom he represents (Heb 5:1–3). According to Ben Sira, Aaron was given the "priesthood of the people" (45:7) in order to "bless his [God's] people" (45:15) and make atonement for them (45:16).

Hebrews 5:9–10 presents the results of Jesus's time on earth. His sufferings are connected to his being made perfect and his offering of salvation. Jesus's humanity is understood as part of a necessary process through which he can serve as high priest. Unlike Aaron or his descendants, Jesus is a source of "eternal salvation" (5:9). Hebrews 5:10 reaffirms Jesus's high priesthood in the order of Melchizedek, which, as the author mentions in 5:6, is an eternal priesthood (cf. 7:1–28).

---

6. So the ESV, KJV, NASB, and NRSV translations.

The details of Jesus's high priesthood and his priestly self-offering in the heavenly tabernacle are taken up later in the epistle (Heb 7:11–10:18). In Hebrews 4:14–5:10, the author starts with the basic requirements for the high priest while using Aaron as the ideal model. Like Aaron, Jesus was fully human and called directly by God to the position. After he establishes these criteria (Heb 5:1–4), the author demonstrates Jesus's divine calling (5:5–6) and details his full humanity (5:7–10). In this passage the author also introduces the high priesthood of Melchizedek (5:6, 10), which becomes important as the author later describes the order and nature of Jesus's high priesthood (7:1–25).

For Further Reading

Additional Ancient Texts

Josephus offers another positive assessment of Aaron and his calling in *Jewish Antiquities* 3.188–92. The account of Aaron saving the Israelites by making atonement for them in the face of God's wrath (Num 18:41–50) is retold in Wisdom of Solomon 18:20–25 and 4 Maccabees 7.11–12.

Melchizedek appears in several Second Temple works, including **Philo**, *Allegorical Interpretation* 3.79–82; Josephus, *Jewish War* 6.438; and, significantly, 11QMelchizedek, discovered at **Qumran**.

English Translations and Critical Editions

Beentjes, Pancratius C. *The Book of Ben Sira in Hebrew: A Text Edition of All Extant Hebrew Manuscripts and a Synopsis of All Parallel Hebrew Ben Sira Texts*. Leiden: Brill, 1997.
New English Translation of the Septuagint
New Revised Standard Version
Ziegler, Joseph. *Sapientia Iesu Filii Sirach*. Septuaginta 12/2. 2nd ed. Göttingen: Vandenhoeck and Ruprecht, 1980.

Secondary Literature

Dyer, Bryan R. "'One Does Not Presume to Take This Honor': The Development of the High Priestly Appointment and Its Significance for Hebrews 5:4." *Conversations with the Biblical World* 33 (2013): 125–46.
Horbury, William. "The Aaronic Priesthood in the Epistle to the Hebrews," *JSNT* 19 (1983): 43–71.
Mason, Eric F. *'You Are a Priest Forever': Second Temple Jewish Messianism and the Priestly Christology of the Epistle to the Hebrews*. STDJ 74. Leiden: Brill, 2008.

Pierce, Madison N. *Divine Discourse in the Epistle to the Hebrews*. SNTSMS 178. Cambridge: Cambridge University Press, 2020.

Rooke, Deborah W. *Zadok's Heirs: The Role and Development of the High Priesthood in Ancient Israel*. OTM. Oxford: Oxford University Press, 2000.

CHAPTER 7

The Community Rule and Hebrews 5:11–6:12: Perfection, Perseverance, and Apostasy

JOHN K. GOODRICH

In Hebrews 5:11–6:12—the third of the epistle's "warning passages" (cf. 2:1–4; 3:7–4:13; 10:19–39; 12:14–29)—the author reprimands his readers for their apathy. Although he has additional insights to share, he is convinced his readers "no longer try to understand" (5:11). His complaint is that they are lazy and should be more developed in their faith than they currently are. Indeed, "by this time you ought to be teachers," yet as things stand "you need someone to teach you the elementary truths of God's word all over again" (5:12). Simply put, "You need milk," and "anyone who lives on milk, being still an infant, is not acquainted with the teaching about righteousness" (5:13). "But solid food is for the *mature*" (5:14), our author declares. Thus, his readers need to "move beyond the elementary teachings about Christ" so they might "be taken forward to *maturity*" (6:1).

The New International Version agrees with most English translations when it renders the key word in 6:1 "maturity." Lying behind this gloss and the related adjective in 5:14 ("mature"), however, are a pair of Greek terms (*teleios, teleiotēs*) whose cognates elsewhere in the epistle normally translate as "perfect(ion)" (cf. 2:10; 5:9; 7:11, 19, 28; 9:11; 10:1, 14, 40; 12:2, 23). Given the abundance of human development terminology in our passage, the New International Version's rendering makes sense. Nonetheless, these key terms, together with the epistolary discourse of which they are a part, are intended to contribute to the author's larger theme about Christian perseverance and perfection.[1]

---

1. Harold W. Attridge, *Hebrews: A Commentary on the Epistle to the Hebrews*, Hermeneia

But how does the author conceive of Christian perfection? And why does he elevate his instructions about growing in perfection above concepts that modern believers often associate with mature Christianity—namely, "repentance," "faith in God," "cleansing rites, the laying on of hands, the resurrection of the dead, and eternal judgment" (6:1–2)? To answer these questions, we will compare what our passage says about human perfection to a related discourse in a contemporary Jewish text (the Community Rule) that instructs pious Israelites to "walk with perfection." We will then explore the theme of perfection elsewhere in Hebrews before explaining how our author uses this concept in our passage.

The Community Rule
"WALK WITH PERFECTION ON ALL THE PATHS OF GOD"

The Community Rule was one of the first and most important finds among the **Dead Sea Scrolls**. It is a **sectarian** document, written by and for a community (or communities) of devout Jews who fancied themselves to be stricter adherents of their ancestral faith than those belonging to what was considered mainstream Judaism. The rule has been transmitted to us in a dozen Hebrew copies discovered in the **Qumran** caves and is best preserved in the first-century BC manuscript known as 1QS, which will serve as our source text.

The Community Rule is significant for many reasons, not least because of its account of the organization and ideological outlook of the community (the Yahad) that produced the Dead Sea Scrolls. Sandwiched between its introduction (1.1–15) and concluding hymn (10.9–11.22), the document includes remarkable details about the Yahad's admission requirements (1.16–3.12), worldview (3.13–4.26), administrative structure (5.1–7.25), desert outpost plans (8.1–9.11), leadership qualifications (9.12–26a), and liturgical calendar (9.26b–10.8). For our purposes, we will highlight the community's basic beliefs and the rule's emphasis on "walking in perfection."

Basic Beliefs. The community responsible for producing this rule consisted of pious Jews who were critical of the priesthood at the Jerusalem temple. The Yahad considered themselves to be an **eschatological** remnant

---

(Minneapolis: Fortress, 1989), 163: "It would be a mistake to deny any connection between the maturity that the addressees are urged to attain and the perfection that Christ affords. Once again, our author is involved in his characteristically subtle word play."

who were faithful to God's commandments and were actively participating in the inauguration of the new **covenant** ("the covenant of kindness," 1.8).[2] They labeled themselves the "sons of light" (1.9; 2.16; 3.13, 24, 25) and believed their hearts had been enlightened (2.3; 4.2) by the "spirit of holiness" (3.7; 4.21; 9.3; cf. 3.8, 18, 25; 4.3–6) so that they might discern and do what is "good" (1.2; 4.26). These were a special people on whom God had "showered . . . his merciful favor" (2.1) and whom he had equipped with "intelligence, understanding, [and] potent wisdom which trusts in all the deeds of God and depends on his abundant mercy" (4.3–4).

The community also had deep convictions about eschatological judgment. As the rule's concluding hymn states, "To God (belongs) the judgment of every living being, and it is he who pays man his wages" (10.18; cf. 10.16). Indeed, at the final reckoning, the wicked will receive "eternal damnation by the scorching wrath of the God of revenges" (4.12), while the righteous receive nothing less than "eternal enjoyment with endless life" (4.7; cf. 11.16).

To be admitted to or reaffirmed in the Yahad, one had to undergo a process of purification. This included, among other things, the rite of ritual bathing, which represented repentance of sin, atonement by God's Spirit, and allegiance to Israel's law:

> [7] And it is by the holy spirit of the community, in its truth, that [the initiate] is cleansed of all [8] his iniquities. And by the spirit of uprightness and of humility his sin is atoned. And by the compliance of his soul with all the laws of God [9] his flesh is cleansed by being sprinkled with cleansing waters and being made holy with the waters of repentance. May he, then, steady his steps in order to walk with perfection [10] on all the paths of God, as he has decreed concerning the appointed times of his assemblies and not turn aside, either right or left, nor [11] infringe even one of all his words. In this way he will be admitted by means of atonement pleasing to God, and for him it will be the covenant [12] of an everlasting Community. (3.7–12)

If undergoing the rite of washing implied purity and participation in God's covenant people, then refraining from such rituals, either as a nonmember or departing member, implied spiritual contamination and rebellion against God's holy law.

---

2. Translations of the Community Rule are adapted from Florentino García Martínez and Eibert J. C. Tigchelaar, eds., *The Dead Sea Scrolls: Study Edition*, vol. 1 (Leiden: Brill, 1997).

[2.26] And anyone who declines to enter [the covenant of Go]d in order to walk in the stubbornness of his heart shall not [enter the Com]munity of his truth, since [3.1] his soul loathes the disciplines of knowledge of just judgments. . . . He shall not be justified while he maintains the stubbornness of his heart, since he regards darkness as paths of light. In the source of the perfect [4] he shall not be counted. He will not become clean by the acts of atonement, nor shall he be purified by the cleansing waters, nor shall he be made holy by seas [5] or rivers, nor shall he be purified by all the water of ablution. Defiled, defiled shall he be all the days he spurns the decrees. (2.26–3.5)

These basic beliefs and practices helped to define the Yahad over against outsiders, whether neighboring Jews or other communities. However, what made the community even more distinct, as we shall now see, was their strict adherence to the Mosaic law.

Perfection. As the above excerpts make clear, one of the essential membership requirements of the Yahad was "walk[ing] with perfection on all the paths of God" (3.9–10)—otherwise referred to throughout the rule as "perfection of behavior" (4.22; 8.10, 18, 21; 9.2, 9; 11.2), "perfection of his path" (5.24; 11.11), "perfect paths" (1.13; cf. 8.25; 10.21), or to "walk in/with perfection" (1.8; 9.6, 8, 19). Each of these phrases combines the Hebrew term "perfect(ion)" (*tamim*) with either "way" (*derek*) or "walk" (*halak*), or both in the case of 3.9–10. Altogether, the repetition of these varied constructions shows how significant the perfection discourse was for the Yahad.

According to the Community Rule, "walking in perfection" amounted to *flawless adherence to the Mosaic commandments.* Moreover, the phrase not so subtly stresses the personal responsibility of each member for their moral purity. To be sure, God is responsible for each member's obedience ("in his hand is the perfection of my behavior," 11.2; cf. 11.10–11). Nevertheless, members were obligated to commit to perfection and were held to account. Admission to the covenant was restricted to "all those who freely volunteer to carry out God's decrees . . . and walk in perfection in his sight, complying with all revealed things concerning the regulated times of their stipulations" (1.7–9). Thus, when a person entered the community, he was required to "swear with a binding oath to revert to the law of Moses, according to all that he commanded, with whole heart and whole soul, in compliance with all that has been revealed of it" (5.8–9). There was even a small group of elite, monastic members of the community for whom maintaining "perfection of behavior" was an even stricter requirement (8.1–9.11).[3]

Perseverance and Apostasy. Given the theological and covenantal significance of maintaining individual perfection, incentives were introduced for encouraging obedience and longevity. On the one hand, membership rank and status became dependent on one's degree of perfection: "And their spirit and their deeds must be tested, year after year, in order to upgrade [in rank] each one to the extent of his insight and the perfection of his path, or to demote him according to his failings" (5.24). Beyond this, consequences were imposed on those in known violation of communal policies and commandments. Minor infractions (e.g., interrupting a fellow member or inappropriate gesturing) resulted in a ten-day penalty, but more severe transgressions received one- or two-year suspensions. Apostasy by long-tenured members, on the other hand, resulted in permanent expulsion, presumably without any possibility for reinstatement: "anyone who has been in the Community council . . . for ten full years. . . . and whose spirit reverts to betray the Community and go away from the presence of the Many in order to walk in the stubbornness of his heart, can never return to the Community council" (7.24–26). An even stricter policy was enforced on the elite group: "All who enter the council of holiness of those walking in perfect behavior as he commanded, anyone of them who breaks a word of the law of Moses impertinently or through carelessness will be banished from the Community council and shall not return again" (8.21–23).

In sum, to be perfect according to the Community Rule is to separate oneself from mainstream Judaism—repenting of past sins, receiving ritual purification, and maintaining flawless obedience to the divine law as a member of the Yahad. Only then could a first-century Jew confidently hope to receive eternal life.

Hebrews 5:11–6:12

"LET US . . . BE TAKEN FORWARD TO MATURITY"

There are numerous points of contact between the Community Rule and Hebrews 5:11–6:12. Both texts focus on a new covenant community, and both envision the community to have developed beyond mainstream

---

3. John J. Collins, *Beyond the Qumran Community: The Sectarian Movement of the Dead Sea Scrolls* (Grand Rapids: Eerdmans, 2010), 69–75.

Judaism. Moreover, both texts address matters of perfection, perseverance, and apostasy. These latter points will concern us here.

Perfection. In our passage, the author of Hebrews chides his readers for their spiritual immaturity, noting that the "elementary teachings" they have thus far received are insufficient for advancement to "maturity/perfection" (6:1). Contrary to the Community Rule, Hebrews boldly claims that "the law made nothing perfect" (7:19). "The law is only a shadow of the good things that are coming—not the realities themselves. For this reason it can never, by the same sacrifices repeated endlessly year after year, make perfect those who draw near to worship" (10:1).

Instead, real perfection is applied only to Christ followers, and only because Jesus was perfected first. Jesus realized perfection as a consequence of his perseverance. Christ himself, though sinless (4:15), learned obedience and was made perfect through the suffering experienced in both his ministry and crucifixion (2:10; 5:7–9).[4] Having endured such shame, Jesus was raised to new life—his resurrection coinciding with his attainment of perfection, the status which then qualified him for appointment as eternal high priest.[5]

With Jesus installed in his heavenly priesthood, he was authorized to make a singular, everlasting, and all-encompassing atonement before taking his seat at God's right hand (10:10, 12). This once-for-all sacrifice presented in the heavenly tabernacle "has made perfect forever those who are being made holy" (10:14). Altogether, Christ's priestly work now allows those who share in his perfection (3:14) to enter, cleansed and with confidence, into the Most Holy Place to draw near to God (10:19–22).

It is this sort of "solid food" (5:12, 14)—this "teaching about righteousness" (5:13) that advances past "the elementary truths of God's word"

---

4. Some scholars argue that Jesus's exaltation and appointment to eternal high priesthood were prerequisites for his attainment of final perfection; see, e.g., David Peterson, *Hebrews and Perfection: An Examination of the Concept of Perfection in the 'Epistle to the Hebrews,'* SNTSMS 47 (Cambridge: Cambridge University Press, 1982); Kevin B. McCruden, "The Concept of Perfection in the Epistle to the Hebrews," in *Reading the Epistle to the Hebrews: A Resource for Students,* ed. E. F. Mason and K. B. McCruden (Atlanta: Society of Biblical Literature, 2011), 209–29; and Seth M. Simisi, *Pursuit of Perfection: Significance of the Perfection Motif in the Epistle to the Hebrews* (Eugene: Wipf and Stock, 2016), 149–55. However, the epistle does not clearly support such a view. Since perfection was a qualification for Jesus's high priesthood, it hardly makes sense for his priesthood also to have been necessary for his perfection. As 5:9–10 makes clear, it was only *after* Jesus suffered and was "made perfect" that "he became the source of eternal salvation for all who obey him and was designated by God to be high priest in the order of Melchizedek." See also the lengthy discourse on faith in resurrection and its climactic statement on being "made perfect" in Hebrews 11 (esp. 11:39–40).

5. David M. Moffitt, *Atonement and the Logic of Resurrection in the Epistle to the Hebrews,* NovTSup 141 (Leiden: Brill, 2011), 194–208; R. B. Jamieson, *Jesus' Death and Heavenly Offering in Hebrews,* SNTSMS 172 (Cambridge: Cambridge University Press, 2019), 23–35.

(5:12–13) and "beyond the elementary teachings about Christ" (6:1)—that Hebrews insists is necessary for training believers "to distinguish good from evil" (5:14). The basics of early Jewish theology—"The foundation of repentance from acts that lead to death, and of faith in God, instruction about cleansing rites, the laying on of hands, the resurrection of the dead, and eternal judgment," all of which we saw were doctrines and practices that adherents of the Community Rule embraced and believed distinguished them from covenant outsiders—are important though insufficient for those intent on realizing perfection.

Perseverance and Apostasy. Perfection, however, requires not only progressing beyond theological basics; it also demands faithful endurance. Hebrews praises its readers for their prior spiritual fruit, ensuring them that God "will not forget your work and the love you have shown him as you have helped his people and continue to help them" (6:10). Thus, it exhorts readers "to show this same diligence to the very end, so that what you hope for may be fully realized" (6:11). Warning against laziness, the sermon calls on its readers "to imitate those who through faith and patience inherit what has been promised" (6:12). The author probably has in view the scriptural heroes (11:1–40) and church leaders (13:7) to be discussed in the letter's finale. Foremost, however, he has in view Jesus himself (12:1–3), whom he has just stated "learned obedience from what he suffered" and was thereby "made perfect" (5:8–9). Perseverance through suffering, therefore, is precisely how perfection is embodied in the present, prior to its consummation at the believer's resurrection.

What readers must finally avoid, then, is apostasy. Just like the Yahad was warned not to forsake their covenant or violate God's law lest they receive expulsion and retribution, so our author alerts his readers, "It is impossible for those who have once been enlightened, who have tasted the heavenly gift, who have shared in the Holy Spirit, who have tasted the goodness of the word of God and the powers of the coming age and who have fallen away, to be brought back to repentance" (6:4–6). Whether the passage teaches that apostates lose their salvation or simply show their participation in Christ and the Spirit to have been inauthentic (cf. 3:1, 14; 6:4), the warning must be heeded. Apostasy is tantamount to re-crucifying Jesus (6:6) and leads to eternal judgment ("cursed," "burned," 6:8). These consequences seem severe, yet "God is not unjust" (6:10), and judgment is rooted in justice, as all who have received a proper "foundation" ought to know (6:2). The path, then, is clear for those aspiring to perfection—"Let us run with perseverance the race marked out for us, fixing our eyes on Jesus, the pioneer and perfecter of faith" (12:1–2).

For Further Reading

Additional Ancient Texts

The concept of perfection is found throughout the works of Philo. See especially *On Agriculture* 2.9, where Philo links the concepts of maturity, milk, and solid/perfect food. See also Wisdom of Solomon 4:13–15. These terms also occur elsewhere in the New Testament (1 Cor 3:1–4; 14:20; Eph 4:11–16; Phil 3:12–15; Col 1:28; Jas 1:2–4).

English Translations and Critical Editions

Charlesworth, James, ed. *The Dead Sea Scrolls: Rule of the Community and Related Documents (Hebrew, Aramaic, and Greek Texts with English Translations).* PTSDSSP. Tübingen: Mohr Siebeck, 1995.

Metso, Sarianna. *The Community Rule: A Critical Edition with Translation.* Early Judaism and Its Literature 51. Atlanta: Society of Biblical Literature, 2019.

Secondary Literature

Bateman, Herbert W., ed. *Four Views on the Warning Passages in Hebrews.* Grand Rapids: Kregel, 2007.

Brower, Kent E., and Andry Johnson, eds. *Holiness and Ecclesiology in the New Testament.* Grand Rapids: Eerdmans, 2007.

Hempel, Charlotte. *The Community Rules from Qumran: A Commentary.* Texts and Studies in Ancient Judaism 183. Tübingen: Mohr Siebeck, 2020.

_____. *The Qumran Rule Texts in Context: Collected Studies.* Texts and Studies in Ancient Judaism 154. Tübingen: Mohr Siebeck, 2013.

CHAPTER 8

Philo of Alexandria and Hebrews 6:13–20: The Purpose of the Divine Oath

DANA M. HARRIS

In many ways, the divine promises to Abraham are the backbone for much of Hebrews, and probably for even the entire Bible! These promises include descendants and land; they are first articulated in Genesis 12:1–7 and are subsequently developed whenever an apparent threat emerges to their fulfillment (e.g., Gen 13:14–17; 15:18–21; 17:1–21). Perhaps the greatest apparent threat was God's command to Abraham to sacrifice his son Isaac. Although Isaac was not Abraham's only son, he alone was the heir of the divine promises, since his conception represented faith in God's supernatural intervention (Gen 18:10–15; 21:1–7; cf. Gal 4:21–23). In this way Isaac was Abraham's unique son. His premature death would have thwarted the transmission of the promises to the next generation. Hence God's provision in Genesis 22:1–19 reveals the divine commitment to ensure the fulfillment of these promises.

The author of Hebrews was profoundly aware of the importance of the Abrahamic promises and their development in Genesis. He carefully distinguished between the promise of descendants (initially obtained with Isaac; Heb 6:15), and of land (unfulfilled until the city that is to come; Heb 11:10, 13). A key passage concerning the Abrahamic promises is Hebrews 6:13–20, where the author makes two key claims regarding God's promises to Abraham, drawing upon Genesis 22:15–18 (and its surrounding context): first, God ensures the fulfillment of his promises by swearing by himself (6:13–15); second, God's oath makes clear the unchanging nature of his purpose (6:16–17), so that the recipients of Hebrews might be greatly encouraged (6:18–20) and might persevere with faith and patience and thus obtain the promises (6:11–12). There are some noticeable parallels to these claims about God making oaths and promises in the writings of the Hellenistic Jewish philosopher **Philo** of Alexandria. Two passages in particular stand out: *Allegorical Interpretation* 3.203–208 and *On the Sacrifices of Cain and Abel* 91–96.

Philo of Alexandria

"AN OATH IS TO ASSIST FAITH"

The biblical account of Abraham, and especially the command to sacrifice Isaac, featured prominently in ancient Jewish writings. Discussion often focused on the divine oath and Abraham's paradigmatic faith.[1] The writings of Philo, however, present the most apparent parallels to Hebrews in this regard.

Allegorical Interpretation. One topic that Philo discusses is the nature of God's words and the apparent problem posed by the addition of a divine oath to those words. Since God's words could be understood to be just as binding as an oath, what was the purpose of the divine oath? Consider Philo's comments on the divine oath uttered in Genesis 22:16 in a three-volume work he wrote on the Pentateuch titled *Allegorical Interpretation (Alleg. Interp.).* After affirming that Abraham was "the perfect man," Philo quotes Genesis 22:16 and comments,

> [203] Good is it both that He confirmed the promise by an oath, and that He did so by an oath befitting God; you mark that God swears not by some other thing, for nothing is higher than He, but by Himself, who is best of all things. [204] Some have said, that it was inappropriate for Him to swear; for an oath is added to assist faith, and only God and one who is God's friend is faithful, even as Moses is said to have been found "faithful in all His house" [Num 12:7]. Moreover, the very words of God are oaths and laws of God and most sacred ordinances; and a proof of His sure strength is that

---

1. See the fuller discussion in James W. Thompson, *Hebrews*, Paideia Commentaries on the New Testament (Grand Rapids: Baker Academic, 2008), 125. Human oaths are discussed in Leviticus 5:4; 19:12; Numbers 6; 30:2–3; Deuteronomy 23:21–23; and Psalm 50:14; curses for swearing falsely occur in Deuteronomy 6:13 and Zechariah 5:3–4.

what He saith cometh to pass, and this is specially characteristic of an oath. (*Alleg. Interp.* 3.203–204)[2]

In this passage, Philo begins by observing that given that God wanted to confirm his promise with an oath, he could only swear by himself, because no one greater exists by whom he could swear (3.203). Philo notes that the reason why God added this oath was to assist human faith, presumably Abraham's, although this is not explicit. This is immediately followed by an emphasis on Moses's faith and status as God's friend.[3]

On the Sacrifices of Cain and Abel. In a second passage, *On the Sacrifices of Cain and Abel* (*Sacrifices*) 91–94, Philo again addresses the apparent problem of why God would even need to make an oath, here drawing upon Exodus 13:11–13:

> [91] But, when he [Moses] tells us that God swore an oath, we must consider whether he lays down that such a thing can with truth be ascribed to God, since to thousands it seems unworthy of Him. For our conception of an oath is an appeal to God as a witness on some disputed matter. But nothing is uncertain or open to dispute with God. [92] He it is who has shown to all others plainly the signs whereby they may know the truth. Truly he needs no witness, for there is no other God to be His peer. (*Sacrifices* 91–92)

Philo then claims that actually it was Moses who presented God as adding an oath: "Why then did it seem well to the Prophet and revealer to represent God as binding Himself by an oath? It was to convince created man of his weakness and to accompany conviction with help and comfort" (*Sacrifices* 94). This passage indicates Philo's discomfort with the idea that God should add an oath to his already irrevocable word, which he explains as divine accommodation to human weakness. This parallels Philo's argumentation in *Allegorical Interpretation* that the oath in Genesis 22:16 was added to assist human faith.

---

2. Translations of Philo are from the Loeb Classical Library. Elsewhere Philo comments, "Now men have recourse to oaths to win belief, when others deem them untrustworthy; but God is trustworthy in His speech as elsewhere, so that His words in certitude and assurance differ not a whit from oaths. . . . For the oath does not make God trustworthy; it is God that assures the oath" (*Sacrifices* 93).

3. Philo makes a similar argument in *On the Life of Abraham* 273, where he claims both that God gave the oath in Genesis 22:16 to Abraham because the latter was God's friend and that all God's words are understood to be oaths.

Hebrews 6:13–20

"GOD WANTED TO MAKE THE UNCHANGING NATURE OF HIS PURPOSE VERY CLEAR"

Hebrews 6:13–20 is the first extended discussion of Abraham in the epistle, although Abraham's descendants are briefly mentioned in 2:16 (where the author implies that the audience is the seed of Abraham). Yet the author has been carefully preparing for his discussion of Abraham. Hebrews 1 focuses on the Son's divinity, with Hebrews 2 focusing on his solidarity with those with whom he shares the same blood and flesh, described as Abraham's descendants. Hebrews 3 uses the faithfulness of Moses as a foil to the wilderness generation, whose faithlessness precipitated God's oath that they would not enter his promised rest in the land. This is followed by a presentation of the Son's faithfulness to endure obedience and suffering and thereby become the perfect high priest who is the source of eternal salvation in Hebrews 5. The author briefly touches upon the unique nature of the Son's priesthood in the order of Melchizedek (5:6, 10), only to interrupt himself and warn his audience about the dangers of their spiritual immaturity and failure to grow (5:11–6:8). This exhortation is followed by assurances concerning their salvation and the presentation of Abraham as the model of faith (6:9–12). The brief mention of Melchizedek also prepares for the focus on Abraham in Hebrews 6. Although Hebrews 5:6 and 5:10 draws upon the priesthood of Melchizedek in Psalm 110:4, Hebrews 7 focuses on the only other Old Testament passage where this enigmatic figure appears, namely, Genesis 14:17–20, which records Abraham's remarkable encounter with Melchizedek. In this way, the focus on Abraham in Hebrews 6:13–20 prepares for the subsequent discussion of Melchizedek in Hebrews 7:1–10.

The Divine Oath in Hebrews 6. In Hebrews 6:13–20, the author begins by commenting on the oath added to the Abrahamic promise in Genesis 22:16. (Notice how the word "promise" links the beginning of this passage to the end of the previous one.) Like Philo, the author of Hebrews notes that God could not swear by anyone greater than himself. Also like Philo, Abraham is the supreme example of persevering faith (Heb 6:15)—indeed, Abraham waited about twenty-five years for the promised birth of Isaac!

The focus on Abraham is followed in 6:16 by the statement of an apparently axiomatic truth: "People swear by someone greater than themselves, and the oath confirms what is said and puts an end to all argument." In their ancient context, the someone (or something) greater could be the Caesar, a deity, a pagan temple, or even the temple. This language echoes

Philo's comments in *On the Sacrifices of Cain and Abel* 92. Unlike Philo, however, Hebrews does not question or view negatively this apparent truism. Instead, the author of Hebrews presents an *a fortiori* (from lesser to greater) argument: If something is true of human beings, how much more is this true of God? Thus, Hebrews does not appear to find the fact that God swore an oath in Genesis 22:16 to be problematic—at least not in the same way Philo does. Furthermore, unlike Philo, the author of Hebrews does not indicate that the oath was some type of divine accommodation to assist human faith. Instead, the author of Hebrews states that "God wanted to make the unchanging nature of his purpose very clear to the heirs of what was promised" (Heb 6:17). In other words, the divine oath did not concern (Abraham's) faith, but rather an assurance of God's unchanging purposes for Abraham's descendants. Given the previous reference to Abraham's descendants in 2:16, the author of Hebrews has his current audience in view, although this assurance is certainly not limited to this original audience. It is also likely that the assurance from the divine oath in Genesis 22:16 was meant to contrast with the divine oath in Psalm 95:11, which is quoted in Hebrews 3:11 and applied to the audience in Hebrews 3 and 4. In Psalm 95, however, the divine oath is associated with judgment for the unbelief of the wilderness generation that prevented them from entering the land. Thus, the author may be intending an implicit comparison between these two divine oaths, which would add to the force of the divine oath in Genesis 22:16 (cited in Heb 6:14) to encourage his audience to persevere.

The function of the divine oath for the epistle's present audience is made explicit in Hebrews 6:18–20, where the author claims that the divine promise and oath (the "two unchangeable things in which it is impossible for God to lie") are for great encouragement. Once again, there is a certain overlap with Philo in the correspondence of God's word and oath, but (once again) this conjunction is not viewed negatively or in need of explanation. Instead, the author links the encouragement that comes from these "two unchangeable things" to a personified depiction of an objective hope that has already entered behind the veil of the heavenly sanctuary, where Jesus, the forerunner, has entered. The reference to Jesus as "a high priest forever, in the order of Melchizedek" anticipates the extended discussion of Melchizedek's priesthood in Hebrews 7, which is also associated with another divine oath—the one found in Psalm 110:4. Thus, the discussion of the divine oath and Abraham in Hebrews 6 prepares the way for the focus on Melchizedek and another divine oath in Hebrews 7.

Assessing the Relationship between Philo and Hebrews. Previously, there have been some scholars, such as Ceslas Spicq, who claimed direct dependence by the author of Hebrews on Philo's writings; some even suggest that the author of Hebrews knew Philo personally. Yet, although both Philo and Hebrews offer extended discussion on the nature of the divine oath, it is important to understand that they do so in very different ways. First, there is no indication in Hebrews that the divine oath was problematic. Second, according to the author of Hebrews, the divine oath in Genesis 22:16 was not given for Abraham's benefit but rather for his descendants (including but not limited to the original audience).

So how can we account for the similarities between these two authors and their discussion of the divine oath in Genesis 22? It is likely that the author of Hebrews was generally familiar with Philo's writings, having heard about them either directly or indirectly. It is also possible that Jews in Rome (the likely destination of Hebrews) either had heard about Philo's teaching or even had heard Philo himself teach when he was there in AD 38–40.[4] Finally, Philo and the author of Hebrews may have been influenced by a common conceptual background or framework that may have emerged from the Hellenistic Jewish community in Alexandria. Both authors seem to have been struck by the remarkable fact that God added an oath to his promise in Genesis 22:16. Even so, they saw different implications from this fact and drew different conclusions from it. In the end, the exact relationship between the two may not be satisfactorily determined, and that may not be ultimately important.

For Further Reading

Additional Ancient Texts

Several works by Philo discuss oaths in general: oaths make a disputed matter secure (*Dreams* 1.12); sworn oaths should be avoided but kept if made (*Spec. Laws* 2.2–8). The eternally enduring nature of God's oath is affirmed by Rabbi Eleazar in the Babylonian Talmud, tractate Berakhot 32a. Finally, several related topics are also considered in Philo's writings: the role of God as the unseen witness to human interactions (*Spec. Laws* 4.31); and the unchangeable nature of God's will (*Unchangeable*, e.g., 1.26; *Alleg. Interp.* 2.89).

---

4. See the discussion in Folker Siegert, "Philo and the New Testament," in *The Cambridge Companion to Philo*, ed. Adam Kamesar (Cambridge: Cambridge University Press, 2009), 178.

English Translations and Critical Editions

Colson, F. H. and G. H. Whitaker, trans. *Philo, with English Translation*. LCL. Cambridge, MA: Harvard University Press, 1929.

Yonge, Charles Duke, and David M. Scholer. *The Works of Philo: Complete and Unabridged*. New updated ed. Peabody, MA: Hendrickson, 1993.

Secondary Literature

Bekken, Per Jarle. "Philo's Relevance for the Study of the New Testament." Pages 226–67 in *Reading Philo: A Handbook to Philo of Alexandria*. Edited by Torrey Seland. Grand Rapids: Eerdmans, 2014.

Siegert, Folker. "Philo and the New Testament." Pages 175–209 in *The Cambridge Companion to Philo*. Edited by Adam Kamesar. Cambridge: Cambridge University Press, 2009.

Sowers, Sidney G. *The Hermeneutics of Philo and Hebrews: A Comparison of the Interpretation of the Old Testament in Philo Judaeus and the Epistle to the Hebrews*. Richmond, VA: John Knox, 1965.

Thompson, James W. *Hebrews*. Paideia Commentaries on the New Testament. Grand Rapids: Baker Academic, 2008.

Williamson, Ronald. *Philo and the Epistle to the Hebrews*. Leiden: Brill, 1970.

CHAPTER 9

11QMelchizedek and Hebrews 7:1–10: The Heavenly Melchizedek

ERIC F. MASON

ebrews 7:1–10 functions as a pivotal link in the overall argument of the Epistle to the Hebrews, connecting the earlier presentations of Jesus as the divine Son and great high priest with the subsequent focus on the nature and implications of his self-sacrifice. In this passage (and in chapter 7 more broadly) the author finally explains an important phrase he has enticingly dangled before his audience in previous chapters: that Jesus is "a priest forever, in the order of Melchizedek."[1] This phrase—which is quoted in Hebrews 5:6; 6:20; 7:17, 21—is from Psalm 110:4 (LXX 109:4).[2] While language from verse 1 of that royal psalm (likely addressed originally to a Davidic king in ancient Israel) is utilized frequently elsewhere in the New Testament, only the author of Hebrews quotes from verse 4.

Discussion of Melchizedek is extremely sparse in the entire biblical tradition. Beyond Hebrews and two passages in the Hebrew Bible (with only slight differences in the Septuagint versions), he is mentioned nowhere else in the New Testament, nor does he appear in any book of the **Apocrypha** or **deuterocanonicals**, despite the fact that some interpreters have sought to link him to the priestly figures who exercised political (and eventually royal) roles in the **Maccabean** and **Hasmonean** eras. As

---

1. Other English translations render the Greek more literally as "according to the order" (CSB, NAB, NRSV) or "after the order" (ESV, KJV, RSV) of Melchizedek.

2. It is possible that the Hebrew wording of Psalm 110:4 could have been read differently by some ancient Jews, who, for example, may have understood "Melchizedek" (which in Hebrew means "my king is righteous") not as a personal name but as a description of a righteous king.

addressed below, however, he is mentioned in several Jewish texts from the **Second Temple period** that were not ultimately included in either the Jewish or Christian Bibles.

The only other reference to Melchizedek in the Hebrew Bible (apart from Ps 110:4) appears in an awkward scene describing his mysterious encounter with Abram (later called Abraham) in Genesis 14:18–20. Abram had returned from battle, in which he (with the men of his household) had rescued his nephew Lot by defeating a coalition of kings who earlier had plundered numerous cities, including Sodom and Gomorrah. One reads in Genesis 14:17 that the king of Sodom traveled to meet the victorious Abram; in 14:21–24 the king asked Abram to give him the people he had liberated but to keep the goods he had recovered. Abram declined the latter, lest he appear financially indebted to the king, and he agreed only that his men should keep their share of the spoils. The scene between Abram and the king of Sodom reads smoothly if one skips directly from 14:17 to 14:21. This prompts most scholars to assume that the contents of 14:18–20—about a mysterious encounter between Melchizedek and Abram instead—are a later insertion into the narrative.

Whereas the reader of verse 17 expects Abram to meet the king of Sodom in the next verse, that is delayed until verse 21. Instead, in verse 18 "Melchizedek king of Salem," who is also "priest of God Most High," appears abruptly. He "brought out bread and wine," and he pronounced God's blessing on Abram (14:19–20). The Hebrew of verse 20 concludes with the comment that "he" gave "him" one-tenth of an undefined quantity. Most interpreters (and English Bible translators) infer from the context that Abram gave a tithe of his war spoils to the king-priest. Melchizedek then disappears completely from the narrative, as the scene promptly shifts back to Abram's conversation with the king of Sodom and the *other* discussion about the recovered wealth in 14:21–24.

When one considers this meager biblical precedent for discussion of Melchizedek, the comments the author of Hebrews makes about the figure in Hebrews 7:1–10 are stunning. Not only does the author playfully argue for the superiority of Melchizedek to the Levitical priesthood on the basis of his creative deductions about the priest-king's encounter with Abraham in Genesis 14:18–20, but he also finally elaborates on what it means that Jesus has a priesthood "in the order of Melchizedek" (NRSV). That discussion engages the remainder of chapter 7 and opens an extended series of comparisons of Jesus (including his priestly work and self-sacrifice in the heavenly sanctuary of the "new **covenant**") with the Levites (and their "old covenant" priesthood and animal sacrifices in the earthly sanctuary) that constitutes most of Hebrews 8–10.

Perhaps the most perplexing comment comes in Hebrews 7:3, where the author says of Melchizedek, "Without father or mother, without genealogy, without beginning of days or end of life, resembling the Son of God, *he* remains a priest forever" (emphasis added).[3] As discussed below, it soon becomes clear in the text of Hebrews 7 *why* the author says what he does about Melchizedek—this occurs chiefly to highlight similar assertions about Jesus that are explained in 7:11–28. But one might also ask *how* the author could say such things about Melchizedek himself. To answer this question, we will consider how the portrait of Melchizedek in Hebrews compares with other Second Temple Jewish discussions of the figure, especially as he is presented in a text from the **Dead Sea Scrolls** called 11QMelchizedek.

11QMelchizedek

"The end of the tenth jubilee, in which atonement is made for . . . the men of the lot of Melchizedek"

The Manuscript, Contents, and Structure. The manuscript 11QMelchizedek (11Q13) is a thematic pesher, an interpretative text on an **eschatological** theme in which the author wove together biblical citations from various sources.[4] The only surviving copy of this Hebrew text was discovered among the Dead Sea Scrolls in 1956, and it was first published in 1965. The fragments (between ten and fifteen, depending on how they are counted) preserve portions of three columns of text, likely from the end of the composition, but only the second of these three columns is substantially intact with twenty-five relatively complete lines. The manuscript likely dates to the first half of the first century BC, though some argue for the second century BC.[5]

The author's pattern was to present an initial biblical text for consideration, to read this in light of one or more additional passages, then to elaborate on the fulfillment of the combined texts under the influence of yet

---

3. Other translations include "but" (NRSV) or "thus" (NABRE) before "resembling" (or its equivalent), reflecting a Greek conjunction that the NIV omits.

4. See Shani L. Berrin, "Pesharim," *EDSS* 644–47.

5. For discussion of these matters, see esp. Florentino García Martínez, Eibert J. C. Tigchelaar, and Adam S. van der Woude, eds., "13. 11QMelchizedek," *Qumran Cave 11, II (11Q2–18, 11Q20–31)*, DJD 23 (Oxford: Clarendon, 1998), 221–41, and pl. 27, esp. 221–23.

another passage. Three cycles can be discerned in column 2, and each cycle appears to engage allusions from Isaiah 61:1–3 in the fulfillment exposition. Lines 2–9 concern Leviticus 25:13 with Deuteronomy 15:2; lines 10–14 concern Psalm 82:1 and both Psalm 7:8–9 and Psalm 82:2; and lines 15–25 concern Isaiah 52:7 and both Daniel 9:25 and Leviticus 25:9.[6]

The Heavenly Melchizedek as Angelic Warrior-Priest. Most (but admittedly not all) scholars understand the extant portion of this text to present Melchizedek—presumably intended as the figure from Genesis 14 and Psalm 110—as an angelic warrior-priest who brings God's eschatological deliverance for the righteous and judgment on the wicked as the fulfillment of these scriptural passages.[7] The first cycle (lines 2–9) begins with scriptural quotations about the Year of Jubilee, return of property, and forgiveness of debts. It then moves to an interpretative fulfillment in the context of a climactic tenth Jubilee period, which begins with a proclamation of freedom for returning "captives" who are identified as the "inheritance" (or "lot") of Melchizedek (II, 4–5; cf. II, 8): "He will proclaim to them an emancipation to release them [from the burden of] all their sins, and [thus] this word [will come to pas]s in the first week of the jubilee after [the] ni[ne] jubilees" (II, 6–7).[8] This tenth Jubilee appears to conclude with Melchizedek's priestly action: "And [the] d[ay of atonem]ent i[s] the end of [the] tenth [ju]bilee, in which atonement is made for all the Sons of [Light and] the me[n of] the lot of Mel[chi]zedek . . . upon [the]m . . . accord[ing to all] their [work]s, because it (is) the time for the year of favor for Melchize[de]k" (II, 7–9).

The Heavenly Melchizedek as Judge. In the second cycle (lines 10–14), the scriptural texts present God acting as judge in a council of gods (or other heavenly beings; Ps 82:1) along with other biblical admonitions for judgment. In the interpretation, however, Melchizedek fills the judicial role of God expressed in the psalm and is said to be assisted by "all the divine

---

6. I have examined 11QMelchizedek and other Second Temple period understandings of Melchizedek more fully in other publications, esp. Eric F. Mason, *'You Are a Priest Forever': Second Temple Jewish Messianism and the Priestly Christology of the Epistle to the Hebrews*, STDJ 74 (Leiden: Brill, 2008), 138–90.

7. Other suggestions for the identity of "Melchizedek" in this text include the Davidic Messiah, the archangel Michael, Yahweh or else the angel of Yahweh, the Logos, a divine human, or an undefined "king of righteousness."

8. Brackets appear in the translations to indicate that they reflect scholarly reconstructions of very fragmentary texts. Unless otherwise noted, translations of 11QMelchizedek are those of J. J. M. Roberts, "Melchizedek (11Q13=11QMelchizedek=11QMelch)," in *The Dead Sea Scrolls: Hebrew, Aramaic, and Greek Texts with English Translations*, vol. 6B, Pesharim, Other Commentaries, and Related Documents, ed. J. H. Charlesworth et al. (Louisville: Westminster John Knox; Tübingen: Mohr Siebeck, 2002), 264–73.

beings . . . all the sons of God" over whom he presides in the assembly (II, 14–15). He "will exercise the veng[ea]nce of the judgments of Go[d]" on "Belial" (or Satan) and the wicked. In the third cycle (lines 15–25), the scriptural texts concern a messenger of peace and salvation and a coming anointed leader. Unfortunately, the text is very fragmentary in the key lines 19–24; scholars debate whether Melchizedek is the messenger here, but he likely is the anointed one and may also be called "God" (using the same Hebrew word for God in Psalm 82:1) in line 24.

Overall, the impression in this text is that Melchizedek is a heavenly— likely angelic—figure with priestly duties of proclamation and atonement who serves on behalf of God and is identified intimately with God.

Hebrews 7:1–10

"RESEMBLING THE SON OF GOD, HE REMAINS A PRIEST FOREVER"

The author of Hebrews finally turns in chapter 7 to explain what it means that Jesus is a priest in (or according to) the order of Melchizedek. Although Melchizedek was mentioned earlier in the text in quotations of Psalm 110:4, and this remains the key verse in Hebrews 7, the author's creative interpretation of Genesis 14:18–20 to support his explanation of Jesus's priestly role is prominent.

Melchizedek as Superior to the Levitical Priests. The chapter begins in 7:1–2 with a brief summary of Melchizedek's encounter with Abraham, followed by etymological ruminations on his name and title that are comparable to similar speculations of **Josephus** (*J.W.* 6.438; *Ant.* 1.180) and **Philo** (*Alleg. Interp.* 3.79). And, moving next to genealogical musings in 7:4–10, the author playfully proclaims the superiority of Melchizedek over the Levitical priests on the basis of his bestowal of blessings on and reception of tithes from Abraham. According to the author's logic, because Abraham is the ancestor of Levi, who himself is the ancestor of the Levitical priests, Abraham's deference to Melchizedek with tithes therefore implies that Levi himself (symbolically present already in Abraham's "body" in the NIV, literally "loins") also participates in the patriarch's act (7:6, 10). The point is to elevate Melchizedek as superior to the Levitical priests, who themselves are authorized by the Jewish law to collect tithes from other descendants of Abraham (7:5). But there is another key difference between Melchizedek and the Levitical priests: while the latter are mortal,

Melchizedek is someone "who is declared to be living" (7:8). This takes us back to 7:3.

The Heavenly Melchizedek as Superior to the Levitical Priests. The language in 7:3 is stunning: "Without father or mother, without genealogy, without beginning of days or end of life, resembling the Son of God, he remains a priest forever." Virtually all interpreters agree that a *major* reason the author describes Melchizedek this way is to relate these lofty attributes to Jesus. Whereas in Hebrews Jesus is usually said to be like Melchizedek (as in the Ps 110:4 quotations), here Melchizedek is presented as "resembling the Son of God." But many scholars are hesitant to relate other things in this acclamation to the figure of Melchizedek himself. The statements instead are deemed yet more examples of Hebrews' exegetical creativity, grounded in a Jewish interpretative tradition that things (here details about Melchizedek's origin and destiny) not explicitly stated in the Torah do not exist. But the statements are explicitly presented in Hebrews as attributes of Melchizedek *himself,* and these declarations about his lack of genealogy, origin, or end are reminiscent of Hellenistic philosophical discussions about characteristics of a deity.[9] Also, the twin affirmations that Melchizedek lacks a (priestly) genealogy and yet is an eternal priest undergird the way the author explains his use of Psalm 110:4 in the rest of Hebrews 7. Jesus, like Melchizedek, is superior to the Levitical priests: both are priests not through physical descent but "on the basis of the power of an indestructible life" (7:16; cf. 7:24, 28). So, for the author of Hebrews, Jesus is "a priest forever" like Melchizedek not only because he is not Levitical but especially because he is eternal.

Thus, the author appears to understand Melchizedek as sharing certain nonhuman characteristics with Jesus, but not to the extent that he becomes a competitor. Perhaps the author of Hebrews thinks of him as angelic, with heavenly rather than human origins and characteristics. We read nothing else about Melchizedek in Hebrews: he has served his exegetical purpose in Hebrews 7, and then the author turns to discuss Jesus's superiority over the Levitical priests and their sacrificial system. Admittedly, legitimate questions remain about how *precisely* the author of Hebrews understood Melchizedek. Yet we should also note that 11QMelchizedek demonstrates that another interpreter in the broader world of Second Temple period Judaism could also think of him in heavenly, angelic terms. This is not to say that the author of

---

9. See esp. Jerome H. Neyrey, "'Without Beginning of Days or End of Life' (Hebrews 7:3): Topos for a True Deity," *CBQ* 53 (1991): 439–55.

Hebrews would agree with *everything* the author of 11QMelchizedek says about the figure (or vice versa), but rather that they might agree on the particular idea that he was a heavenly, angelic priest.

FOR FURTHER READING

Additional Ancient Texts

Melchizedek's portrait in 11QMelchizedek may be supported by understandings of Melchizedek in two other very fragmentary **Qumran** texts that must be heavily reconstructed, but it differs significantly from the presentation in many other Second Temple period texts. Songs of the Sabbath Sacrifice (especially 4Q401 11 3; 4Q401 22 3; 11Q17 3 II, 7) may present Melchizedek as a heavenly priest—perhaps even head of the entire angelic priesthood, maybe in the context of eschatological warfare. Elsewhere, the namesake of Visions of Amram (4Q543–549, but especially 4Q544 3 IV, 2–3), the grandson of the priestly progenitor Levi, dreams of two angelic figures fighting over him. The lines that identify the two figures are very poorly preserved, but the standard reconstruction identifies the protagonist as one figure variously called Michael, the Prince of Light, and Melchizedek. The later (and much-debated) text of 2 Enoch (69–73) also takes a speculative approach to Melchizedek but moves in different directions.

The more common view of Melchizedek in Second Temple period texts, however, presents him as the mortal priest-king of Genesis 14:18–20. Josephus (*J.W.* 6.438; *Ant.* 1.179–81), Philo (*Abraham* 235; *Prelim. Studies* 99; *Alleg. Interp.* 3.79–82), Pseudo-Eupolemus (in Eusebius, *Praep. ev.* 9.17.5–6), and the Genesis Apocryphon (1QapGen ar XXII, 12–17) provide numerous creative (and for Philo, allegorical) retellings of his encounter with Abraham with little to no corresponding interest in Psalm 110:4. As noted above, the author of Hebrews also seemed to know these kinds of traditions; so, too, the author of Jubilees (13:25), though there is a gap in that account where one would expect Melchizedek's name.

English Translations and Critical Editions

García Martínez, Florentino, Eibert J. C. Tigchelaar, and Adam S. van der Woude, eds. "13. 11QMelchizedek." Pages 221–41 in *Qumran Cave 11, II (11Q2–18, 11Q20–31)*. DJD 23. Oxford: Clarendon, 1998.

Kobelski, Paul J. *Melchizedek and Melchireša'*. CBQMS 10. Washington, DC: Catholic Biblical Association of America, 1981.

Roberts, J. J. M., ed. "Melchizedek (11Q13=11QMelchizedek=11QMelch)." Pages 264–73 in *The Dead Sea Scrolls: Hebrew, Aramaic, and Greek Texts with English Translations*. Vol. 6B, Pesharim, Other Commentaries, and Related Documents. Edited by James H. Charlesworth et al. Louisville: Westminster John Knox; Tübingen: Mohr Siebeck, 2002.

Secondary Literature

Dalgaard, Kasper. *A Priest for All Generations: An Investigation into the Use of the Melchizedek Figure from Genesis to the Cave of Treasures*. Copenhagen: Faculty of Theology, 2013.

Mason, Eric F. *'You Are a Priest Forever': Second Temple Jewish Messianism and the Priestly Christology of the Epistle to the Hebrews*. STDJ 74. Leiden: Brill, 2008.

Chapter 10

The Damascus Document and Hebrews 7:11–28: Messianism and the Aaronic High Priesthood

Dominick S. Hernández

S ystemic problems within the Aaronic high priesthood produced a dilemma for first-century Jewish people, according to the author of Hebrews. On the one hand, the Torah depicts God providing the people of Israel a sacrificial system that required the exclusive involvement of Levitical priests to mediate between the community and God (Lev 8; Num 3:6–51; 8:5–19). On the other hand, these priests time and again grappled with the same imperfections as those for whom they interceded. This problem vexed Israel and, time and again, derailed them from properly carrying out their divinely ordained system of religious practice throughout their history.

Thereby hangs a tale.

The struggle of the priesthood to maintain good standing as an intermediator is exemplified through the eventual forefather of all high priests, Aaron (Exod 28–29; cf. Lev 8–9), and the infamous scandal in which he crafted the golden calf idol for Israel to worship at the base of Mount Sinai (Exod 32:1–8). This notorious narrative in the Torah presages other acts of impropriety that were to come through the lineage of Aaron. Aaron's two sons, Nadab and Abihu, also high priests, were enigmatically slain by God for offering unlawful fire before the Lord (Lev 10).

The inability of the Aaronic high priesthood to mediate perfectly on behalf of its community was particularly conspicuous on Yom Kippur (the annual Day of Atonement), when the high priest was commanded to offer sacrifices for his own misdeeds prior to offering atonement on behalf of the people (Lev 16:5–6, 11). The Aaronic high priest was, in essence, counted as a guilty party and, thereby, a provisional and blemished intermediator. Thus, the very instructions of Yom Kippur insinuate that consummate intercession on behalf of the people could not occur between the Aaronic mediators and God. For ideal mediation to be possible, a more exceptional priesthood needed to arise that would no longer require the high priest to make offerings for himself prior to interceding for the people.

Given the unsettling incidents that were caused by the behavior of members of the Aaronic high priesthood (e.g., Eli's household in 1 Sam 2:12–36), the paragon of the high priesthood was not likely to arise from the lineage of Aaron. This suggestion, however, is problematic for the ancient Israelites and the later Jewish community, since no person from any tribe other than Levi could serve as priest, and only those priests from Aaron's lineage could function in the capacity of high priest within the cultic system ordained by God. Since the imperfections of the Levitical priesthood—and more specifically, of the Aaronic high priesthood—were plainly detailed in the Torah's narrative, it is no surprise that the writer of Hebrews indicates that Jesus appeared as a high priest within a different class—namely, the order of Melchizedek (Heb 5:1–10).

In Hebrews 7 the author returns to the priesthood of Melchizedek, and in 7:11–28 specifically contrasts the Aaronic high priesthood with the sublime order of Melchizedek. In doing so, the author explicitly addresses a theological problem of his day—that is to say, the idea that Jesus could serve as the ultimate high priest as a descendant of Judah and not Levi. Nevertheless, not all Jewish people in Israel during the late Second Temple period argued for an upgrade in the Aaronic priesthood. The elevation of the new Melchizedekian priesthood above the Aaronic priesthood reflects a view of the Aaronic priesthood that seems to be incongruous with the opinion that was accepted by the community responsible for the Damascus Document. While the writer of Hebrews asserts that the Aaronic priesthood is flawed and thereby in need of replacement by a more perfect order, the Damascus Document reflects a high view of a messianic figure from Aaron's lineage who would ultimately participate in improving their community's circumstances. Briefly reviewing the optimism relating to an Aaronic messiah in the Damascus Document helps to illustrate how the writer of Hebrews thoroughly emphasizes the necessity for the Aaronic priesthood to be superseded by the order of Melchizedek.

The Damascus Document
"A MESSIAH OF AARON AND ISRAEL"

A plethora of documents were found in the caves near the Qumran settlement in the 1940s–50s. However, the primary section of one of these compositions was found in a neighboring country and attained prominence for having been discovered prior to the famous breakthrough on the northwest shore of the Dead Sea. In the late 1890s, Solomon Schechter came upon what later became known as the Damascus Document while researching the illustrious Cairo Geniza documents.[1] Schechter believed the work to be a product of Zadokites (i.e., perhaps the "Sadducees") and thus, published it in 1910 in a book titled *Documents of Jewish Sectaries, Vol. 1: Fragment of a Zadokite Work*.[2] When the Dead Sea Scrolls were later discovered following the Second World War, several other fragments of the Damascus Document were found among them, dating to approximately the first century BC, thereby vindicating Schechter's understanding of this work to be an ancient Jewish text.[3]

A Priestly Community. Curious readers may question why the conventional name of the composition bears the location "Damascus" (Syria), given that it was discovered in Cairo (Egypt) and further recovered at Qumran (Israel). The answer can be found in column 6, lines 2–5, of Cairo manuscript A (CD 6.2–5) and bears weighty implications with regard to how the Qumran community perceived themselves to be a devoted remnant of the people of God who faithfully interpreted and adhered to the Torah: "They are the penitents [lit. 'returners'] of Israel who depart from the land of Judah and dwell in the land of Damascus" (see also 7.15, 19; 8.21; 19.34).[4] The dedicated among the sect relocated from Judah and came into "the new covenant in the land of Damascus" (CD 6.19; cf. 8.21; 20.12). In Damascus the religious group was able to live properly in community and practice the true religion of Israel, "to offer up the holy

---

1. For the impact of the Cairo Geniza documents, see Adina Hoffman and Peter Cole, *Sacred Trash: The Lost and Found World of the Cairo Geniza* (New York: Schocken, 2016).

2. Reprinted by Ktav Publishing House in 1970 with a prolegomenon by Joseph A. Fitzmyer.

3. The abbreviation CD represents the two "Cairo Damascus" documents (manuscripts A and B) that were found in the Egyptian *geniza* (i.e., a repository for Hebrew documents, especially for those that contain the divine name). The typical numbering of the Dead Sea Scrolls is used when citing from the fragments that were found in the caves by the Qumran settlement (e.g., 4Q266–73 or 4QD^a-h; 5Q12; 6Q15). The numbering of the texts and fragments in this chapter is adopted from Joseph L. Angel, "Damascus Document," in *Outside the Bible: Ancient Jewish Writings Not Included in Scripture* (vol. 3), ed. L. H. Feldman, J. L. Kugel, and L. H. Schiffman (Philadelphia: Jewish Publication Society, 2013), 2975–3035.

4. All translations of the Damascus Document are my own, carried out with attentive consultation with the translations listed at the end of this essay.

things according to their interpretations, to love each man his brother like himself, to strengthen the hand of poor, destitute, and foreign [people] . . . and to seek each man the peace of his brother" (CD 6.20–7.1). Irrespective of whether the toponym "Damascus" literally refers to the environs of the Syrian capital or is a symbolic allusion to another locale (e.g., Qumran), these passages clarify both the document's current name and the Qumran community's view of themselves as the supreme interpreters and practitioners of the Torah during their time.

A Priestly Messiah. In addition to the belief that their interpretations and practice of the law were superior to their contemporaries, the Qumran sect was convinced that they lived in an era during which wickedness temporarily reigned. However, they espoused that the period of wickedness would end upon the arrival of an eschatological messianic period. This hope is implied at the beginning of the Damascus Document, which, though fragmentary, appears to communicate a fundamental purpose of the composition— namely, for "the 'Sons of Light' [i.e., the sectarian community] to keep apart from the way[s of wickedness] until the completion of the appointed time for visitation upon [wickedness]" (4QD^a 1 a–b 1). The inauguration of the messianic age would bring the iniquity and religious treachery of those outside of the community to an end (cf. 4.8–9; 6.10, 14; 15.7; 4QD^f 2 12).

The Qumran community believed that it would ultimately be vindicated in a messianic age featuring a messiah of Aaron and Israel. The Damascus Document states, "And this is the rule of the settlement of the camps, those who walk in them during the era of wickedness until the arising of a messiah of Aaron and Israel" (CD 12.22–13.1). The connection between the priesthood of Aaron and the concept of a messiah (i.e., "anointed one") stems from the consecration of Aaron as high priest of Israel through the application of oil on his head, which illustrated that he was an anointed intermediary (Lev 8:12). This action contributed to the belief that the messiah would be a uniquely anointed, priestly figure. The idea that there would be a twofold messiah, or even perhaps two messiahs, is seemingly derived from the sectarians' interpretation of Numbers 24:17, which states, "A star will come out of Jacob; a scepter will rise out of Israel." The star that was to come from Jacob was interpreted by the community as a priestly messianic figure ("a messiah of Aaron"), whereas the scepter apparently represented a prince who prefigured a royal messiah of Israel.[5]

---

5. Angel, "Damascus Document," 3024. Compare, for example, the reference to the messianic "star" of Numbers 24:17 in CD 7.18–20 and Revelation 22:16.

Several admonitory passages of the Damascus Document corroborate the hope that a messiah of Aaron would participate in realizing eschatological, divinely appointed retribution upon those who do not honor God's commands in contrast to those "poor of the flock" who properly keep the divine ordinances: "These [i.e., the poor of the flock] will escape in the era of visitation. But the remaining ones will be handed over to the sword in the coming of a messiah of Aaron and Israel" (CD 19.9–10, Genizah B).

There is another reference to a messiah of Aaron and Israel in the fragmentary concluding remarks of CD 14. This segment asserts that the Damascus Document consists of the precepts by which the community was to be governed during the age of wickedness until the advent of a messiah from Aaron and from Israel: "And this is the meaning of judgments by which . . . [they shall be judged] until the [coming of a mess]iah of Aaron and of Israel, and their iniquity will be atoned" (CD 14.18–19). The final portion of this reference, if understood properly, is particularly relevant to the study of Hebrews because it seems to suggest that the Qumran community combined an eschatological atonement for sin with the advent of a messiah from the high priestly line of Aaron. The author of Hebrews apparently develops this expectation as it relates to Jesus the Messiah. Hebrews validates the Torah's staging of a priestly intermediator while also presenting the necessity of a high priesthood that transcends the mediation of the lineage of Aaron.

Hebrews 7:11–28

"A PRIEST FOREVER, IN THE ORDER OF MELCHIZEDEK"

The transfer of the Levitical high priesthood from the lineage of Aaron would presumably have been revolutionary to the Jewish community of the late Second Temple period. Jewish people revered the law, and the priesthood prescribed therein was essential to the administration of the divinely ordained cult from the inception of their people. Thus, the only way to alter such a fundamental aspect of the rituals prescribed in the Torah would be for God to assert divine prerogative. This is precisely what the author of Hebrews claimed God did when declaring that Jesus was appointed as a priest according to the superior order of Melchizedek by a divine oath (Heb 7:12; cf. 5:6, 10; 7:18).

A Priest of a Superior Order. Jesus descended from the royal tribe of

Judah (Matt 1:3; 2:6; Luke 3:33) and, according to the law, was not appointed to serve as a priest since the Torah made no mention of the descendants of Judah functioning in this capacity (Heb 7:12–14). Jesus was in a position to carry out the royal messianic expectations that were seemingly in vogue during the late Second Temple period as a descendant of Judah (Rev 5:5; 22:16; cf. Gen 49:10; 1 Sam 7:14; Isa 11:1). However, the presumption that a messianic Aaronic priest could have emerged from the tribe of Judah would have been utterly illegitimate (cf. 2 Chr 26:18–20; Exod 30:1–10; Num 16:40).

The fact that the Torah does not permit members of the tribe of Judah to serve as priests introduces a problem for early Christians: if Jesus was unauthorized to serve as a priestly intermediator between humankind and God, then it was not proper for him to offer any type of sacrifice that could benefit humankind's standing before God. How could believers in Jesus—and especially early Jewish believers in Jesus—claim that he served in a priestly function and offered the ultimate sacrifice once and for all for the forgiveness of sin (cf. Heb 7:27; 10:10)?

As if expecting this objection, the author of Hebrews immediately presents a solution that was forecast in the Hebrew Scriptures. Jesus is a priest of a *superior order to that of Aaron*—a divinely appointed order that was foreshadowed but never fully realized until Jesus's advent. Jesus is a priest *according to the order of Melchizedek*, which is a priesthood not based on ancestry but, rather, inextricably linked to the power of Jesus's indestructible life (Heb 7:16).

Whereas the mention of Jesus's indestructible life might prompt the expectation of a discussion related to Jesus's resurrection power (cf. 1 Cor 15:12–58), the topic of Hebrews 7 abruptly shifts to a citation of Ps 110:4 and reconsiders Melchizedek: "You are a priest forever, in the order of Melchizedek." To understand this rhetorical maneuver, it is necessary to briefly trace the personage of Melchizedek and the imagery derived from this mysterious figure.

Genesis 14 bears curious language relating to Melchizedek's identity. The narrator indicates that Melchizedek was a priest of the Most High God while simultaneously functioning as the king of Shalem (or Salem). The Hebrew word *Shalem* relates to the idea of being at "peace," and is closely related to the commonly known Hebrew word *shalom*, meaning "peace, wholeness." Genesis 14:18–20 briefly presents a scene in which a tithe is offered between the Israelite forefather Abraham and Melchizedek. In the literary context of Genesis, it is unclear who offers the tithe and who receives it, given that the Hebrew text ambiguously states, "and he gave to him a tenth of everything."

Later, Psalm 110:4 presents Melchizedek as an exalted figure, but it is not until Hebrews 7:4 that readers are explicitly informed that Abraham tithed to Melchizedek. The fact that Abraham tithed to Melchizedek, king of Salem, who simultaneously functioned as king and priest, demonstrates that the seed of Abraham is inferior in its function of priest (and king) to this curious figure (Heb 7:4–10). However, the power of Jesus's indestructible life displays that he could uniquely fulfill the roles of both priest (and king) forever, like the exalted personage, Melchizedek. None of the former priests attained this credential. Jesus established perfect mediation, unlike the Aaronic priesthood, and rendered inoperative the former regulations for the priesthood, so that through him human beings might draw near to God (Heb 7:19; cf. 4:16; 7:25; 10:1, 22; Jas 4:8).

An Eternal Priesthood. Jesus's Melchizedekian appointment transcends the flesh and blood connection to an imperfect, temporary priesthood that was subject to death like all other humanity. Because of Jesus's eternal life, he is able to constantly intercede on behalf of the people who approach God through him (Heb 7:23–25). In this manner, Jesus became the guarantor of the better, everlasting covenant that was established by his work as the Melchizedekian high priest who spilled his own blood as the utmost sacrifice (Heb 9:23–26).

Whereas the Aaronic high priest was "able to deal gently with those who [were] ignorant and [were] going astray, since he himself [was] subject to weakness" (Heb 5:2), Jesus was able to empathize with human weakness in every way yet remained without sin (Heb 2:17; 4:15). Not needing to sacrifice for his own sin, and himself being the only perfect sacrifice, Jesus functioned in the role of high priest and sacrifice, offering himself once and for all. Therefore, Jesus, who was appointed to the Melchizedekian high priesthood by divine oath, who lived a perfect life, who perfectly carried out the cultic responsibilities of ancient Israel, who is the exact representation of God, is worthy of veneration (Heb 7:27; cf. Heb 1:3; Eph 5:2; Col 2:9).

Conclusion. The Torah-observant Jewish community responsible for the Damascus Document believed that they were entering into a new covenant by properly obeying the law in Damascus until the messianic age, in which a messiah of Aaron and of Israel would appear and rectify their predicament. The writer of Hebrews recast this line of thinking by detailing the miraculous credentials making Jesus the perfect, if unexpected, Messiah. Jesus the Messiah arrived from the royal line of David and jointly carried out the priestly role that was anticipated by some people during his day by serving as the ultimate high priest according to the sublime order of

Melchizedek. All who come to God through the person and work of Jesus, the Melchizedekian high priest, will not endure the judgment during the eschaton but rather be united with Jesus (Heb 9:28). Jesus is the most excellent facilitator of the new covenant, bridging the gap between humankind and God by emerging from a new order and sealing the covenant with his blood (Luke 22:20).

FOR FURTHER READING

Additional Ancient Texts

A survey of some of the other extrabiblical texts that were found in Qumran will provide a fuller sense of the messianic expectation of the Qumran community: The Community Rule (1QS 9:11) also mentions a messiah of Aaron and Israel; 4QFlorilegium (4Q174), 4Q252, and 4Q285 allude to the Branch of David as a messianic figure; 11QMelchizedek (11Q13) apparently endows this enigmatic personage with a divine nature.

The University of Cambridge Digital Library has high-resolution images of both MS A of the Damascus Document (https://cudl.lib.cam.ac.uk/view/MS-TS-00010-K-00006/1) as well as MS B of the Damascus Document (https://cudl.lib.cam.ac.uk/view/MS-TS-00016-00311/1).

English Translations and Critical Editions

Angel, Joseph L. "Damascus Document." Pages 2975–3035 in *Outside the Bible: Ancient Jewish Writings Not Included in Scripture*. Vol. 3. Edited by Louis H. Feldman, James L. Kugel, and Lawrence H. Schiffman. Philadelphia: Jewish Publication Society, 2013.

Baumgarten, Joseph. *Qumran Cave 4. XIII: The Damascus Document (4Q266–273)*. Discoveries in the Judean Desert 18. Oxford: Clarendon, 1996.

Cook, Edward. "The Damascus Document." Pages 49–74 in *The Dead Sea Scrolls: A New Translation*. Edited by Michael Wise, Martin Abegg Jr., and Edward Cook. New York: HarperCollins, 1996.

García Martínez, Florentino, and Eibert J. C. Tigchelaar. *The Dead Sea Scrolls Study Edition*. Vol. 1, pages 551–627. Leiden: Brill, 1997.

Secondary Literature

Collins. John J., *The Scepter and the Star: Messianism in Light of the Dead Sea Scrolls*. 2nd ed. Grand Rapids: Eerdmans, 2010.

Hempel, Charlotte. *The Damascus Texts*. Companion to the Qumran Scrolls 1. Sheffield: Sheffield Academic, 2000.

_____. *The Laws of the Damascus Documents: Sources, Tradition and Redaction.* STDJ 29. Leiden: Brill, 1998.

Novenson, Matthew V. *The Grammar of Messianism: An Ancient Jewish Political Idiom and Its Users.* Oxford: Oxford University Press, 2017.

Wacholder, Ben Zion. *The New Damascus Document: The Midrash on the Eschatological Torah of the Dead Sea Scrolls: Reconstruction, Translation, and Commentary.* STDJ 56. Leiden: Brill, 2007.

CHAPTER 11

The Damascus Document and Hebrews 8:1–13: The New Covenant

RADU GHEORGHITA

Hebrews 8 stands at a pivotal turn in the epistle's argument. "Now the main point of what we are saying is this" (8:1) suggests both a summary of the preceding exposition and a transition to the climactic stages still to be presented. The opening verses, 8:1–2, link the chapter to other key passages, namely 4:14–16 and 10:19–22. Like the discernible subject in a musical fugue, all three passages restate in similar fashion the main theme of the epistle: Jesus, the exalted Son at the right hand of God, is the high priest of the new **covenant** people. He opened a pathway for them into God's presence and summons them to approach God with confidence. Though the Son's coregency emerges in other passages (e.g., 1:13; 12:2), these three summaries, strategically placed, form the structural backbone of the epistle.

Hebrews 8 also plays a significant thematic role in the epistle's thought. Throughout the middle section (7:1–10:19), the author addresses the foundational components of Judaism: *the Levitical priesthood, the first covenant,* and *the Mosaic law.* He asserts boldly that in the wake of Jesus's life and ministry, these three pillars needed to be reassessed. Each one had been found deficient and in need of a radical upgrade. Their systemic interrelationship also required a recalibration under a "new order" (9:10). He expresses his assessment in syllogistic fashion. When he ponders, "If perfection could have been attained through the Levitical priesthood" (7:11), he affirms implicitly that the *priesthood* could not offer perfection. Similarly, when he asserts, "For if there had been nothing wrong with that first covenant" (8:7), he underscores the faulty nature of the *first covenant.* As to *the law,* his phrasing is akin to saying, "If the law had been the reality of the good things," implying that it was only a shadow (10:1).

Starting with Hebrews 8, the author turns his attention to the Mosaic covenant, specifically to an assessment of its status. If God found something at fault with that covenant, was it still an operating, valid covenant? Alternatively, if a replacement had to be found, what should be put in its place? To answer these questions, the author focuses on one key prophetic oracle of Scripture, which he interprets in light of the completed work of Christ. Barely a century prior to the writing of Hebrews, in the Judean desert another community wrestled with the same cardinal issue and invoked similar axioms and terminology to describe their position with regard to the Mosaic covenant.

The Damascus Document

"THOSE WHO ENTERED THE NEW COVENANT IN THE LAND OF DAMASCUS"

The paucity of references to the new covenant in the **Second Temple Jewish** literature has long been acknowledged. The most notable exception is the collection of writings associated with the **Dead Sea Scrolls**. Martin Abegg lists approximately 250 occurrences of "covenant" in the **sectarians'** writings.[1] Among them, the Damascus Document provides the highest tally, with about one-sixth of all the references.[2] It is also, with the exception of Pesher Habakkuk (1QpHab), the only writing that uses the phrase "new covenant," a concept of paramount importance in Hebrews. The Damascus Document (CD) is a constitutive document for the community of the covenant. While the content is primarily devoted to exhortations, admonitions, and the community laws, it also delves sketchily into the history of the community and its understanding of God's plan for Israel.[3]

God's Covenant with the Forefathers. The references reveal a close

---

1. Martin Abegg et al., *The Dead Sea Scrolls Concordance: The Non-Biblical Texts from Qumran*, vol. 1 (Leiden: Brill, 2003). The literary data and the theological profile of the sectarian's understanding of covenant have been analyzed thoroughly. See esp. Craig A. Evans, "The Covenant in the Qumran Literature," in *The Concept of the Covenant in the Second Temple Period*, ed. S. E. Porter and J. C. R. de Roo (Leiden: Brill, 2003), 55–80; and Martin G. Abegg, "The Covenant of the Qumran Sectarians," in *The Concept of the Covenant in the Second Temple Period*, ed. S. E. Porter and J. C. R. de Roo (Leiden: Brill, 2003), 81–97.

2. The Damascus Document was discovered a half century earlier in the Cairo Geniza, from where it derives its name, the Cairo Damascus Document (CD); see also, Cecilia Wassen, "Damascus Document," in *T&T Clark Encyclopedia of Second Temple Judaism*, vol. 1, ed. D. Gurtner and L. Stuckenbruck (London: T&T Clark, 2020), 143–47.

3. Joseph A. Fitzmyer, *A Guide to the Dead Sea Scrolls and Related Literature* (Grand Rapids: Eerdmans, 2008), 189–90.

similarity between the Jewish Scriptures and the sectarian's understanding of covenant. The Damascus Document repeatedly refers to it as "God's/his covenant" (1.17; 3.11), instituted (4.9) and protected by God (19.1), and as reflecting God's faithfulness toward his people (19.2).[4] From "the very beginning" (1.4), the covenant was established with "the forefathers" (8.18), but in time it had been extended to include "all Israel" (15.9). This covenant was enacted through the "agency of Moses" (15.8), gathering the people already bound by the "Abrahamic covenant" (12.11). The people's responsibility was obedience to the covenant laws and regulations, mindful of the covenantal blessings and curses. The covenant, resilient and lasting forever (3.4), had to be reenacted periodically. By means of an oath (15.6), the Israelites took upon themselves annually the responsibility of obedience and adherence to the covenant's demands.

The Covenant Renewed. Against this backdrop, there are four explicit references to the "new covenant," a concept that holds a unique place in the sectarian's understanding of the covenant (CD 6.19; 8.21; 19.33; 20.12). The new covenant is always qualified as the covenant in the "land of Damascus" (e.g., "those who entered the new covenant in the land of Damascus," 8.21), making the two notions virtually synonymous.

The exact nature of the Damascus covenant, hence, of the sectarians' new covenant, continues to be disputed.[5] The emerging picture suggests a conceptual overlap between the periodic renewal of the Mosaic covenant and the Damascus covenant. As E. J. Christiansen correctly observes, "the term 'new covenant' is never opposed to an 'old covenant.' Consequently, the 'new covenant' cannot be understood simply as replacement of an old covenant."[6] The language seems to imply that the Mosaic covenant needed restoration, not abolition. Michael Knibb even suggests that the CD in its final form "was intended for use at the annual ceremony of the renewal of the covenant."[7]

The implicit similarities between the Mosaic covenant and the Damascus covenant likewise suggest renewal rather than replacement. For example, the unfaithful members who reject the Damascus covenant are described in terminology reserved for those who forsook the Mosaic covenant. Similarly,

---

4. All translations of the Cairo Damascus Document are my own unless stated otherwise.

5. E. J. Christiansen, "The Consciousness of Belonging to God's Covenant," in *Qumran between Old and New Testaments*, ed. F. H. Cryer and T. L. Thompson (Sheffield: Sheffield Academic, 1998), 82–84.

6. Christiansen, 83.

7. Michael A. Knibb, *The Qumran Community* (Cambridge: Cambridge University Press, 1987), 14.

any transgression of either covenant had severe consequences on Israel's commonwealth: the people, their kings, and their land (3.9–11).[8] Most compellingly, the idea of covenant renewal is suggested by the fact that God's punishment for covenantal unfaithfulness, terrible as it was, triggered the very opportunity for a renewal movement, the emerging of a remnant with whom God was about to renew the covenant.[9]

Hebrews 8:1–13

"THE COVENANT OF WHICH HE IS MEDIATOR IS SUPERIOR TO THE OLD ONE"

While it is difficult to conclude unequivocally whether the sectarians considered the new covenant a brand-new covenant or, most likely, a (periodically) renewed Mosaic covenant, Hebrews settles the matter with less ambiguity. In Hebrews the new covenant is inseparably linked with the prophetic oracle in Jeremiah 31 (LXX Jer 38) and its fulfillment in Christ. Unlike the sectarian writing, which offers only a meager lexical point of contact to the passage,[10] Hebrews quotes the prophecy twice in its central exposition as it explores Jeremiah's meaning in light of the **Christ event**.[11]

Two Covenants Contrasted. The terminology indicates that the author develops an argument based on a contrast between two covenants. One of them, the "first covenant" (8:7), is the mosaic covenant, the covenant God "made with their ancestors" (8:9). It stands in contrast to the "eternal covenant" (13:20), the **eschatological** covenant whose mediator is Christ (8:6). The contrast is accentuated by another pair of opposites: the "new covenant" (8:8; cf. 12:24), which stands in opposition to the "old covenant"—inferred from "what is obsolete" (8:13). The new covenant is also the "better

---

8. Evans, "Covenant in the Qumran Literature," 58.

9. Evans, 58. The Habakkuk pesher adds one important dimension. The new covenant is associated with the activity of the Teacher of Righteousness, whose rejection was condemned as a covenant break and an insult to God's holy name.

10. The Cairo Damascus Document's dependence on the Jeremiah passage is debated; see Evans, "Covenant in the Qumran Literature," 59. The name of the prophet Jeremiah is mentioned in 8.20, right before the damage at the bottom of the page. Any inference is at best tentative; see Harold Attridge, "The Epistle to the Hebrews and the Scrolls," in *When Judaism and Christianity Began*, vol. 2, ed. A. Avery-Peck et al. (Leiden: Brill, 2004), 315–42.

11. The LXX Jeremiah passage enables a middle point between the Hebrew *beryt* (CD and MT) and the Greek *diathēkē* (LXX and Heb.). For a thorough review of the textual traditions and variants, see Gert J. Steyn, *A Quest for the Assumed LXX Vorlage of the Explicit Quotations in Hebrews* (Göttingen: Vandenhoeck and Ruprecht, 2011), 248–72.

covenant" (7:22), not least because it is established on the "better promises" (8:6) foretold by Jeremiah.

The New Covenant Inaugurated. The essential nature of the new covenant, however, resides not in these descriptive epithets but in the reality inaugurated by Jesus the **Messiah**, the originator, mediator, and perfecter of the new covenant. The function of the quotation in Hebrews 8 is to associate inextricably the new covenant foretold by Jeremiah with the person and ministry of Jesus.

A notable feature in the Jeremiah passage is the conglomeration of future verbs. The first two—"I will make" (8:8) and "I will establish" (8:10)—set the framework for the new covenant, while the others—"I will . . . write" (8:10), "I will be" (8:10), "they will be" (8:10), and "they will . . . know" (8:11)—reveal its features. Three other verbs in the Greek text—one participle ("put," 8:10) as well as two double negative subjunctives ("no longer will they teach," 8:11; and "will remember . . . no more," 8:12)—all carry future force. The future-oriented passage did not escape the theological acumen of the author, a biblical interpreter bent on exploring the eschatological implications of biblical prophecy.[12] These verbs may be grouped in four verbal pairs, set in synonymous parallelism, which unpack the essential aspects of the new covenant.

1. "I will put my laws in their minds // and write them on their hearts" (8:10a)
2. "I will be their God // they will be my people" (8:10c)
3. "No longer will they teach . . . or say . . . 'know the Lord' // because they will all know me" (8:11)
4. "For I will forgive their wickedness // and will remember their sins no more" (8:12)

Space allows for only a cursory analysis. The opening pair, "I will put my laws in their minds and write them on their hearts" (8:10a), designates the locus where God grafts his law under the new covenant. This act marks an inner transformation that enables the member of the new covenant to do God's will. Christ himself exemplified and patterned this principle, especially in his resolve to do God's will. The essence of the incarnation is Christ's determination "to do your will, my God" (10:7). The epistle's closing

---

12. G. B. Caird, "The Exegetical Method of the Epistle to the Hebrews," *Canadian Journal of Theology* 5 (1959): 44–51.

prayer extrapolates the same principle to include all the believers, by petitioning God to enable them "for doing his will" (13:21).

The second pair, "I will be their God, and they will be my people" (8:10c), stands theologically at the very core of the new covenant. While the covenantal relationship between God and the people was equally foundational under the Mosaic covenant, Hebrews interprets the new covenant as an allegiance built on faith, not ethnicity.[13] Already Hebrews 2 introduces the family formed around the Messiah no longer as an ethnic concept but as a faith-, trust-, and worship-based alliance. The constitutive pattern is Jesus's filial relationship to God, described in similar terms: "I will be his Father, and he will be my Son" (1:5).

The following pair addresses the importance of the knowledge of God: "No longer will they teach their neighbor, or say to one another . . . because they will all know me" (8:11). The new covenant broadens the scope of this knowledge, encompassing with "me" the person of the Son, the very imprint of God's character and the radiance of God's glory (1:3). Moreover, the new covenant knowledge of God is no longer limited to ethnic Israel; the neighbor, no less than the brother, will know God.

The fourth pair, "For I will forgive their wickedness and will remember their sins no more" (8:12), receives the lengthiest attention. It underlines the most developed exposition of the high-priestly ministry of Christ. The forgiveness promised under the new covenant rests on the unique competence of Jesus as high priest. He ensures a quality of forgiveness, holiness, and perfection that was simply unachievable under the first covenant. God's willingness to show mercy and to forgive sins are corollaries of the new covenant, revealing that which is "new" in the "new covenant." The stipulations of this covenant are vastly superior because of the unique person and work of the high priest. Unlike the weak and prone-to-sin Aaronic high priest of the first covenant, the new covenant boasts a sinless, perfect high priest. Unlike the repeated sacrifices and offerings under the Mosaic covenant, this high priest offers one sacrifice, "once for all" (10:10). Unlike a covenant ratified with blood of sacrificed animals, this covenant is put into effect by the blood of the high priest, the Offeror who offers his own blood. Unlike the man-made sanctuary in which the ritual was performed, the high priest of the new covenant entered the heavenly tabernacle. Unlike a sacrificial

---

13. Though the Jeremiah passage in Hebrews 8 mentions the "house of Judah and the house of Israel," the reprise in Hebrews 10 leaves out the references, implicitly annulling the ethnic boundaries of the new covenant.

system unable to perfect the conscience of the worshiper, the one perfect sacrifice of the new covenant accomplished precisely that.

In their own way, the Damascus Document and Hebrews are theological reflections on "matters related to God," among which the new covenant holds a unique role. While there are similarities between the two perspectives, theologically the two documents could not be further apart. Their authors as well as the addressees appeal to the new covenant concept in order to define their community's relationship to God and to live with the responsibilities and the privileges attached therein. For the sectarian community, the qualifier "new" belongs to the realm of "renewal," a return to the original, restored covenant. For the author of Hebrews, that approach was not only against the grain of the Jewish Scriptures but also contrary to the unparalleled work of God in the person of the Son. He inaugurated the new covenant by his sacrificial death and thus established that which is radically "new" in the "new covenant." After all, there is something new under the sun. To reject this new covenant, to turn away from it, to ignore it, to minimize it, or to abandon it, is the gravest possible offense against God.

FOR FURTHER READING

Additional Ancient Texts

While the new covenant language is absent, the Community Rule (1QS), in its various installments, offers a parallel treatment of the covenant theme among the sectarians' writings. The hymnic material 1QH^a sets the theme of the covenant within the context of the liturgical prayers and praises of the community. The Habakkuk pesher 1QpHab is particularly helpful for reconstructing the triadic relationship between the community, the new covenant, and the Teacher of Righteousness. As to the New Testament, the synoptic parallels (Matt 26:26–29; Mark 14:22–25; Luke 22:17–20) and the Pauline Corinthians correspondence (1 Cor 11:23–32; 2 Cor 3:7–18) stand alongside Hebrews as prime expositions of the new covenant theme.

English Translations and Critical Editions

Garcia Martínez, Florentino, and Eibert J. C. Tigchelaar, eds. *The Dead Sea Scrolls: Study Edition*. Vol. 1. Grand Rapids: Eerdmans, 1997.

Eisenman, Robert. "The Damascus Document." Pages 355–78 in *The Dead Sea Scrolls and the First Christians: Essays and Translations*. Edison, NJ: Castle, 2004.

Secondary Literature

Christiansen, Ellen Juhl. "The Consciousness of Belonging to God's Covenant." Pages 69–97 in *Qumran between the Old and New Testaments*. Edited by F. H. Cryer and T. L. Thompson. Sheffield: Sheffield Academic, 1998.

_____. "Covenant Conditions and Ritual Boundaries in the Temple Scroll and the Damascus Document." Pages 104–44 in *The Covenant in Judaism and Paul*. Leiden: Brill, 1995.

Davies, Philip R. *Damascus Covenant. An Interpretation of the "Damascus Document."* Sheffield: Sheffield Academic, 1983.

Knibb, Michael A. "The Damascus Document." Pages 13–76 in *The Qumran Community*. Cambridge: Cambridge University Press, 1987.

Lehne, Susanne. *The New Covenant in Hebrews*. London: T&T Clark, 1990.

Porter, Stanley E., and Jacqueline C. R. de Roo, eds. *The Concept of the Covenant in the Second Temple Period*. Leiden: Brill, 2003.

Talmon, Shemaryahu. "The Community of the Renewed Covenant: Between Judaism and Christianity." Pages 3–24 in *The Community of the Renewed Covenant*. Edited by E. Ulrich and J. C. VanderKam. Notre Dame, IN: University of Notre Dame Press, 1994.

CHAPTER 12

Philo of Alexandria and Hebrews 9:1–10: The Passing and the Permanent

KENNETH L. SCHENCK

While the sermon we call Hebrews has many enigmatic features, it is clear that its author was arguing for the superiority of Christ over all Levitical means of atonement. The exact reason for this argument is somewhat elusive. Assuming the author was a man, he clearly wished to bolster his readers' faith in Christ. Some think he was trying to dissuade them from relying on the still standing Jerusalem temple in some way. Others think he was consoling them in the absence of the temple after it had been destroyed. Whatever the case, he went about his argument by demonstrating the superiority of Christ's atonement to any Levitical means of being right with God.

Hebrews constructs this argument in three key ways. It argues that Jesus is (1) a superior high priest, (2) who brought a superior sacrifice and offering, (3) into a superior sanctuary. Hebrews 7 and 8 present Jesus as a superior priest who is in the order of Melchizedek, which the author argues is superior to the Levitical priesthood. Then much of Hebrews 9 and 10 address Christ's death and heavenly offering as superior to the "blood of bulls and goats" (e.g., Heb 10:4).

Hebrews 9:1–10 is the passage where the author begins to unfold the superiority of the heavenly sanctuary to any earthly one. He has already introduced the topic in the previous chapter (8:1–6). Interestingly, he does not talk about the Jerusalem temple. Instead, he goes back to Exodus when Israel had a portable "tent" or "tabernacle" in the desert. He indicated that from the very beginning, that earthly sanctuary was only meant to foreshadow and point to the *real* sanctuary in heaven (8:5), where Jesus offered his sacrifice (9:24).

The beginning of Hebrews 9 dives into greater detail. What is interesting is that the author does not merely present a literal analysis of the wilderness tabernacle. He considers the two rooms of the tabernacle to be a "parable" of two ages of time (9:9). The first, outer room of the tent represents the present age that is passing away with its never-ending earthly sacrifices. The second room represents the once-and-for-all sacrifice and offering of Jesus.

This "parabolic" treatment of the wilderness tabernacle reminds us a little of **Philo of Alexandria**, a Jewish thinker and commentator of the Pentateuch who lived in Alexandria, Egypt, at the very time that Jesus lived. Philo interpreted the Jewish law extensively by way of allegory, where various aspects of the biblical text were taken to be symbolic of other concepts, and the tabernacle served his thinking well. While he was far more prone to allegory than any New Testament author, he offers a helpful backdrop to the interpretation of Hebrews in these verses, not least because Hebrews' language about the tabernacle at least superficially resembles Philo's.

Philo of Alexandria

"THOSE THINGS WHICH ARE BELOW HEAVEN ARE MUTABLE AND CHANGEABLE"

Philo seems to have written or at least started three great commentary series during his lifetime. One, called *The Exposition of the Law,* aimed at the entry-level reader. It stayed fairly close to the literal or surface meaning of biblical texts in the Jewish law. Another series was *Allegorical Commentary.* It unfolded hidden and symbolic meanings Philo and others saw in the text, often connecting main passages of interest in Genesis to other texts in the Pentateuch and beyond. A third series, from which the least has survived, was *Questions and Answers.* As one might expect, it uses a question-and-answer format. It delves deeply into allegorical meanings as well but is much less extensive in scope than the *Allegorical Commentary.* Philo's treatment of Exodus in this third work will be our focus.

The Tabernacle as Allegory. Since Exodus 25–27 gives instructions on the wilderness tent and its equipment, it is interesting to compare this section of *Questions and Answers on Exodus* (2.51–106) with Hebrews 9:1–10. In particular, *Questions and Answers on Exodus* 2.83 asks, "What is the tabernacle?" Philo has several perspectives on the wilderness sanctuary that Israel had before they entered the promised land. First, he accepted the literal sense of the book of Exodus. He believed Israel really did have a tent that God gave them instructions to build and that Israel took it around with them in the desert as they wandered for forty years.

However, Philo also agreed with many other Jews that the tabernacle had symbolic and allegorical meanings. For example, like others he believed that the tabernacle symbolized the cosmos, as evidenced in his words "The highest temple and the temple of God in truth . . . is the whole universe, having as its sanctuary the most holy part of existence of the things that exist, namely, heaven" (*Spec. Laws* 1.66). Still another perspective on the tabernacle, more unique to Philo, was that the heavenly tabernacle represented a very particular type of pattern that the earthly tabernacle copied. For Philo, the heavenly tabernacle was a Platonic archetype, an ideal sanctuary of which the earthly tent was only a copy and a shadow.

Plato was a philosopher who lived about four hundred years before the New Testament. He taught that the world we see and touch around us is not the most real world. Rather, the real world is a world of ideas and patterns that we can contemplate with our minds. The material world around us is only a copy and shadow of that ideal world. Looking at Exodus 25:40, Philo applied this understanding to the Exodus tabernacle: "See that you make them according to the pattern shown you on the mountain" (cf. Heb 8:5). The earthly tent, he believed, was a shadowy copy of the heavenly ideal.

The Two Rooms. Combining his Platonism with his penchant for allegory, Philo also found hidden significance in the various items in the tabernacle. In *Questions and Answers on Exodus* 2.83, he believed the ark of the covenant represented the heavenly world of ideas, the world we know through our minds, a world without bodies. It is a world that does not change. It is clear from his responses to other questions (*QE* 2.68; 2.94) that he considered the innermost chamber of the tent, the Most Holy Place, to relate especially to the ideal realm.

By contrast, the outer room, the Holy Place, has items that represent the world of our senses. The table of presentation especially represents the world of our senses (cf. *QE* 2.69). The lampstand, also in the outer room, represents the visible heavens (cf. *QE* 2.73; 2.95), with each lamp representing a different planet. In the outer chamber and beyond, we move to the realm of those things that are below the moon, things made of the four basic substances—earth, air, fire, and water. The veil symbolically separates the two realms from each other (cf. *QE* 2.91, 94).

One key difference between the inner and outer chambers of the tabernacle is that the inner chamber represents that which does not change. It symbolizes the unchanging ideal truths on which everything else is based. By contrast, the outer room represents all that is mutable and changeable in the visible world. In fact, the portable tabernacle of Israel as a whole embodies the transitory and passing nature of this visible world. "For the tabernacle is a portable temple of God and not a stationary or fixed one. And (similarly) those things which are below heaven are mutable and changeable, while heaven alone is unchangeable and self-consistent and similar to itself" (QE 83).

We immediately see at least some superficial similarities between Philo's interpretation of the wilderness tabernacle and that of Hebrews. Hebrews also sees the earthly tabernacle as a shadow, perhaps even a copy of a heavenly "archetype" or pattern. Both the writer of Hebrews and Philo invoke Exodus 25:40—they even quote the verse in the same unique way. Both give a sense that the earthly realm involves the transitory and ever-changing while Christ's actions are once and for all and unchanging (e.g., Heb 7:27). The question is whether these similarities are merely superficial or more substantial.

Hebrews 9:1–10

"THIS IS AN ILLUSTRATION FOR THE PRESENT TIME"

Hebrews alternates between "teaching" (exposition) and "preaching" (exhortation). As this sermon approaches its middle, we get the central and most pointed warning to the audience in 5:11–6:12. The author gives a stern warning that the audience may not be able to return if they walk away from Christ at this point. That admonition then gives way to the central exposition of the book in 7:1–10:18, where the author gives them the key theological reason for not giving up. Hebrews 7 is where we learn about Jesus as a superior priest. Hebrews 8 talks about the superior covenant he has inaugurated. Then we reach the verses on which we are focusing, Hebrews 9:1–10, where the argument explores in more depth the nature of the heavenly sanctuary and sacrifice.

The Two Tents. The first paragraph, 9:1–5, lays out the basic structure of the earthly sanctuary. The wilderness tabernacle had two rooms, an outer one known as the holies or Holy Place. Then it had an inner room known as the holy of holies or Most Holy Place. What is intriguing about Hebrews' presentation of this structure is that the original Greek text does not talk about *rooms* but about two *tents*. The Old Testament refers to the whole structure as a tent, but Hebrews speaks of these two rooms as two tents with two curtains. This is a key observation if we are to understand the verses that follow.

"The first tent" of Hebrews 9:2 is what we might more normally call the first room of the whole tabernacle. It is the room in which we find the lampstand, the table of presentation with bread always kept on it. Then the "second tent" after the "second curtain" leads to the Most Holy Place in which Hebrews places the altar of incense and the ark of the covenant (9:4). Interestingly, while Exodus seems to locate the altar of incense in the outer room (Exod 30:6–7), Hebrews places it in the Most Holy Place in the "second tent."

After laying out the structure of the two "tents," Hebrews 9:6–7 describes the function of that structure. The priests went into "the first tent" throughout the year, accomplishing their appointed service (9:6). Only the high priest was permitted to go into "the second tent" and only once a year (9:7). On that day, the Day of Atonement, the high priest took blood into the Most Holy Place to offer it on behalf of himself and the people of God who had committed sin in ignorance.

The Tabernacle as Allegory. Now the author comes to the point. This two-tent structure is a parable. The Holy Spirit is revealing a message through the structure and operations of these two tents. The way into the Most Holy Place only becomes apparent when the "first tent" has lost its standing. The New International Version has translated this comment as "as long as the first *tabernacle* was still functioning" (9:8) and thus moves in a different direction from the one that seems most obvious from the train of thought. The NIV switches its sense of the word "tent" from what it has been throughout the chapter so far—the first room of the tabernacle—to the "tabernacle" as a whole. However, the context gives us no indication of such a switch.

The train of thought thus pushes us to think that Hebrews is building an allegory of the two parts to the wilderness tabernacle. The author seems to be saying that the "first tent," the outer room of the sanctuary, is a parable or "illustration" for this present age. Accordingly, the "second tent" or inner room represents the age that Jesus inaugurated with the new covenant. This present age is passing away. In this age, gifts and sacrifices are constantly being offered, but they are not able to clear the conscience of a person or truly take away sins (9:9; 10:4). They are just "ceremonial washings" and "external regulations" (9:10).

By contrast, the "new order," the time of the new covenant, involves actual cleansing of sins through the blood of Christ (10:10, 14). Whereas the first covenant involved the continual offering of ineffective sacrifices, the new covenant involves a once-and-for-all offering of Christ. This point follows closely on the fact that priestly activity was continual in the outer room but only occurred once a year in the inner sanctum. The first covenant only foreshadowed the real atonement through Christ. It involved priestly activity on earth, while Christ entered heaven itself (9:24).

When we follow the "two tent" train of thought in Hebrews 9:1–10, we find that Hebrews has made an allegory of the sanctuary's structure not unlike the ones Philo makes. Philo, of course, has his own unique concerns and interpretations. While Hebrews uses language that sounds vaguely Platonic (e.g., Heb 8:5), any similarity seems rather superficial upon closer examination. The majority of interpreters also do not interpret the heavenly sanctuary of Hebrews in a cosmological sense (as Philo did), although some do.

Nevertheless, the form of Philo's allegories is not dissimilar to that of Hebrews. For example, *Questions and Answers on Exodus* does align the inner room with the unchanging and the outer room with the transitory. We do not know whether the author of Hebrews interpreted other elements of the sanctuary allegorically as well. He makes the oblique comment that "we cannot discuss these things in detail now" (9:5). It is at least possible that he means he could expand on their allegorical significance but simply does not have space in the sermon to do so. Although the nature of the tabernacle in Hebrews remains a matter of debate, the similarities to Philo may support a more metaphorical approach to Hebrews' tabernacle imagery. Rather than a literal structure in heaven, Hebrews uses varying metaphors of a heavenly tabernacle to demonstrate that an earthly sanctuary is no longer necessary.

FOR FURTHER READING

Additional Ancient Texts

For other places where Philo discusses the sanctuary, see *On Planting* 50; *Who Is the Heir?* 75; *On Dreams* 1.215; *On the Special Laws* 1.66–79. Josephus also knew the cosmological interpretation of the temple: *Jewish War* 5.213–18; *Jewish Antiquities* 3.123, 181–83. See also the Wisdom of Solomon 9:8–10; 18:24. For Paul's metaphorical use of the temple, see 1 Corinthians 3:16–17; 6:19.

English Translations and Critical Editions

Philo. Translated by F. H. Colson et al. 12 vols. LCL. Cambridge, MA: Harvard University Press, 1929–62.

Secondary Literature

Church, Philip. *Hebrews and the Temple: Attitudes to the Temple in Second Temple Judaism and in Hebrews*. SNT 171; Leiden: Brill, 2017.

Klawans, Jonathan. *Purity, Sacrifice, and the Temple: Symbolism and Supersessionism in the Study of Ancient Judaism*. Oxford: Oxford University, 2006.

Koester, Craig R. *The Dwelling of God: The Tabernacle in the Old Testament, Intertestamental Jewish Literature, and the New Testament*. CBQMS 22. Washington, DC: Catholic Biblical Association, 1989.

Regev, Eyal. *The Temple in Early Christianity: Experiencing the Sacred*. New Haven: Yale University Press, 2019.

Schenck, Kenneth. *A Brief Guide to Philo*. Louisville: Westminster John Knox, 2005.

_____. *Cosmology and Eschatology in Hebrews: The Settings of the Sacrifice*. SNTSMS 143. Cambridge: Cambridge University Press, 2007.

Seland, Torrey, ed. *Reading Philo: A Handbook to Philo of Alexandria*. Grand Rapids: Eerdmans, 2014.

CHAPTER 13

Songs of the Sabbath Sacrifice and Hebrews 9:11–28: Heavenly Sanctuary, Priest, and Sacrifice

BENJAMIN RIBBENS

Hebrews 9:11–28 depicts Christ as a high priest who enters a heavenly sanctuary where he presents himself as a heavenly offering. While other New Testament authors describe Christ's redemptive work with sacrificial imagery, Hebrews is unique in locating Christ's priestly actions in a heavenly locale, which raises questions about how the heavenly sanctuary and sacrifice function in Hebrews' argument. To answer those questions, it may help to turn to **Second Temple Jewish** writings that also describe a heavenly sanctuary where heavenly priests offer heavenly sacrifices, because these writings provide context for how heavenly sacrifices would have been understood by the author of Hebrews and his audience. While several texts offer parallels to Hebrews' description of heavenly sacrifice (esp. 1 En. 14; T. Levi 3.1–8; cf. Jubilees), we will look at the Songs of the Sabbath Sacrifice because of its sustained discussion of a heavenly sanctuary where heavenly priests offer heavenly sacrifices. Reading Hebrews 9:11–28 alongside Songs of the Sabbath Sacrifice will highlight that Christ's sacrifice is the heavenly ideal that corresponds to the earthly Levitical practice.

Songs of the Sabbath Sacrifice

"PRIESTS OF THE INNER SANCTUM WHO SERVE BEFORE THE KING"

Most extant manuscripts of the Songs of the Sabbath Sacrifice (henceforth, Songs) come from **Qumran** and date from the first century BC. Some of these manuscripts are quite fragmentary. One manuscript containing material from Songs Five and Six was found at Masada and likely dates to the middle of the first century AD. Since one manuscript was found outside Qumran, the Songs may not have been **sectarian** in terms of original authorship, but they were clearly part of the faith, life, and self-understanding of the Qumran community.[1]

Songs is a liturgical work consisting of thirteen songs written for the first thirteen Sabbaths of the liturgical calendar. Each song begins with a three-part introduction: (1) "For the instructor," (2) "song for the sacrifice on the Sabbath" followed by the number of the Sabbath for which the song was written, and (3) the command "praise" directed toward the angels in heaven.[2] The songs describe the contents of the heavenly sanctuary and the worship of the angels, including their investiture or consecration as priests and the sacrifices they offer.

Heavenly Sanctuary, Priest, and Sacrifice. The heavenly *sanctuary* is prevalent throughout the Songs, which uses terms such as *tabernacle, sanctuary, temple,* and *holy of holies* to identify the heavenly worship space. The heavenly temple is the backdrop for the angelic worship and liturgy, and at times aspects of the temple are accentuated and described. In fact, Song Seven invokes not only the angels but also parts of the temple—the foundations, columns, and corners—to join in the praise (4Q403 I, 41–42).

The heavenly sanctuary has heavenly *priests.* Song One describes the investiture of the angelic priesthood. The song states that God "established for himself priests of the inner sanctum" (4Q400 1 I, 19; cf. I, 10). The angels are "ministers of the presence in his glorious sanctuary" (I, 4) and "priests of the inner sanctum who serve before the King" (I, 8). During the angelic investiture, the angels are sanctified and purified so that they may "propitiate his favor for all who turn from sin" (I, 15–16). Since those who "turn from sin" are likely the earthly Qumran community (see CD II, 5; 1QHᵃ VI, 24; X, 9; XIV, 6), the angelic priesthood achieves atonement, or propitiation of God, for human beings as a response to their sin.

While Songs describes at length a heavenly sanctuary with a heavenly priesthood, the mention and discussion of heavenly *sacrifice* in the extant manuscripts is more limited. Sacrificial language is found throughout the Songs, but the most explicit mention of sacrifices that parallel the earthly practice occurs in Song Thirteen, which is unfortunately quite fragmentary.

---

1. Carol A. Newsom, *Songs of the Sabbath Sacrifice: A Critical Edition*, HSS 27 (Atlanta: Scholars Press, 1985), 1–4.

2. All translations of Songs of the Sabbath Sacrifice are my own.

It refers to the "sacrifices of the holy ones," the "aroma of their offerings," and the "aroma of their drink offerings" (11Q17 21–22 IX, 3–5). Although explicit descriptions of angels performing sacrifices are limited, the sacrificial practice of the angelic priesthood is assumed throughout the Songs. The angelic priests must obey and carry out all God's ordinances, precepts, and regulations that he wrote down for them (4Q400 1 I, 5–15), and the heavenly ordinances likely correspond to the earthly ordinances in the Torah, which include sacrifice. Song One also describes the angelic priests atoning for the sins of the people, so one can presume that the ordinances that the heavenly priests follow include the sacrificial regulations that atone. Because the heavenly sacrifice is the ideal sacrifice, the angelic priests must be holy and perform the regulations precisely. There is no tolerance for any perversion or impurity (I, 14). Song Twelve reiterates this theme, noting that "there is none among them who omits a law" (4Q405 23 i 10). In sum, Songs depicts an angelic priesthood in the heavenly sanctuary achieving atonement or propitiation through sacrifices, offerings, and libations.

The Connection between the Earthly and Heavenly Sacrifice. In Second Temple literature, the heavenly sanctuary, priesthood, and sacrifices are the ideals. The earthly sanctuary, priesthood, and sacrifices are patterned after the heavenlies, and the earthly sacrifices are valid when they properly imitate the prototypical model and synchronize the earthly worship with the heavenly. For instance, Song One was intended to be read on the first Sabbath of the year, so that—according to the liturgical calendar of the Qumran community—the heavenly investiture of the angelic priesthood would take place at the same time the community consecrated its own priesthood.[3] There were many debates in the Second Temple period concerning the proper administration of the temple, and the Qumran community rejected the contemporary sacrificial practice and withdrew from the temple. Liturgical texts like Songs that describe the ideal heavenly worship and sacrifice as matching that of the community served to validate their worship, priesthood, and sacrifice (in contrast to the impure priesthood of Jerusalem) and helped to address the need to perform Torah-mandated sacrifices while apart from the temple. Earthly worship that corresponded to the heavenly worship was the true and valid worship, participated in some way with the heavenly worship, and received the benefits of the heavenly worship (e.g., consecration and atonement).

---

3. Newsom, *Songs of the Sabbath Sacrifice,* 72.

Hebrews 9:11–28

"HE ENTERED THE MOST HOLY PLACE ONCE FOR ALL BY HIS OWN BLOOD"

Heavenly Sanctuary, Priest, and Sacrifice. Hebrews 9:11–28 compares and contrasts Christ's sacrifice to the sacrifices performed under the first covenant, which are described in 9:1–10. The first covenant had regulations (9:1) for an earthly sanctuary (9:2–5), in which priests carried out their sacrificial ministry for the sins of the people, and Hebrews summarizes the Levitical sacrifices by describing the Day of Atonement when the high priest enters the Most Holy Place (9:6–10). Hebrews 9:11–28 then depicts Christ's sacrifice in similar terms: Christ is a high priest who enters the Most Holy Place where he makes an offering for sins.

Table 13.1. Similarities between Christ's Sacrifice and Levitical Sacrifice

	Levitical sacrifice	Christ's sacrifice
High priest	9:7	9:11
Enters Most Holy Place	9:7, 25	9:11–12, 24–25
Makes an offering	9:7, 25	9:14, 25–26, 28
For sins	9:7	9:15, 26, 28
Blood	9:7, 12, 25	9:12, 14

In the midst of outlining the correspondences between Christ's sacrifice and Levitical sacrifice, Hebrews highlights key differences in (1) sanctuary, (2) offering, and (3) benefits: Christ entered a (1) *heavenly* sanctuary where he offered (2a) *himself* (2b) *once for all* in order to achieve (3) *eternal redemption*.

When accounting both for the similarities and differences, one sees that just as the Songs depicts a heavenly priesthood in a heavenly sanctuary presenting offerings to atone for humanity's sins, so Hebrews depicts Jesus as a heavenly priest in a heavenly sanctuary presenting an offering to take away humanity's sins. Yet, Hebrews' description of heavenly sacrifice differs from the Songs in a few important ways. First, Christ is not an angel but is God incarnate (Hebrews 1–2). Second, Christ's heavenly offering is himself, while the angelic priesthood of Songs presents offerings extrinsic to themselves. Third, while Songs and other Second Temple literature have lengthy descriptions of the heavenly sanctuary, Hebrews spends very little time describing the heavenly sanctuary. Fourth, whereas heavenly sacrifice in the Songs is perpetual (just like the earthly Levitical sacrifice; Heb 9:25; cf. 7:27; 10:1, 3, 11), the author of Hebrews repeatedly stresses that Christ's sacrifice is once for all (9:12, 26, 28; cf. 7:27; 10:10, 12, 14).

Table 13.2. Differences between Christ's Sacrifice and Levitical Sacrifice

	Levitical sacrifice	**Christ's sacrifice**
Sanctuary	*Earthly* "earthly sanctuary" (9:1) "copies of the heavenly things" (9:23) "a sanctuary made with human hands that was only a copy of the true one" (9:24)	*Heavenly* "the greater and more perfect tabernacle that is not made with human hands, that is to say, is not a part of this creation" (9:11) "the heavenly things themselves" (9:23) "the true one . . . heaven itself" (9:24)
Offering	*Blood of animals* "blood of goats and calves" (9:12) "blood that is not his own" (9:25) *Repeated* "again and again . . . every year" (9:25)	*Himself, his own blood* "by his own blood" (9:12) "blood of Christ" (9:14) "offer himself" (9:25) "sacrifice of himself" (9:26) *Once for all* "once for all" (9:12, 26, 28)
Benefits	*Limited* "not able to clear the conscience" (9:9) "sanctify . . . outwardly clean" (9:13)	*Expansive* "eternal redemption" (9:12) "cleanse our consciences" (9:14) "eternal inheritance" (9:15) "set them free from the sins" (9:15) "do away with sin" (9:26) "take away the sins of many" (9:28)

The Connection between the Earthly and Heavenly Sacrifice. The differences listed above demonstrate how Hebrews depicts Christ's sacrifice as superior to Levitical sacrifices, and Hebrews drives this point home in 9:23 ("better sacrifices than these"). Based on the superiority of Christ's sacrifice, interpreters often conclude that Hebrews considers Levitical sacrifices to be useless and ineffective. However, when one reads Hebrews in the context of Second Temple literature like the Songs that depict a heavenly sanctuary where heavenly sacrifices take place, the relationship between the earthly and heavenly practice becomes more nuanced, because heavenly sanctuaries and sacrifices did not diminish their earthly counterparts. Rather, the heavenly realities validated particular earthly spaces and practices. The earthly sanctuary that corresponded to the heavenly was the true sanctuary where God dwelled, and the earthly sacrifice that corresponded to the heavenly was the true practice that received salvific benefits. Songs depicts the heavenly sacrifice to demonstrate the validity of its community's earthly practice.

Hebrews 9:11–28 argues that Christ's sacrifice is *better* than Levitical sacrifice. Yet Hebrews' argument is not simply that Christ's offering is better, because a superior sacrifice could be completely unrelated to the Levitical practice. Rather, in a way that no other New Testament text does, Hebrews 9:11–28 depicts Christ's sacrifice as a heavenly counterpart to the Levitical Day of Atonement. Whereas Songs describes heavenly sacrifice in order to validate a particular earthly practice, Hebrews describes the Levitical sacrifice in order to identify Christ's sacrifice as the *heavenly ideal*. Christ's sacrifice is not just better, it is also the ideal. While the ideal is better, it does not diminish and devalue the shadow—that is, the Levitical practice. Rather, the correspondence is what gives the earthly shadow its validity and salvific benefits. Since Second Temple texts assume that proper earthly sacrifice follows the pattern of the heavenly, Hebrews' description may imply (a) that the Levitical sacrifices were valid because they imitated Christ's offering and (b) that the Levitical sacrifices participated in a limited way in the salvific benefits of the heavenly reality (9:15).[4]

Still, there is at least one significant way in which Hebrews' description of the connection between the earthly and heavenly sacrifice differs from the Songs and other Second Temple literature. The Songs depicts perpetual heavenly sacrifice that corresponds to and affirms the continued and perpetual earthly sacrifice. Not only does Hebrews describe the heavenly sacrifice

---

4. For a fuller discussion of this relationship, see Benjamin Ribbens, "The Sacrifice God Desired: Psalm 40.6–8 in Hebrews 10," *NTS* 67 (2021): 302–4; idem, *Levitical Sacrifice and Heavenly Cult in Hebrews*, BZNW 222 (Berlin: de Gruyter, 2016), 136–40, 236–40.

as a singular sacrifice, but the singular heavenly sacrifice also means that the earthly sacrifice is no longer necessary for the forgiveness of sins (10:18). Christ's heavenly sacrifice does not affirm the ongoing earthly sacrificial practice; rather, it inaugurates a new covenant (9:15) that brings an end to the first covenant practice (9:10; cf. 10:9).

By reading Hebrews in the context of Songs, we come to see Hebrews' depiction of Christ's sacrifice in a more nuanced way. Not only is Christ's sacrifice *better* than Levitical sacrifice (9:23), but it is also the *heavenly ideal* that is connected to and corresponds with the Levitical practice.

FOR FURTHER READING

Additional Ancient Texts

For depictions of angelic priests offering heavenly sacrifices in a heavenly sanctuary, see 1 Enoch 14; Testament of Levi 3.1–8; 3 Baruch 11–12; Life of Adam and Eve 33; b. Ḥagigah 12b; b. Menaḥot 110a; and b. Zebaḥim 62a. Jubilees describes angels performing worship in the heavenly realm that corresponds to Israel's worship. As part of these descriptions, the angels are identified as priests, and the earthly worship that corresponds to the heavenly includes sacrifice, though there is not a description of angels performing sacrifices (Jub. 2.17–33; 6.17–31; 15.25–27; 30.18–20; 31.11–17; 50.6–13).

English Translations and Critical Editions

Garcia Martinez, Florentino, and Eibert J. C. Tigchelaar, eds. *The Dead Sea Scrolls: Study Edition*. 2 vols. Leiden: Brill, 2007.

Newsom, Carol A. *Songs of the Sabbath Sacrifice: A Critical Edition*. HSS 27. Atlanta: Scholars Press, 1985.

Secondary Literature

Alexander, Philip S. *Mystical Texts*. CQS 7. London: T&T Clark, 2006.

Barnard, Jody A. *The Mysticism of Hebrews: Exploring the Role of Jewish Apocalyptic Mysticism in the Epistle to the Hebrews*. WUNT 2/331. Tübingen: Mohr Siebeck, 2012.

Calaway, Jared. *The Sabbath and the Sanctuary*. WUNT 2/349. Tübingen: Mohr Siebeck, 2013.

Davila, James R. *Liturgical Works*. Eerdmans Commentaries on the Dead Sea Scrolls. Grand Rapids: Eerdmans, 2000.

Mackie, Scott D. "Heavenly Sanctuary Mysticism in the Epistle to the Hebrews." *JTS* 62 (2011): 77–117.

Newsom, Carol A. "'He Has Established for Himself Priests': Human and Angelic Priesthood in the Qumran Sabbath *Shirot.*" Pages 101–20 in *Archaeology and History in the Dead Sea Scrolls.* Edited by Lawrence H. Schiffman. JSPSup 8. Sheffield: JSOT, 1990.

Ribbens, Benjamin. *Levitical Sacrifice and Heavenly Cult in Hebrews.* BZNW 222. Berlin: de Gruyter, 2016.

CHAPTER 14

Philo of Alexandria and Hebrews 10:1–18: The Sacrifices of the Righteous

ZOE O'NEILL

Hebrews 10:1–18 concludes a long discussion on Jesus's high priestly offering in the heavenly holy of holies that began in 8:1. Like the previous chapters, Hebrews 10:1–18 is concerned with the superiority of Christ's sacrifice to Levitical sacrifices: it is once for all and complete, unlike Levitical offerings, which require repetition (10:1, 11–12; cf. 9:12, 25–28), and it perfects the conscience of the worshiper, whereas Levitical sacrifices only perfect the flesh (10:2, 10, 14; cf. 9:13–14). Yet Hebrews 10 goes further than the preceding chapters and leaves the reader in no doubt that old covenant sacrifices are ineffective with the declaration: "It is impossible for the blood of bulls and goats to take away sins" (10:4). According to Hebrews, animal sacrifices only remind one of sin (10:3); Christ's sacrifice, however, removes both sins and the memory of those sins, making further sacrifices unnecessary (10:18).

The topic of sacrifice, central to this text, is also dealt with in many Jewish writings; however, significant parallels emerge when we read this passage in Hebrews alongside **Philo**'s work, *On Planting (De plantatione)* 107–109. In particular, both Hebrews and Philo contrast unacceptable sacrifices that only bring to mind sin with acceptable sacrifices that God desires. These shared themes make Hebrews and Philo significant dialogue partners as we seek to understand Jewish and early Christian attitudes to sacrifice in the first century AD. Yet when we delve into these texts, it becomes clear that their common themes regarding sacrifice are treated very differently.

Philo of Alexandria

"A SACRIFICE THAT BRINGS TO MIND SIN"

Philo's work *On Planting* is the ninth book in his *Allegorical Interpretation*, which provides an allegorical interpretation of Genesis. The primary aim of *On Planting* is to explain Genesis 9:20 ("Noah, a man of the soil, proceeded to plant a vineyard"), but it also draws upon and expounds other biblical texts as it seeks to understand this verse from Genesis. The first half of the work deals with this planting metaphor in three parts. First, in *On Planting* 1–72, God is described as a planter and the world as his plant. Second, Abraham is discussed as a planter in imitation of God (*Planting* 73–93). The third section looks at human beings as planters and how they are to be righteous and free from unrighteous desires (*Planting* 94–138).

The second half of the book considers the work of philosophers on drunkenness to give a rationale for how a wise person like Noah could get drunk (*Planting* 139–177). The text we are considering here (*Planting* 107–109) occurs within a discussion that seeks to understand what it means "to remove the uncleanness of what has been planted" (drawing on Lev 19:23) but focuses on the sacrifices conducted by righteous and unrighteous people.[1]

Sacrifices That Are Unacceptable to God. Philo begins by describing two growths. The first is a noble growth of "ritual observances and sacrifices of service." The second, however, springs up alongside it and is "an evil growth, a superstition, which it is profitable to cut away before the first shoots spring up" (*Planting* 107). Philo explains that this evil growth represents those who offer sacrifices in immorality, concerned with appearing religious on the outside rather than developing godly character. As Philo describes, "For some are convinced that the offering of cattle is godly, and they assign parts of these to the altars, whether through theft, lying, fraud, robbery or plunder" (*Planting* 107). These "unclean people" think that sacrificing stolen animals on altars will negate their evil deeds, the intention behind these sacrifices being "to avoid punishment for their wrongdoing" (*Planting* 107). Philo criticizes such people and acknowledges that their sacrificial offering is useless: "O you people, the tribunal of God is incorruptible, thus he rejects those with guilty intent, even if they offer a hundred cattle every day" (*Planting* 108). "A hundred cattle" is a reference

---

1. Translations of Philo are my own.

to a general sacrificial offering. The thrust of the statement here is on the repetition of the sacrifice, rather than its size.[2] For Philo, no sacrifice offered unrighteously is desirable to God.

God Desires Obedience, Not Sacrifice. Contrasted with those whom God rejects are the innocent whom God accepts. Philo underscores that God receives the righteous, "even if they offer no sacrifice at all" (*Planting* 108). The empty altars of the virtuous are worth rejoicing in, not full altars that "burn with the unconsecrated sacrifices of the unholy" (*Planting* 108). It is tempting to assume from this statement that Philo denounces literal sacrifices. However, Philo stops short of claiming that animal sacrifices are unnecessary. The focus of *On Planting* 107–109 is not on the sacrifices themselves but on the character of the one presenting the sacrifice: holy people present the most suitable sacrifices, whereas sacrifices presented in hypocrisy are dismissed.[3] Philo himself even traveled from his home city of Alexandria to Jerusalem to offer sacrifices, indicating that he understood sacrificial offerings to be important to his own religious life.[4]

Philo then discusses the sacrifices of the unholy that God rejects. It is these sacrifices that "Moses has spoken of somewhere" (cf. Num 5:15): "a sacrifice that 'brings to mind sin'" (*Planting* 108). While in Numbers 5:15 the sacrifices refer to the offering given by the husband of an adulterous wife, in Philo's mind any sacrifice offered by the unholy brings to mind sin. The one to whom sin is brought to mind is initially unclear. Yet most likely Philo is referring to God as this citation occurs in response to Philo's assertion that "God rejoices in altars without fire around which the virtues dance."

In *On Planting* 109 Philo concludes that the improper offering of sacrifices causes "damage." Philo claims that "it is necessary to remove and cut away [such things] following the divine oracle, in which it is commanded 'to remove the uncleanness of the tree that has been planted, which is suitable for consumption.'" Here Philo reiterates his main concern that the manner of life of the one offering sacrifices is more important than the sacrifices they provide.

---

2. Albert C. Geljon and David T. Runia, *Philo of Alexandria, On Planting: Introduction, Translation, and Commentary*, PACS 5 (Leiden: Brill, 2019), 223.

3. Daniel C. Ullucci, *The Christian Rejection of Animal Sacrifice* (New York: Oxford University Press, 2012), 49–50.

4. *On Providence* 2.107. For more on Philo's attitude to sacrifices, see Jutta Leonhardt, *Jewish Worship in Philo of Alexandria*, TSAJ 84 (Tübingen: Mohr Siebeck, 2001), 214–55.

Hebrews 10:1–18

"SACRIFICES ARE AN ANNUAL REMINDER OF SINS"

Sacrifices That Are Unacceptable to God. Our passage in Hebrews, as in Philo's writing, begins by devoting attention to sacrifices that are inadequate and only serve to bring sin to memory. Hebrews 10:1–3 acknowledges that because the law is a shadow of the good things to come and not the reality, Levitical sacrifices are not able to perfect worshipers. The author of Hebrews reasoned that if animal sacrifices could perfect the worshiper, they would have stopped being offered. Instead, "those sacrifices are an annual reminder of sins," a phrase reminiscent of Philo's "sacrifice that brings to mind sin," which likely also alludes to Numbers 5:15. As in Philo, the reference is to animal sacrifices, not to an offering for an adulterous wife. Who is reminded of sins here is difficult to determine: God or the sinner? If we read Hebrews alongside Philo, we could understand God to be the one who is reminded of sins,[5] which then provides a contrast with the statement that God remembers sins no more (10:17; cf. 8:12). However, the Day of Atonement ritual is alluded to here, where the people remember their sins as the high priest confesses their sins over the scapegoat and sends it into the wilderness (Lev 16:21). This favors a reference to the sinner's remembrance, suggesting that the writer of Hebrews understands the memorial function of sacrifices differently from Philo.

Table 14.1. Memorial Offerings in Numbers, Philo, and Hebrews

Numbers 5:15	Philo, *Planting* 108	Hebrews 10:3
He must not pour olive oil on it or put incense on it, because it is a grain offering for jealousy, <u>a reminder-offering to draw attention to wrongdoing</u>.	Indeed, Moses has said somewhere that there is <u>a sacrifice that brings to mind sin</u>.	But those sacrifices are an <u>annual reminder of sins</u>.

Hebrews also diverges from Philo in its insistence that all Levitical sacrifices are ineffective: "It is impossible for the blood of bulls and goats to

---

5. Stefan Svendsen, *Allegory Transformed: The Appropriation of Philonic Hermeneutics in the Letter to the Hebrews*, WUNT 2/269 (Tübingen: Mohr Siebeck, 2009), 186.

take away sins" (10:4). On initial reading, it looks like the author dismisses animal sacrifices completely. However, is it possible that Hebrews' thought is much closer to Philo's than is typically recognized? An alternative reading takes Hebrews to imply that sacrifices provided by unrighteous priests are displeasing to God. Justin Duff has argued that the LXX of Isaiah 1:11 is a significant background text for Hebrews 10:4.[6] The Isaiah passage is concerned with the offering of sacrifices in hypocrisy:

> What to me is the multitude of your sacrifices?
>> says the Lord;
> I am full of whole burnt offerings of rams
>> and I do not want the fat of lambs
>> nor the blood of bulls and goats. (Isa 1:11 NETS)

If this Old Testament text is relevant for Hebrews' argument here, then Hebrews disregards the sacrifice of the lawless priests in favor of the perfect high-priestly sacrifice of Christ. Given that Philo acknowledges that God rejects the sacrifice of the lawless, Hebrews may understand that the only acceptable Levitical sacrifice is offered in righteousness. Likewise, Hebrews' emphasis on Christ coming to do the will of God could imply that Levitical priests at that time were not following God's will.

However, it is more likely at this point that Hebrews moves away from existing Jewish traditions, including that of Philo. Hebrews' language is explicit that animal sacrifices are unable to take away sin, without exception, regardless of the character of the offerer. Nor does God desire sacrifices offered following the law (10:8), irrespective of whether they are given by the godly or ungodly. Reading Hebrews in light of Philo may soften the critique of Levitical sacrifices here, but Hebrews' argument does not have the same nuance that Philo's has: the blood of goats and calves cannot effectuate total forgiveness of sin. Indeed, Hebrews' thought here is innovative among Second Temple Jewish writings.

God Desires Obedience, Not Sacrifice. Hebrews also argues, as Philo did, that God does not delight in the offering of burnt sacrifices but is pleased with obedience. In Hebrews, however, it is Christ's obedience to God's will, exemplified in his sacrificial self-offering, that God desires. The author cites Psalm 40:6–8 as the words of Christ:

---

6. Justin Harrison Duff, "The Blood of Goats and Calves . . . and Bulls? An Allusion to Isaiah 1:11 LXX in Hebrews 10:4," *JBL* 138 (2018): 765–83.

> Sacrifice and offering you did not desire,
>> but a body you prepared for me;
> with burnt offerings and sin offerings
>> you were not pleased.
> Then I said, "Here I am—it is written about me in the scroll—
>> I have come to do your will, my God." (Ps 40:6–8 in Heb
>> 10:5b–7)

Hebrews then restates elements from the psalm, dividing it into two parts. First, God did not desire sacrifices or various offerings, nor was he "pleased with them"—even though they were offered according to the law (10:8). Second, Christ proclaimed, "Here I am, I have come to do your will." This two-part division leads Hebrews to acknowledge that Christ "sets aside the first to establish the second" (10:9). Christ's sacrificial offering, which established a new covenant, displaced the old covenant sacrificial system. This idea that Levitical offerings were no longer necessary would have been foreign to Philo, who, as we noted above, saw a continuing role for animal sacrifices.

Hebrews goes on to specify in more detail how Christ's sacrifice is superior to Levitical sacrifices. Levitical sacrifices, because they cannot remove sins, must be repeatedly offered by priests who stand day after day performing their religious duties (10:11). Christ, on the other hand, has supplied "for all time one sacrifice for sins," and is now seated at the right hand of God, having "made perfect forever those who are being made holy" (10:12, 14; cf. 10:10). The Holy Spirit then testifies to Christ's perfecting of believers in Jeremiah 31:33–34: in this new covenant, the law of God is written on the hearts and minds of believers, and their sins and lawless acts are remembered no more. Consequently, further sacrifices are unnecessary (10:18). Therefore, unlike Philo, who saw the sacrifice of the guiltless as acceptable, even if there was no physical offering on the altar, the author of Hebrews understood Christ to provide a sacrifice to end all other sacrifices. Nevertheless, Hebrews' author does acknowledge later in his argument, in a thought paralleling Philo's, that believers, who have the law of God internalized, are to offer a sacrifice of praise and worship that is pleasing to God (12:28–29; 13:15). The focus of Hebrews' argument here in 10:1–18, nonetheless, is on Christ's sacrifice, not the spiritual sacrifice of believers.

Conclusion. Reading Hebrews alongside Philo's *On Planting* 107–109 shows that a concern to explain what makes a sacrifice acceptable to God existed in the first century AD. However, it also demonstrates how Hebrews draws insights that differ from Jewish tradition based on its knowledge of the Christ event. Philo, like many Jewish writers, understood that sacrifices offered in hypocrisy will be rejected by God, while God accepts the righteous regardless of their sacrificial offerings. For Hebrews, it is Christ's obedient self-offering that God desires, not further Levitical sacrifices.

For Further Reading

Additional Ancient Texts

Philo discusses which sacrifices are acceptable to God elsewhere—*On the Life of Moses* 2.106–8; *On the Special Laws* 1.215, 272; *Questions and Answers on Exodus* 2.98. Many Second Temple texts acknowledge that God decides whether a sacrifice is suitable and rejects the sacrifices of immoral people— for example, 2 Enoch 45.3; 61.3; 66.3; Sirach 7:9; 34:23; 35:8–9, 14–15; Jubilees 5.15–17; 1QS 3.1–11.

English Translations and Critical Editions

Geljon, Albert C., and David T. Runia. *Philo of Alexandria, On Planting: Introduction, Translation, and Commentary.* PACS 5. Leiden: Brill, 2019.

Philo. Translated by F. H. Colson et al. 12 vols. LCL. Cambridge, MA: Harvard University Press, 1929–62.

Secondary Literature

Duff, Justin Harrison. "The Blood of Goats and Calves . . . and Bulls? An Allusion to Isaiah 1:11 LXX in Hebrews 10:4." *JBL* 138 (2018): 765–83.

Leonhardt, Jutta. *Jewish Worship in Philo of Alexandria.* TSAJ 84. Tübingen: Mohr Siebeck, 2001.

Petropoulou, Maria-Zoe. *Animal Sacrifice in Ancient Greek Religion, Judaism, and Christianity, 100 BC to AD 200.* Oxford Classical Monographs. Oxford: Oxford University Press, 2008.

Svendsen, Stefan. *Allegory Transformed: The Appropriation of Philonic Hermeneutics in the Letter to the Hebrews.* WUNT 2/269. Tübingen: Mohr Siebeck, 2009.

Ullucci, Daniel C. *The Christian Rejection of Animal Sacrifice.* New York: Oxford University Press, 2012.

CHAPTER 15

Mishnah Yoma and Hebrews 10:19–39: Deliberate Sin and Atonement

JASON MASTON

Hebrews 10 divides into two sections. The first section (10:1–18) concludes the lengthy argument about Jesus as high priest that begins in 7:1. The second section (10:19–39) is a call to perseverance. As this section begins in verses 19–25, the author encourages his readers to draw near to God, to hold fast to their confession, and to continue meeting together for mutual encouragement, especially in light of the coming day of judgment (10:25). Likewise, verses 32–39, recalling the sufferings they have already endured, challenge the audience to persevere in the face of a new set of persecutions.

Sandwiched between these two encouraging paragraphs on perseverance is one that causes the reader some consternation. In 10:26–30 the author warns that "if we deliberately keep on sinning after we have received the knowledge of the truth," we should expect judgment. The reason there is only judgment is because "no sacrifice for sins is left." To support his claim, he argues that since those "who rejected the law of Moses" were found guilty, then surely those who "trampled the Son of God" will also be held accountable.

One might think that God's judgment in these verses is directed toward unbelievers, but we should notice that the author speaks here of "we" (10:26, 30). The threat of judgment is not reserved for unbelievers alone. This passage is meant for those who have acknowledged the truth that Jesus is the high priest and has offered himself as an atoning sacrifice once for all. The author does not mince words: for those who acknowledge such truth, there is no sacrifice left if they "deliberately keep on sinning" (10:26). But what exactly does this mean? Is the author suggesting that post-baptismal sin will bring judgment? Or does this statement simply warn against a more permanent act of sin, like apostasy? Thankfully, the writer of Hebrews was not the only ancient author to issue such a warning or to address the matter of ineffectual sacrifices. Rabbinic Jewish works were especially concerned to address such questions. To bring more clarity to this matter, we will therefore compare our passage in Hebrews to the rabbinic text Mishnah Yoma (m. Yoma).

Mishnah Yoma

"THE DAY OF ATONEMENT EFFECTS NO ATONEMENT"

Consisting of the Mishnah, the Tosefta, and the two Talmuds, rabbinic literature is a rich source for understanding how Jewish teachers interpreted and applied the Hebrew Scriptures. The Mishnah, which was compiled about AD 200–220 and is the basis for the later rabbinic literature, is the written record of the oral teachings of rabbis from the Tannaitic period (ca. 50 BC–AD 200). The Mishnah is organized into six divisions, which are subdivided into tractates. Our comparator text comes from the second division, Mo'ed, which addresses the Jewish feasts. The tractate of interest to us, Yoma, deals with practices and beliefs associated with the Day of Atonement.

The sacrificial acts for the Day of Atonement are originally set out in Leviticus 16 (cf. Num 29:7–11). As with many of the laws in the Old Testament, though, the instructions provided do not address every matter. Later Jews reflected on this material and developed practices that clarified or filled out individual commandments. Most of m. Yoma clarifies the instructions found in Leviticus 16. Sections 1–7 describe in some detail the procedures leading up to and on the Day of Atonement. Section 1, for example, addresses the steps taken by the high priest to prepare himself for bringing the sacrifice to God. Other sections explain how the blood was sprinkled (section 5) or how one ensured that the goat "For Azazel" made it outside the camp (section 6). While the majority of the tractate deals with the procedures associated with the Day of Atonement, section 8 changes directions by addressing what was expected of the common Israelite (8.1–7) and what sins were atoned for on the Day of Atonement (8.8–9). Concerning this atonement, we read,

[8] The Sin-offering and the unconditional Guilt-offering effect atonement; death and the Day of Atonement effect atonement if there is repentance. Repentance effects atonement for lesser transgressions against both positive and negative commands in the Law; while for graver transgressions it suspends punishment until the Day of Atonement comes and effects atonement.

[9] If a man said, 'I will sin and repent, and sin again and repent', he will be given no chance to repent. [If he said,] 'I will sin and the Day of Atonement will effect atonement', then the Day of Atonement effects no atonement. For transgressions that are between man and God the Day of Atonement effects atonement, but for transgressions that are between a man and his fellow the Day of Atonement effects atonement only if he has appeased his fellow. This did R. Eleazar b. Azariah expound: *From all your sins shall ye be clean before the Lord* [Lev 16:30]—for transgressions that are between man and God the Day of Atonement effects atonement; but for transgressions that are between a man and his fellow the Day of Atonement effects atonement only if he has appeased his fellow. R. Akiba said: Blessed are ye, O Israel. Before whom are ye made clean and who makes you clean? Your Father in heaven; as it is written, *And I will sprinkle clean water upon you and ye shall be clean* [Ezek 36:25]. And again it says, *O Lord the hope* (mikweh) *of Israel* [Jer 17:13]—as the *Mikweh* cleanses the unclean so does the Holy One, blessed be he, cleanse Israel.[1]

Repentance and Deliberate Sinning. Mishnah Yoma 8.9 begins by presenting two different scenarios. There is, first, the person who declares that he will sin and then repent. The double statement suggests that a person who knowingly sins does so boldly and repetitively. The person assumes that forgiveness will be extended so long as he repents. For such a person, however, "no chance to repent" will be offered. This could mean one of two things. It could mean that the person will eventually become so entangled in his sin that he will forget to repent. Alternatively, it could imply that the person will die, perhaps as a form of God's judgment, prior to being able to repent. Whichever of these is intended, the basic point is clear: this person incorrectly assumes that mere words of confession will be sufficient to avoid punishment for their deliberate acts of evil.

---

1. All translations of the Mishnah are from Herbert Danby, ed., *The Mishnah* (Oxford: Oxford University Press, 1933), 172. In the name R. Eleazar b. Azariah, "R." stands for "Rabbi" and "b." for "*ben*," the Hebrew word for "son of."

The Day of Atonement and Deliberate Sinning. The second scenario pres-ents a person who chooses to sin and assumes that the Day of Atonement will effect atonement. Again, the assumption is mistaken: "The Day of Atonement effects no atonement." The thought here is similar but different from the first scenario. Underlying the person's claim is the assumption that the Day of Atonement brought atonement for any and all sins. But the teaching here counters this in two ways. First, we are given the explana-tion that the Day of Atonement effects atonement only for sins committed against God. Transgressions against other humans require restitution. This conclusion is supported by the statement from R. Eleazar b. Azariah. A sec-ond reason that the Day of Atonement will not effect atonement was stated in the previous paragraph (8.8). Repentance is a requirement for the Day of Atonement to effect atonement. The Day of Atonement is not some myste-rious rite that simply cancels out one's sins. Rather, the Day of Atonement works precisely because the sinner has confessed and repented. The Day of Atonement assumes that people will sin, and its effectiveness is found in the combination of the ritual and repentance.

These two scenarios describe persons who utilize God's grace as a license for sin. These are not individuals who accidently break the law or commit apostasy. Instead, these are people who knowingly engage in trans-gression and *assume* that forgiveness will always be available to them. For such persons, however, there will be no atonement.

With these comments in place, we are now in a position to return to Hebrews to see how m. Yoma can help clarify the meaning of Hebrews' warning.

Hebrews 10:19–39

"IF WE DELIBERATELY KEEP ON SINNING . . . NO SACRIFICE FOR SINS IS LEFT"

The warning in Hebrews 10:26 is strongly stated: "If we deliberately keep on sinning after we have received the knowledge of the truth, no sacrifice for sins is left." What exactly does "deliberately keep on sinning" mean? According to many scholars, deliberate sinning is specifically the sin of apos-tasy.[2] Grant Osborne states, "The closest thing to a definition of apostasy in

---

2. Harold W. Attridge, *Hebrews: A Commentary on the Epistle to the Hebrews*, Hermeneia (Minneapolis: Fortress, 1989), 292–95; Luke Timothy Johnson, *Hebrews: A Commentary*, NTL (Louisville: Westminster John Knox, 2006), 262.

Hebrews is found in 'we willfully keep on sinning after we have received the knowledge of the truth' (v. 26)."[3] This is the person who, having previously experienced God's mercy in Christ, now rejects the claim that Jesus is the high priest whose offering has effected atonement. The willful sin is a deliberate and permanent turning away from Christ. Gareth Cockerill puts it this way: "Those who persist in such laxity and neglect due to inertia, the threats or promises of an unbelieving society, or any other reason, are headed for such a destiny. They may approach it gradually, but, if unchecked, they will come to the point of definitively, willfully, and indeed probably publicly repudiating the One whose cleansing power they have experienced."[4]

Despite the popularity of this reading, commentators do not present arguments in favor of it; rather, they merely assert that apostasy is the sin. But notice that the author does not say that the persons described have rejected or denied the truth. To the contrary, his warning to them only makes sense if they have accepted the truth about Christ, have been sanctified, and have experienced the grace of God. That is, the author's warning against willful sin only has merit if the audience really believes what he has argued about Jesus. So what might the author be warning against? Here the perspective of m. Yoma 8.8–9 can help.

Christ's Sacrifice and Deliberate Sinning. As we have seen, m. Yoma depicts two scenarios in which a sinner continues in sin—deliberately, we might say—while assuming that God's mercy is all-encompassing and that the sacrifice given on the Day of Atonement will indeed effect atonement for any and all sins. Willful and persistent sin is the problem, not the rejection of the truth claims about God.

The same concern is present in Hebrews 10:26. In the previous sections of Hebrews, the author argues from multiple angles that Christ's sacrifice supersedes the sacrifices offered under the old **covenant**. One point that he stressed is the "once-for-all" nature of Christ's offering. This idea runs throughout chapters 7–10, with the high point being chapter 9. This once-for-all offering secures an eternal redemption (9:12). Additionally, the author claims, "We have been made holy through the sacrifice of the body of Jesus Christ once for all" (10:10). Such statements could easily be understood to indicate that Christ's sacrifice has effected atonement not only for past sins but also for future ones. After all, he says in 9:26 that Jesus "has appeared

---

3. Grant R. Osborne, "A Classical Arminian View," in *Four Views on the Warning Passages in Hebrews*, ed. H. W. Bateman (Grand Rapids: Kregel, 2007), 120.
4. Gareth Lee Cockerill, *The Epistle to the Hebrews*, NICNT (Grand Rapids: Eerdmans, 2012), 491.

once for all at the culmination of the ages to do away with sin by the sacrifice of himself."

These statements could create a mindset in which a reader is duped into thinking that one's disobedience no longer matters. If Christ's sacrifice was truly a once-for-all event, if it really does cleanse one completely, then there is no longer a need to worry about sin, punishment, or judgment. Although sacrifices had to be repeatedly offered under the old covenant because no single sacrifice could fully effect atonement once for all, Christ's sacrifice does not suffer from this limitation. His offering has secured an eternal redemption. Sin no longer is a concern, for Christ has resolved the problem.

This outlook on Christ's sacrifice mirrors the attitude of the second person in m. Yoma 8.9 who presumes that the Day of Atonement will effect atonement irrespective of how one lives. A further connection is made when one recalls that the author of Hebrews sets his description of Jesus in the context of the Day of Atonement rituals. He reminds his audience that the priest can enter the inner room only once a year (9:7), and he must do so every year (9:25), which is a reminder that the blood of goats and bulls can never truly atone for sin (10:3–4). Read from the perspective of m. Yoma, when the author of Hebrews warns his audience not to engage in deliberate sin, he is cautioning against presuming on the once-for-all nature of Christ's sacrifice.[5]

In 10:28–29 the author employs an argument from lesser to greater: if one was put to death for "rejecting" the Torah, then one can expect something even worse for those who know the truth about Jesus and yet deliberately sin. The idea of rejecting points to a person who lives in disobedience to the commandments of the Torah. This is not a person who rejects the truth claims of the Torah about God but rather one who accepts the Torah's testimony to God's mercy and the validity of the sacrifices. The problem here is precisely the problem addressed by the prophets: they challenged their fellow Israelites who, despite their sinful lives, assumed that God would show mercy so long as they offered sacrifices (e.g., Isa 1:10–17; Mal 2:10–17). Similarly, in Hebrews, the author confronts an outlook that assumes that because Christ's sacrifice has effected an eternal atonement and cleansed completely, one does not need to be concerned with disobedience.

Drawing a comparison with m. Yoma 8.8–9 helps place the warning in

---

5. Although it is often claimed that there was no sacrifice for willful sins, some ancient sources indicate that the Day of Atonement effected atonement for *all* sins, including willful (Lev 16:16; Philo, *Spec. Laws* 1.234–238; *Posterity* 48; cited by Craig Koester, *Hebrews: A New Translation with Introduction and Commentary*, AB [New York: Doubleday, 2001], 451).

Hebrews 10:26–31 in a historical context and connects it with several elements of the preceding argument. Seen from this perspective, the author warns his audience against continuing in sin despite having come to a correct knowledge of the truth. He is not referring to a person who abandons the Christian faith by denying and rejecting Jesus as God's high priest. He has in view, instead, the person who presumes that God will always be merciful, that Jesus's sacrifice extends to all sins without repentance. Hebrews, like m. Yoma, stresses the opposite: God will hold accountable those who willfully engage in sinful actions. Jesus's once-for-all offering does not give a license for disobedience any more than the Day of Atonement effected atonement without repentance.[6]

For Further Reading

Additional Ancient Texts

Philo mentions the distinction between willful and involuntary sins in several places (e.g., *Spec. Laws* 1:234–38; *Posterity* 10–11) and suggests that sacrifices can atone for all sins (*Posterity* 48). For additional texts, see Craig Koester, *Hebrews: A New Translation with Introduction and Commentary*, AB (New York: Doubleday, 2001), 451. Later Christians debated whether forgiveness could be attained for post-baptismal sins, and Hebrews was at the center of it (see Herm. Vis. 2.2.4–5; Tertullian, *Modesty* 20).

English Translations and Critical Editions

Blackman, Philip. *Mishnayoth*. 2nd ed. 6 vols. New York: Judaica, 1990.

Danby, Herbert, ed. *The Mishnah*. Oxford: Oxford University Press, 1933.

Neusner, Jacob. *The Mishnah: A New Translation*. New Haven, CT: Yale University Press, 1988.

Secondary Literature

Bateman, Herbert W., ed. *Four Views on the Warning Passages in Hebrews*. Grand Rapids: Kregel, 2007.

Maccoby, Hyam. *Early Rabbinic Writings*. Cambridge: Cambridge University Press, 1988.

Strack, H. L., and G. Stemberger. *Introduction to the Talmud and Midrash*. Translated by Markus Bockmuehl. Edinburgh: T&T Clark, 1991.

---

6. Another connection between m. Yoma 8.9 and Hebrews 10:22 occurs in R. Akiba's statements about cleansing through water. Space does not permit an analysis of this here.

CHAPTER 16

2 Maccabees and Hebrews 11:1–22: Faith, Creation, and Resurrection Hope

MATTHEW C. EASTER

Hebrews 11 is the famous "hall of faith" chapter, where the author lists a number of heroes from Israel's story. These heroes are the "cloud of witnesses" surrounding us (12:1). Curiously, the author does not mention some heroes we might expect (such as Elijah, Ruth, Esther, or Josiah), and mentions others who do not play as large of a role in the Old Testament (such as Abel and Rahab). Other times he mentions a hero we might expect but does not tell the story the hero might be most known for. For example, the author mentions Joseph (11:22) but nothing about his fleeing temptation, interpreting dreams, or leading Egypt through famine. Similarly, he mentions Moses (11:23–28) but nothing about him as lawgiver. It seems, then, that the author chose his heroes and their accomplishments for a particular reason.

Faith in the Face of Death. The author of Hebrews likely chose the heroes he did because each of them showed faith in the face of death (see table 16.1).

Table 16.1. Heroes and Death in Hebrews 11

Hero	Relation to Death	Reference
Abel	"still speaks, even though he is dead"	11:4
Enoch	"taken from this life, so that he did not experience death"	11:5
Noah	prepared ark and so saved his household from death	11:7

Hero	Relation to Death	Reference
Sarah	at an old age gave birth to Isaac through a man "as good as dead"	11:11–12
"All these"	"were still living by faith when they died"	11:13
Abraham	"reasoned that God could even raise the dead, and so in a manner of speaking he did receive Isaac back from death"	11:17–19
Isaac	"blessed Jacob and Esau in regard to their future" (referring to their lives after his impending death)	11:20
Jacob	"when he was dying, blessed each of Joseph's sons"	11:21
Joseph	"when his end was near . . . gave instructions concerning the burial of his bones"	11:22
Moses	saved from the king's death edict; kept the Passover, saving the firstborn from the destroyer	11:23, 28
Israelites	escaped death at the Red Sea	11:29
Rahab	"was not killed with those who were disobedient"	11:31
Unnamed	"shut the mouths of lions, quenched the fury of the flames, and escaped the edge of the sword;" "became powerful in battle;" "women received back their dead, raised to life again;" "were tortured, refusing to be released so that they might gain an even better resurrection;" "put to death by stoning;" "sawed in two;" "killed by the sword"	11:33–37

Some exhibited faith by accepting death (11:36–37), others by faith avoided death in the face of dangerous threats (11:7, 17–19, 23, 28, 29, 31, and

33–35), and still others in faith looked beyond their own deaths to offer hope to the living (11:20–22). In each case faith is clearly situated in the context of death.

Death and Persecution. Why the focus on faith in the face of death? This is the message the hearers of Hebrews needed to hear. They had faced persecution in the past (10:32–34), and members of their fellowship were being mistreated and imprisoned now (13:3). While they had not yet resisted sin to the point of shedding their blood (12:4), the implication is that such a time might come, especially given that the race they would be running was one of suffering to the point of death, like Jesus did (12:1–3). So, whether the community was currently facing persecution, perceived themselves to be persecuted, or anticipated persecution in the future, the message of faith in the face of death spoke pastorally to their situation.

If faith in the face of death is the unifying theme in Hebrews 11, why did the author begin his "by faith" statements in 11:3 with a reference to creation ("By faith we understand that the universe was formed at God's command, so that what is seen was not made out of what was visible")? A comparison with 2 Maccabees 7 will help us to see that even Hebrews 11:3 is about faith in the face of death. Like Hebrews, 2 Maccabees narrates faith in the face of persecution. Both texts address the question, "If the righteous are faithful even to the point of death, then what hope do they have?"

2 Maccabees

"THE CREATOR OF THE WORLD . . . WILL GIVE BREATH AND LIFE BACK TO YOU AGAIN"

Second Maccabees is a theological history compiled by an unknown editor, condensing a five-book volume written in Greek by Jason of Cyrene (2 Macc 2:19–32). The book was likely completed around 124 BC, when Judea was under the leadership of the **Hasmonean** John Hyrcanus. The events in 2 Maccabees, however, recall the earlier struggle of Judea under the brutal rule of the **Seleucid** king **Antiochus IV Epiphanes** from 168–164 BC. Antiochus Epiphanes sought to Hellenize the Jews, making them adopt Greek customs and behavior.

Persecution under Antiochus Epiphanes. Antiochus's Hellenization campaign included serious persecution of Jews. The Jewish people were ordered to live no longer by the laws of God and to worship Zeus in the temple in Jerusalem (2 Macc 6:1–2). Gentiles overtook the temple, behaved debaucherously, and sacrificed animals that were "unfit"—namely, swine (6:3–5).

The persecution took a particularly gruesome turn when the colonizers tried to force Jews to eat swine's flesh. They started with Eleazar, an elderly high-ranking scribe. He refused even to eat a different clean meat and pretend it was pork because he wanted to die as an example to younger Jews (6:18–31). Next, seven brothers and their mother were arrested and tortured until they would eat swine's flesh. Each of them refused and were murdered for their refusal (7:1–42).

Hope of Resurrection in the Face of Death. The mother and her seven sons died hoping to be raised again. The second son confidently told his torturer, "You accursed wretch, you release us from this present life, but the king of the world will raise us up into eternal resurrection life after we die for his laws" (7:9).[1] Likewise, the third brother eagerly offered his tongue and limbs for removal (7:10), because he expected to get them back again: "I received these from heaven, and I am disregarding these on account of his laws, and I hope to receive these again from him" (7:11). Likewise, the fourth son expected to be raised: "It is desirable while dying by human hands to hold out hope from God to be raised up again by him. But for you there will be no resurrection into life" (7:14).

Creation and Resurrection Hope. The mother's words are most relevant to Hebrews 11:3. She based her resurrection hope in God's creative power. She believed that the God who creates life in the womb can re-create life:

> I do not know how you appeared in my womb. I neither gave you breath and life, nor did I arrange the elements in each of you. Therefore, the creator of the world, the one who formed the beginning of humanity and crafted the beginning of all things, will give you breath and life back again with mercy, since now you are disregarding yourselves for his laws. (7:22–23)

Similarly, the mother based her resurrection hope in God's creation of all things:

> I beg you, child, after looking to heaven and earth, and after seeing everything in them, to recognize that God did not make them out of things that existed. And in the same way the human race

---

1. All translations of 2 Maccabees are my own.

was created. Do not fear this executioner, but proving worthy of your brothers, welcome death in order that in God's mercy I might receive you back with your brothers. (7:28–29)

Even though the torturers mutilated the bodies of the martyrs, the God who created the world can resurrect these destroyed bodies into a whole state. The hope of resurrection, therefore, is rooted in God's creative power. These martyrs could have faith in the face of death because the creator God can re-create their bodies through resurrection (see also 2 Macc 12:43–45; 14:46). Returning to Hebrews, we see a similar hope for the faithful.

Hebrews 11:1–22

"BY FAITH WE UNDERSTAND THAT THE UNIVERSE WAS FORMED AT GOD'S COMMAND"

There are several parallels between 2 Maccabees 7 and Hebrews 11. Once we recognize these parallels, Hebrews' comments about death, resurrection, and creation come into a new light.

Table 16.2. Suffering and Hope in 2 Maccabees 7 and Hebrews 11

2 Maccabees 7	Hebrews 11
The mother expected her sons to be raised (7:22–29).	"Women received back their dead, raised to life again" (11:35).
tortured on "the rack" (6:19, 28)	"were tortured" (11:35)
Eleazar refused to be released, even though he could have been saved from death (6:23–30); the seven brothers refused to be released (7:2, 7–8, 24–30).	"refusing to be released" (11:35)
The seven brothers hoped to be vindicated by resurrection (7:9, 11, 14, 23, 29).	"so that they might gain an even better resurrection" (11:35)
teased the second brother for the sport (7:7)	"faced jeers" (11:36)
tortured with whips (7:1)	"flogging" (11:36)

Like the Maccabean martyrs, each of the heroes in Hebrews 11 showed faith in the face of death. The Maccabeans viewed suffering as discipline (2 Macc 6:12–16; 7:18–19, 32–33), similar to Hebrews' exhortation to endure trials as God's parental discipline (Heb 12:5–11). This was a comforting message to the persecuted community of Hebrews. The author remained convinced that this community would not shrink back to destruction but would be faithful to the preservation of their lives (10:39). The next verse says, "Now faith is confidence in what we hope for and assurance about what we do not see" (11:1). In other words, the nature of faith is one that should conclude assuredly in the preservation of life, as the previous verse says.

Unfulfilled Hope of Resurrection. The "ancients were commended for" this faith (11:2), but none of them received what had been promised (11:13, 39). Although the author did not explicitly say what the promises were, he likely had the hope of life after death in mind. In fact, the author named a number of temporal promises the heroes *did* receive, and yet he maintained that they died without receiving the promises. Abraham received the promises (11:17), the content of which are likely numerous descendants, given that the author described Abraham as the one to whom God said, "It is through Isaac that your offspring will be reckoned" (11:18, quoting Gen 21:12). The author made a similar claim about Abraham's realization of the promised descendants in 11:11–12, where he noted that "by faith even Sarah, who was past childbearing age, was enabled to bear children" (11:11), and "from this one man [Abraham], and he as good as dead, came descendants as numerous as the stars" (11:12; see also 6:15). Given that the author clearly believed Abraham received the promises and yet at the same time maintained that he and others died without receiving the promises in 11:13, these promises in 11:13 must refer to something he failed to receive in his temporal life. The reason they failed to receive these promises is not because God is a poor promise keeper who did not deliver on his earthly promises (10:23 and 11:11 say quite the contrary), but because God's promises are reserved for after death. The author of Hebrews maintains that they have not received these **eschatological** promises, but he still maintains hope that they will receive them at some point in the future (as insinuated especially by "together with us" in 11:40).

Creation and Resurrection Hope. These heroes of faith, who exemplified an "assurance about what we do not see," still died in faith without experiencing the promise of life. Where is the hope for Hebrews' persecuted community? Hebrews 11:3 gives the answer. The first "by faith" in Hebrews 11 is not attributed to a hero, but to *us*: "By faith *we* understand that the universe was formed at God's command, so that what is seen was not made out of what was visible." Given the number of parallels to 2 Maccabees 6–7 in Hebrews 11–12, the author's introduction of God as creator in Hebrews 11:3 likely parallels the Maccabean mother's words. If Hebrews 11:3 parallels this scene of martyrdom in 2 Maccabees 7, then the author introduced God as creator to substantiate the hope of resurrection we see later in Hebrews 11. Like the Maccabean mother, the hearers of Hebrews need not fear what may happen to their bodies. God created the world from nothing, so resurrecting a body is no big deal. Even though none of the heroes in Hebrews 11 have yet received the promises, the creator God will re-create all of the faithful through resurrection. This "is confidence in what we hope for and assurance about what we do not see" (11:1)!

This hope of resurrection explains why the author began his encomium with our understanding of God as creator in Hebrews 11:3. All the heroes of faith in Hebrews 11 exercised faith in the face of death, and the author began this list by noting that God can re-create the lives of those who die in faith. At present, however, none of the heroes have been "made perfect" (11:40), likely another reference to resurrection. The final hope of resurrection is intertwined with the destiny of another faithful one yet to come: Jesus, the one who will "perfect" faith (12:2). His resurrection gives the faithful hope of the same (2:5–13; 5:6–10; 7:11–28; 13:20).

For Further Reading

Additional Ancient Texts

For other **Second Temple Jewish** texts on the resurrection, see 1QS 11.5–8; 4Q385; 4Q386; 1QH[a] 19.13–17; 2 Baruch 49–51; Jubilees 23.31; Wisdom of Solomon 3; Testament of Judah 25:4; Liber antiquitatum biblicarum 19.12–13; 23.13; and **Josephus** (*Ag. Ap.* 2.217–18; *J.W.* 2.163–65; *Ant.* 18.14–16). For creation, see Wisdom of Solomon 1:12–15; Sirach 24:8; 4 Maccabees 11.5 (part of the larger story of the seven brothers in 8.3–13.1, but with a hope of immortality rather than resurrection). Outside of Hebrews 11, other potential references to resurrection in Hebrews are found in 2:9–13; 3:12, 19; 4:2–3; 5:7–9; 6:1; 7:16, 28; and 13:19–20. For God as creator in Hebrews, see also 1:2.

English Translations and Critical Editions

Hanhart, R. *Maccabaeorum Liber II*. Septuaginta 9.2. Göttingen: Vandenhoeck and Ruprecht, 1976.

New English Translation of the Septuagint
New Revised Standard Version

Secondary Literature

Easter, Matthew C. *Faith and the Faithfulness of Jesus in Hebrews*. SNTSMS
  160. Cambridge: Cambridge University Press, 2014.
Eisenbaum, Pamela Michelle. *The Jewish Heroes of Christian History:
  Hebrews 11 in Literary Context*. SBLDS 156. Atlanta: Scholars, 1997.
Moffitt, David M. *Atonement and the Logic of Resurrection in the Epistle to the
  Hebrews*. NovTSup 141. Leiden: Brill, 2011.
Nickelsburg, George W. E. *Resurrection, Immortality, and Eternal Life in
  Intertestamental Judaism*. HTS 26. Cambridge, MA: Harvard University
  Press, 1972.
Segal, Alan F. *Life after Death: A History of the Afterlife in the Religions of the
  West*. New York: Doubleday, 2004.
van Henten, Jan Willem. *The Maccabean Martyrs as Saviours of the Jewish
  People: A Study of 2 and 4 Maccabees*. JSJSup 57. Leiden: Brill, 1997.

CHAPTER 17

The Biblical Antiquities and Hebrews 11:23–40: Israel's History as a Call to Faith

---∞∞∞---

SUSAN DOCHERTY

ebrews 11:23–40 is the second half of a longer unit in which a cast of scriptural characters are held up as models of faith (11:1–40). The author understands "faith" in a very specific way, as "confidence in what we hope for and assurance about what we do not see" (11:1). In this section, therefore, he shapes his selective presentation of figures from Moses to the Maccabean martyrs to fit this definition. He encourages his audience to imitate their example of trust in future salvation, but also to view their lives as pointing ultimately to the climactic coming of Jesus: "These were all commended for their faith, yet none of them received what had been promised, since God had planned something better for us" (11:39–40; cf. 6:9–20; 10:32–39; 12:1–4; 13:12–14).

The interpretation of Israel's Scriptures is central to the argument of Hebrews as a whole, and the exegetical traditions and techniques employed in the letter have often been compared with early Jewish writings from the Qumran Scrolls to Philo. Another potentially fruitful conversation partner is the Biblical Antiquities, or LAB (from the initials of its Latin title, Liber antiquitatum biblicarum).

The Biblical Antiquities

"FOR GOD . . . DID NOT EMPTILY ESTABLISH A COVENANT WITH OUR FATHERS"

The Biblical Antiquities is one of a small group of texts that retell the scriptural narratives using a combination of abbreviation and expansion of the original material.[1] It reworks parts of the books of the Pentateuch and Former Prophets, with a special emphasis on the covenant and on the role of Israel's leaders in maintaining this unique relationship between the people and their God.[2] Originally composed in Hebrew, it has survived only in a Latin version based on a Greek translation. Its unknown author probably lived in Palestine in the late first century AD and is sometimes referred to as Pseudo-Philo because the work was traditionally—although mistakenly—attributed to Philo of Alexandria.[3] The work offers, therefore, a Jewish reading of Israel's history contemporary with the New Testament. Its coverage of the period of the judges and early kings is especially comprehensive, accounting for almost two-thirds of the text (LAB 25–65), so its content overlaps with Hebrews 11:29–34. Its interpretation of two scriptural episodes in particular illuminates their treatment in the letter: the birth of Moses (LAB 9:1–16; cf. Exod 2:1–10) and Joshua's sending of scouts into Jericho (LAB 20:1–7; cf. Josh 2:1–24).

The Birth of Moses and the Covenant Promises. The pentateuchal account of the birth of Moses, and the decision by his parents to save him from the pharaoh's murderous decree, is notably embellished in the Biblical Antiquities. In a style characteristic of its author, the role of the minor characters in this narrative is enhanced, and dramatic speeches are created to express central theological themes. The Scriptures themselves provide no information about the response of the Hebrew slaves to the edict that their children are to be killed or taken away as Egyptian concubines, so Pseudo-Philo fills in this gap. He imagines a scene in which the people gather together with their elders to discuss this threat, and resolve collectively that from now on "a man should not approach his wife lest the fruit of their wombs be defiled and our offspring serve idols. For it is better to die without children, until we know what God does" (LAB 9:2).[4]

One man dissents from this proposed course of action, though—Moses's father, named here as Amram. He urges his fellow-Israelites to show greater

---

1. This genre of so-called "rewritten Scriptures" also includes the *Book of Jubilees*, the Qumran Genesis Apocryphon, and Josephus's *Jewish Antiquities* 1–11. For further discussion of it, see Molly M. Zahn, *Genres of Rewriting in Second Temple Judaism: Scribal Composition and Transmission* (Cambridge: Cambridge University Press, 2020).

2. On the major themes of Liber antiquitatum biblicarum, see Frederick J. Murphy, *Pseudo-Philo: Rewriting the Bible* (Oxford: Oxford University Press, 1993).

3. For further detail on date and provenance, see Daniel M. Gurtner, *Introducing the Pseudepigrapha of Second Temple Judaism* (Grand Rapids: Baker Academic, 2020), 256–75.

4. All English translations of the Biblical Antiquities are taken from Howard Jacobson, *A Commentary on Pseudo-Philo's Liber Antiquitatum Biblicarum with Latin Text and English Translation*, 2 vols., AGJU 31 (Leiden: Brill, 1996), 1:89–194.

confidence in the power of God to protect them, and in so doing, to fulfill the assurances about innumerable descendants made to Abraham: "Sooner will the world be destroyed forever or the universe sink into the immeasurable or the heart of the deep touch the stars than that the race of the sons of Israel will be destroyed. Some day the covenant will be fulfilled, that he established with Abraham.... I will not abide by what you decree, but I will go in and take my wife and produce children so that we will multiply upon the earth" (LAB 9:3–4).

Amram's arguments persuade the elders to change their minds, and they also receive divine approval: "Because Amram's plan has pleased me, and he has not put aside the covenant established between me and his fathers, behold therefore now he who will be born from him will serve me forever ... and I will perform through him signs and wonders for my people that I have not done for anyone else" (LAB 9:7). Moses's very conception becomes, then, an act of faith in the permanency of the covenant. His unique role as an instrument of future salvation is confirmed in a dream vision experienced by his sister, Miriam, just before his birth, in which an angelic figure announces: "I will work signs through him and save my people, and he will exercise leadership always" (LAB 9:10). When the child grows up, he becomes "glorious above all other men, and through him God freed the sons of Israel as he had said" (LAB 9:16).

Joshua's Conquest of Jericho. The scriptural narratives about the conquest of the land of Canaan are also retold in the Biblical Antiquities with numerous additions and amendments. Pseudo-Philo begins with an account of the transfer of leadership from Moses to Joshua, a choice unequivocally confirmed in a speech by God: "This one will lead my people after you, and into his hand will I deliver the kings of the Amorites" (LAB 20:2). Joshua's first act as Moses's successor is to send scouts into Jericho (LAB 20:6), but the account of this episode is heavily summarized. No reference is made to Rahab's role in sheltering these Israelite spies (Josh 2:1–21) or to the later circling of the city walls that led to their collapse (Josh 6:12–21). The only information given is that "they went up and spied out the city. After they brought back word, the people went up and stormed the city and burned it with fire" (LAB 20:7).

This exploratory mission into Jericho is, however, purposefully connected with an earlier time, when Moses similarly sent out a party of twelve men to survey the land of Canaan before its occupation (LAB 15:16; cf. Num 13:1–14:10). Pseudo-Philo names the two spies sent into Jericho as Cenaz and Naam, the sons of Caleb, and states explicitly that they were given this task because of the part played by their father in the earlier expedition:

> I and your father were sent by Moses in the wilderness, and we went up with ten other men. On their return they spoke ill about the land and disheartened the people, and they and the heart of the people with them were discouraged. But I and your father alone fulfilled the word of the Lord, and behold we are alive today. Now I will send you to spy out the land and Jericho. Imitate your father, and you also will live. (LAB 20:6; cf. 15:1–4).

Caleb and Joshua are praised, then, for trusting in God's power to deliver the Israelites, and are cited as models of faith and righteous action to be imitated by those who come after them.

Two features of the retelling of these narratives about Moses and Joshua in the Biblical Antiquities are especially relevant for the interpretation of the same scriptural material in Hebrews. First, connections and correspondences between different episodes and characters (Abraham and Amram; Moses and Joshua; Caleb and his sons; two analogous spying missions) are highlighted to show that God's dealings with Israel follow a consistent pattern. Second, a greater emphasis is placed on the positive example of certain individuals—especially leaders—who stand out in times of crisis for their unwavering faith in the certainty of the covenant promises and whose hopes are vindicated. It is possible that Pseudo-Philo was deliberately presenting Israel's early rulers as exemplars of the kind of bold, faithful leadership that he considered necessary in his own context.[5] Certainly his work illustrates the long history of exegetical reflection on scriptural figures on which the New Testament writers were also able to draw.

Hebrews 11:23–40

"ONLY TOGETHER WITH US WOULD THEY BE MADE PERFECT"

At this point in his review of Israel's history, the focus of the author of Hebrews turns to Moses, whose status as God's faithful servant has already

---

5. For this view, see esp. George W. E. Nickelsburg, "Good and Bad Leaders in Pseudo-Philo's *Liber Antiquitatum Biblicarum*." in *Ideal Figures in Ancient Judaism: Profiles and Paradigms*, ed. G. W. E. Nickelsburg and J. J. Collins (Chico, CA: Scholars, 1980), 49–66.

been considered earlier in the letter (3:1–6; cf. 8:5–6). He then discusses more briefly two episodes from the conquest narratives: the toppling of the walls of Jericho (Josh 6:1–21) and the help offered at that time to Israel's spies by Rahab (Josh 2:1–24; 6:22–25; cf. Jas 2:25). This section closes with a chain of allusions to other scriptural characters who have demonstrated the virtues of faith and perseverance (11:32–38). Some of these are named (Gideon, Barak, Samson, Jephthah, David, and Samuel), while others are identified only in general terms, as prophets (11:32), or as unnamed women (11:35). Extrabiblical traditions are also incorporated into these verses, such as the accounts of the sawing in two of the prophet Isaiah (Mart. Isa. 5:11–14) and the perseverance under torture of the Maccabean martyrs (2 Macc 6:18–7:42).

Moses as an Exemplar of Faith. Given the importance of Moses within Judaism, his inclusion in this catalog of exemplars is not at all remarkable. More surprising, though, are the specific aspects of his life chosen here to illustrate his "faith." The first episode cited, for example, seems to offer more insight into the character of his mother and father than of Moses himself: "By faith Moses' parents hid him for three months after he was born, because they saw he was no ordinary child, and they were not afraid of the king's edict" (11:23). The Biblical Antiquities, however, attests to a tradition of reading back into the narrative of Moses's birth both a recognition of his extraordinary qualities and an understanding of his preservation from death as an act of courageous confidence by his family in the fulfillment of God's promises to Israel. The adult Moses would himself face dangers with a steadfast faith like that of his parents: "By faith he left Egypt, not fearing the king's anger; he persevered because he saw him who is invisible" (11:27). This is the attitude that the members of the community to which the letter is addressed should aspire to emulate as they endure their own times of adversity (10:32–35; 13:13).

As in the Biblical Antiquities, then, Moses's life is connected in Hebrews with the theme of future promise. Unlike Pseudo-Philo, however, this author regards Jesus as the one who will truly fulfill all the scriptural hopes (11:39–40). He interprets the figure of Moses through this lens, therefore, presenting his experiences of opposition and rejection as somehow foreshadowing or predicting the more significant sufferings of Christ, for whose sake he willingly accepted "disgrace" (11:26; cf. 12:2; Ps 69:7–9; Rom 15:3).[6]

The Faith of Israel's Early Leaders. Like Pseudo-Philo, the author of

---

6. The possible meanings of this verse are discussed more fully in Harold W. Attridge, *Hebrews: A Commentary on the Epistle to the Hebrews*, Hermeneia (Philadelphia: Fortress, 1989), 341–42.

Hebrews also relates the period of the judges and early kings in a very selective way, directing attention to the role of certain successful rulers. As the parallels between figures like Gideon (LAB 35:1–36:4), Jephthah (LAB 39:1–40:8), Samson (LAB 42:1–43:8), and Samuel and David (LAB 50:1–65:5) are accentuated in LAB, so in Hebrews these figures are presented as part of a connected chain, "a great cloud of witnesses" (12:1) to the ideal of faithful perseverance.

Hebrews differs from the Biblical Antiquities, however, in including more detail about the toppling of the walls of Jericho and in appealing specifically to the example of Rahab. Pseudo-Philo focuses only on the people of Israel and their national leaders, but the outsider Rahab is of more interest to New Testament interpreters.[7] She appears again alongside Abraham as an exemplar of faith in action in the Letter of James (Jas 2:25), for instance, and is named as an ancestor of Jesus in the genealogy in Matthew's Gospel (Matt 1:5). Her status as a pagan foreigner was perhaps important for debates about the legitimacy of the inclusion of gentiles into the early Christian churches.

Conclusion. This chapter has highlighted some of the interpretative traditions and techniques common to the Biblical Antiquities and Hebrews 11:23–40. Both authors read Israel's history as an overarching story of unshakable divine promises and highlighted scriptural characters who continued to trust in the fulfillment of those promises, even in times of oppression and danger. This reuse of the scriptural narratives within Hebrews has theological implications as well as rhetorical power. It calls on the followers of Jesus to see themselves as part of the one community of God's people as they wait for the full realization of their common hopes, since it is "together" that we, both Jews and Christians, are "made perfect" (11:40).

FURTHER READING

Additional Ancient Texts

Josephus's *Jewish Antiquities* is another extensive rewriting of the Scriptures dating from the late first century CE; Books II–VII cover the period treated in Hebrews 11:23–40. For other early Jewish reviews of scriptural history and its major figures, see 1 Maccabees 2:51–61; 4 Maccabees 16; Wisdom of Solomon 10:1–11:16; Sirach 44–50; Philo, *On Rewards and Punishments* 11–14 and *On the Virtues* 198–205. Stephen's speech in Acts 7:2–53 offers a comparable New Testament example of this form.

---

7. See further Pamela M. Eisenbaum, *The Jewish Heroes of Christian History: Hebrews 11 in Literary Context*, SBLDS 156 (Atlanta: Scholars, 1997).

English Translations and Critical Editions

Harrington, Daniel J. "Pseudo-Philo: A New Translation and Introduction." Pages 297–377 in *The Old Testament Pseudepigrapha Vol. 2*. Edited by James H. Charlesworth. Garden City, NY: Doubleday, 1985.

Jacobson, Howard J. *A Commentary on Pseudo-Philo's* Liber Antiquitatum Biblicarum: *With Latin Text and English Translation*. 2 vols. Leiden: Brill, 1996.

James, Montague R. "The Biblical Antiquities of Philo." http://www.earlyjewishwritings.com/pseudophilo.html.

Secondary Literature

Bauckham, Richard et al., eds., *The Epistle to the Hebrews and Christian Theology*. Grand Rapids: Eerdmans, 2009.

Eisenbaum, Pamela M. *The Jewish Heroes of Christian History: Hebrews 11 in Literary Context*. SBLDS 156. Atlanta: Scholars, 1997.

Fisk, Bruce N. *Do You Not Remember? Scripture, Story and Exegesis in the Rewritten Bible of Pseudo-Philo*. JSPSup 37. Sheffield: Sheffield Academic, 2001.

Murphy, Frederick J. *Pseudo-Philo: Rewriting the Bible*. Oxford: Oxford University Press, 1993.

Zahn, Molly M. *Genres of Rewriting in Second Temple Judaism: Scribal Composition and Transmission*. Cambridge: Cambridge University Press, 2020.

CHAPTER 18

Psalms of Solomon and Hebrews 12:1–17: The Paternal Discipline of God

AMY PEELER

Near the end of this weighty "word of encouragement," the author returns to an image of God with which he began his address: God as Father (Heb 1:5; 12:9). In this occurrence in chapter 12, his interest lies not in God's relationship with *the Son*, Jesus the Messiah, as was the case at the beginning of the sermon, but in God's paternal relationship with the readers of this letter. He cites explicitly Proverbs 3:11–12 in this section and, in so doing, shows that his reflections on the benefits of being on the receiving end of divine parenting techniques found resonance with many other ancient authors, including quite close parallels with another Jewish text of the Second Temple period, the Psalms of Solomon.

Psalms of Solomon answers a question that the New Testament cannot: How did Jews respond to the desecration of the temple? It might be the case that some of the literature of the New Testament—and Hebrews is a leading contender for this possibility—provides evidence of Jewish reflection on the fall of the temple to the Romans in AD 70. The New Testament never mentions this event explicitly, however. Consequently, scholars have yet to reach a consensus that it can provide insight into this question.

Psalms of Solomon, on the other hand, is widely agreed to have been written in response to the desecration of the temple in an earlier generation. A heart-wrenching example of theodicy that dares to ask about the presence of God amid evil, Psalms of Solomon offers the very same comfort as the author of Hebrews, even if it is not in response to the same event. Although it might be a difficult argument to make because it seems so counterintuitive, both authors stand by the claim that suffering is a sign of God's presence, not a sign of God's absence and, even more weighty, that suffering is evidence of God's paternal education. Listening well to this text helps contemporary readers of Hebrews place the sermon in its own cultural milieu and discover how different authors wrestled with the common human experience of suffering.

Psalms of Solomon

"HAPPY IS THE ONE THE LORD REMEMBERS WITH REBUKING AND PROTECTS FROM THE EVIL WAY WITH A WHIP"

The text of the Psalms of Solomon, although originally written in Hebrew, has been preserved in fifteen manuscripts, mostly Greek and a few Syriac. The events depicted in the Psalms of Solomon indicate that the author (or authors if the Psalms of Solomon are a compilation, as many experts suggest) mourned the presence of a ruler from the West who had sieged the temple. To the grief of the Jewish people, this happened several times throughout their history, but the invasion of Pompey in 63 BC best matches the details of the Psalms. When Israel was poised on the brink of a civil war between the factions supporting the Maccabean brothers Hyrcanus and Aristobulus, Pompey, a Roman general stationed in the East, intervened to establish order. His initially peaceful entrance turned deadly and resulted in his egregious infractions inside the temple.

The theme of God's discipline is especially clear in the tenth chapter of the Psalms of Solomon, and therefore this is a fitting place to begin a comparison with Hebrews. There, with the use of some of the same words, likely due to a common reading of Proverbs, both authors affirm the goodness of God's discipline even when painful. This, however, is not the only place of overlap. Psalms of Solomon discusses God's discipline throughout the collection. Thus, it leaves the reader with a deeper understanding of how faithful Jews of the Second Temple period understood God's involvement with suffering.

Discipline, Not Destruction, for the Righteous. The psalmist was careful to delineate the limits of God's discipline. It may be intense, but it is not destructive. Chapter 7 mentions death itself: "For if you [God] sent death you would give him instructions about us. For you are kind and will not be angry enough to destroy us" (7.4).[1] God's children may experience brushes even with death, but they will not experience annihilation.

The author could be confident of this preservation because throughout the book the psalmist held a tension between corporate and individual discipline. God is the one who disciplines Israel (8.26), yet the author recognizes differences in the nation. The fate of sinners will be different from the fate of the righteous. Hence this collection also recognizes that "the Lord's righteous judgments are according to the individual and the household" (9.5).

Although God's treatments are tailored to the particular child, the Psalms frequently affirm that everyone deserves discipline. For the psalmist, none is righteous; no, not one. The discipline that he and the fellow righteous are experiencing indicate some secret sins that God, through discipline, exposes and then corrects. The righteous person does "stumble" and therefore "proves the Lord right" (3.5). The discipline that God gives comes because of sin. As the righteous "constantly searches his house to remove his unintentional sins" (3.7), the Lord, too, is "cleansing every devout person and his house" (3.8) and doing that cleansing through discipline.

Hence, although all may experience difficulty, the discipline of the (mostly) righteous is for hidden sins and is therefore less destructive than that of sinners. Psalms of Solomon 13.7–8 reads, "For the discipline of the righteous (for things done) in ignorance is not the same as the destruction of the sinners. In secret the righteous are disciplined lest the sinner gloat over the righteous." This is the nature of God's paternal discipline, meted out with the care a father would show for a firstborn son, even an only child (18.4), in order to "divert the perceptive person from unintentional sins" (18.4b).

Discipline for One's Good. Consequently, the Lord's attention—even when it comes in the form of rebuke (*elegkos*)—is a good thing. The aim of God's discipline is to root out something detrimental to the person. The author draws from the intense language of Proverbs 3:11, which depicts God using a whip (*mastigos*). These are parenting sensibilities with which many would no longer find themselves comfortable, but contemporary readers must realize that a belief in corporal punishment in parenting was a widespread assumption.

Discipline from the Messiah. As a manifestation of God's presence with

---

1. Translations of Psalms of Solomon are from R. B. Wright in *Old Testament Pseudepigrapha*, vol 2., ed. J. H. Charlesworth (New York: Doubleday, 1985).

them in the midst of this historical challenge, the Psalms of Solomon look forward to God's promise of a messiah, a Son of David who would root out the invaders and restore godly virtues. Psalms of Solomon unites the affirmations of divine discipline with the hope for a messiah. In chapter 17 the Son of David whom God raises up to rule Israel knows the standing God's people have, namely, that they are God's children (17.27). As many other portions of the book have established that God's children are the recipients of God's discipline, here it is the Lord Messiah who metes out that discipline (17.42). He will lead them in the way of holiness, which includes the purification of discipline. The author celebrates the good fortune of those born in the time of Messiah's reign because they will get to be under "the rod of discipline of the Lord Messiah" (18.4). He will lead them in "the fear of his God, in wisdom of spirit, and of righteousness and strength, to direct people in righteous acts" (18.7–8). The discipline they need to interpret as coming from God will then be implemented by the heir of David who sits on Israel's throne.

Hebrews 12:1–17

"ENDURE TRIALS FOR THE SAKE OF DISCIPLINE. GOD IS TREATING YOU AS CHILDREN"

Chapter 12 of the sermon-letter to the "Hebrews" holds within it the rhetorical high point of the whole. The complex Christology—in which the Son of God is at the same time the sympathetic human high priest—and the passionate exhortations of both challenge and comfort here merge. This is accomplished through the author's varied imagery of struggle and its reward. The athletic contests of the first half of the chapter arrive at the towering mountains of the second half. An overview of the chapter provides the context in which to understand the author's portrayal of God's discipline.

The author encourages the congregation to run the race (12:1) because they are surrounded by all the faithful whose stories he brings to mind in the poetic eleventh chapter. Surrounded by such faithful people, the audience can find encouragement to keep running. If Israel's heroes faced shame, hardship, and even death, and God remained faithful to the promises, this was good assurance that God would act in the same way with the congregation in the first century. Chiefly, though, they could be encouraged by keeping their eyes on Jesus, the ultimate example of faith. He was faithful to endure shame and death, even death on the cross, and was now seated at the right hand of God. If their brother had made it, they could too.

It is at this point that the author focuses on the need for endurance in another way by shifting from the picture of a race to that of parental discipline. In this section it becomes clear that Hebrews shares many of the same themes as Psalms of Solomon concerning God's discipline but applies them in distinct ways.

Punitive vs. Educative Discipline. Scholars have debated if Hebrews is discussing a punitive aspect of God's discipline in Hebrews 12, where God uses discipline to punish for a particular sin. Like the Psalms of Solomon, the author of Hebrews cites Proverbs to demonstrate that God uses a whip to show love to his children (Heb 12:6; citing Prov 3:11–12), and he acknowledges that discipline is not full of joy, but of grief (12:11). On the other hand, other interpreters argue that the author is focusing on more of an educative aspect, in which God's discipline trains children unto maturity. Hence, the concept of "hidden sins" in Psalms of Solomon may resonate with the author of Hebrews' assertion that this community is not as far along in their life of faith as they should be (see esp. Heb 5:11–14). God's discipline (especially with the benefit of the author of Hebrews' helpful interpretation of it) may reveal to them "sins" of immaturity within their community for which they need to repent.

Children vs. Enemies. This educative or revelatory sense of discipline reveals another point of similarity between Hebrews and Psalms of Solomon. Hebrews similarly draws a line between God's discipline of children and God's wrath against enemies. The author frequently refers to everything being brought under the feet of the Son with his allusions to Psalm 110:1, but the author is explicit that God has particular punishments for those who are opposed to the work of God (Heb 2:2; 10:27–28), and so he employs the intense imagery of fire. This might be purgative, but it could also be destructive.

On the other hand, the author makes clear, much like Psalms of Solomon, that God's discipline of the children will never weigh them down to the point of their being destroyed. The author compares God to responsible parents, all of whom use discipline. Whereas human parents do so without complete knowledge, indeed only in ways that seem best to them (12:10), God utilizes discipline with complete knowledge of what is truly beneficial. If the congregants endure God's discipline, they will not only grow in maturity but also come to share in the qualities that make living with God forever a possibility, including holiness, peace, and righteousness (12:11).

At the same time, the experience of discipline might have been more intense for the author of Hebrews than for the psalmist. Psalms of Solomon 15 claims that famine, sword, and death shall be far from the righteous (15.7). They may have encounters with death but not finally be put under its power (7.4–5). Even poverty seems to be beyond what God would use for discipline (16.13). For the author of Hebrews, however, his community had already had their goods taken away (Heb 10:34), and members of their community had already died (Heb 13:7). Yet with such a robust belief in a future life with God, even these things do not translate as destruction.

Communal vs. Individual Discipline. Hebrews also maintains a balance between both corporate and individual discipline. God's discipline is for the community as a whole. God's parental address comes to them all; they all receive it as sons of God (12:5). Each of them, the author asserts, has already participated in this discipline (12:8). This is the proof that they are members of God's family.

After the citation of and reflection upon the verses from Proverbs 3, the author of Hebrews continues to emphasize the importance of the communal dimension of God's discipline, but he does so in such a way that recognizes the distinctions among the community members. Some of them may have been stronger than others—some may have had weak knees and drooping hands—and may have needed to strengthen those who were particularly tempted to fall (12:13–14). They needed to watch over themselves and their fellow congregants so that no one would wander from the family or cause harm within the family. Images of weeds in gardens and Esau's selling of his birthright provided examples of the kinds of dangers they should avoid personally and corporately.

Messianic Presence. If the first half of the chapter highlights the struggle, the second half highlights the reward. If they accept and endure God's invitation to struggle—to keep running and to embrace the discipline of God's training—then they would reach their goal, the mountain of God. They had not come to Mount Sinai, where the law was given in a way that elicited terror (12:18–21). The goal of their race is Mount Zion, where God dwells in celebration with angels and humans (12:22–24). They could approach this mountain because Jesus, the mediator, is there. He had finished his struggle, and so they could finish theirs.

Hence, Hebrews, too, joins God's paternal presence with messianic conviction, the only, yet major, difference being that the Psalms of Solomon greet this messiah from a distance—he is a shadowy future figure—whereas the author of Hebrews invites his readers to approach the throne where the messiah resides. He is Jesus who has lived, died, risen again, and ascended to the right hand of God.

Conclusion. God's parental discipline is one of the several threads the author employs in Hebrews 12 and throughout the sermon to communicate his passionate plea for this congregation to endure. In so doing, the author echoes many other thinkers in the ancient world in his assertions that God disciplines his children. While best practices in parenting have changed since the ancient world, the conviction that God is superior to any parent grants assurance for ancient as well as contemporary communities of faith that whatever methods God employs in the lives of those he loves can be trusted as ultimately wise and beneficial.

FOR FURTHER READING

Additional Ancient Texts

The following texts from both Jewish and Roman authors show how common the belief was that a good God will allow hardship in the lives of his children for their benefit: Philo, *On the Preliminary Studies*, 177; Wisdom of Solomon 12; 2 Maccabees 6; 4 Maccabees 10; Seneca, *On Providence* 1.

English Translations and Critical Editions

Kim, H. C. *Psalms of Solomon: A New Translation and Introduction.* Highland Park, NJ: Hermit Kingdom, 2008.

Wright, Robert B. "The Psalms of Solomon." Pages 639–70 in *The Old Testament Pseudepigrapha*. Vol. 2. Edited by James H. Charlesworth. Garden City, NY: Doubleday, 1985.

———, ed. *The Psalms of Solomon: A Critical Edition of the Greek Text.* Jewish and Christian Texts 1. New York: T&T Clark, 2007.

Secondary Literature

Abel, Frantisek. *The Psalms of Solomon and the Messianic Ethics of Paul.* WUNT 2/416. Tübingen: Mohr Siebeck, 2015.

Atkinson, Kenneth. *I Cried to the Lord: A Study of the Psalms of Solomon's Historical Background and Social Setting Creation to New Creation: Old Testament Perspectives.* JSJSup. London: Brill, 2003.

Bons, Eberhard, and Patrick Pouchelle, eds. *The Psalms of Solomon: Language, History, Theology.* Early Judaism and Its Literature 40. Atlanta: Society of Biblical Literature, 2015.

Croy, Clayton N. *Endurance in Suffering: Hebrews 12:1–13 in Its Rhetorical, Religious, and Philosophical Context.* SNTSMS 98. Cambridge: Cambridge University Press, 1998.

Webb, William J. *Corporal Punishment in the Bible: A Redemptive-Movement Hermeneutic for Troubling Texts.* Downers Grove, IL: IVP Academic, 2011.

CHAPTER 19

The Samaritan Pentateuch and Hebrews 12:18–29: Moses on the Mountain

MICHAEL H. KIBBE

The climactic pronouncement of Hebrews is that we approach God on the heavenly Mount Zion, not on the earthly Mount Sinai (12:18–24). And the final point of comparison between those two locations—the climax of the climax, we might say—is that on one mountain stands Moses, weak-kneed and white-faced before the Holy One of Israel (12:21), and on the other we find Jesus, seated and at ease at the right hand of his Father (12:24). You can hardly blame Moses—a thunderstorm combined with an earthquake combined with a volcano is enough to scare anyone.[1]

But this isn't just anyone. This is *Moses*. Moses, the greatest prophet and lawgiver and mediator and judge and king and shepherd. Early Jewish writers (think the **Dead Sea Scrolls**, **Josephus**, **Philo**, the **Pseudepigrapha**, and all the rest) tripped over themselves trying to outdo one another in praise of Moses. Supremely confident, supremely skilled, he stands quite distinct from the rest of Israel. In one account, he actually turns into an angel on Mount Sinai (1 En. 89.36). Good luck, in other words, finding criticism of Moses in the literature of **Second Temple Judaism**.

---

1. This is my meteorological interpretation of whatever exactly happened when God descended on Mount Sinai. Cf. Exodus 20:18–19 and Psalm 68:8 for some of the more dramatic biblical descriptions of that moment.

The Samaritan Pentateuch

"I WILL RAISE UP FOR THEM A PROPHET LIKE YOU"

The Samaritan Pentateuch (SamP) weaves a unique thread into the tapestry of Moses's greatness. Most readers of the Bible probably know of the Samaritan community through Jesus's interaction with the Samaritan woman at the well (John 4:1–42). Our earliest external analysis of their history comes from Josephus, who identified them as a people of Persian descent forcibly migrated to "Samaria" (northern Israel) when the northern ten tribes were conquered and removed by Shalmaneser in 722 BC (*Ant.* 2.278–91). The Samaritan version of the story is rather different—they are the true Israel, having built the temple on Mount Gerizim in fulfillment of Deuteronomy 27:4.[2] And it is their opposition to the Jerusalem temple, and their special interest in Deuteronomy, that are most crucial for correlating their literature to Hebrews.

The Samaritan Pentateuch, a "version" of the first five books of the Old Testament, was probably written (at least in the form we now have it) in the late second century or early first century BC.[3] One of its most fascinating features is the use of Deuteronomy 34:10 as a "theological principle governing the entire Samaritan tradition."[4] Deuteronomy 34:10 says (in the Hebrew text), "Never since has there arisen a prophet like Moses," which is a pretty big claim. But the Samaritan Pentateuch Deuteronomy 34:10 does it one better: "Never again will there arise a prophet like Moses."[5] *Never*

---

2. Magnar Kartveit, *The Origin of the Samaritans*, VTSup 128 (Leiden: Brill, 2009), 17–18. If you look at your Bible's version of Deuteronomy 27:4, you'll see two disconnects here. First, the mountain named is Mount Ebal rather than Mount Gerizim. Second, the command is to build an altar, not a temple. But the Samaritan version of Deuteronomy 27:4 has Mount Gerizim, and that community took "build an altar" to mean "build a temple," because throughout the Samaritan version of Deuteronomy the place where God would cause his name to dwell (i.e., where he would live in the temple) was Mount Gerizim.

3. I use the term *version* here in a nontechnical sense. Scholars continue to wrestle with the boundaries—if there were any—between translation, commentary, and what we now call "rewritten Bible." One key difference between rewritten Bible and the Samaritan Pentateuch is that, "While the rewritten Bible texts inserted new elements into the previously known biblical text, [the Samaritan Pentateuch] copied existing biblical passages in new locations" (Emanuel Tov, "Rewritten Bible Compositions and Biblical Manuscripts, with Special Attention Paid to the Samaritan Pentateuch," in *Hebrew Bible, Greek Bible, and Qumran: Collected Essays*, TSAJ 121 (Tübingen: Mohr Siebeck, 2008), 60). This is precisely what happens in the Samaritan Pentateuch version of Exodus 20, as we will see shortly.

4. S. Lowy, *The Principles of Samaritan Bible Exegesis*, StPB (Leiden: Brill, 1977), 452.

5. Robert T. Anderson and Terry Giles, *The Samaritan Pentateuch*, SBLRBS 72 (Atlanta: Society of Biblical Literature, 2012), 90.

again. "Who can compare with Moses, the prophet, the likes of whom has not arisen and will never arise?"[6] And yet there is a tension in the Samaritan community, because although they exalted Moses more highly than any other Jewish community of the Second Temple period, they also emphasized the need for "prophets like Moses" (Deut 18:15–18) to keep them on track. One of the ways they did this—and herein lies another point of interest for reading Hebrews 12:18–29—was by inserting the Deuteronomic prediction of such prophets into the Exodus Sinai narrative. Here, then, is the text of Exodus 20:15–18 as contained in the Samaritan Pentateuch, with Hebrew Old Testament texts being cited given in parentheses and the versification of the Samaritan text given in square brackets:[7]

[20:15] And all the people heard the voices, and the ram's horn voice, and saw the lightning flashes, and the mountain smoking. And when all the people saw, they trembled and stood at a distance (Exod 20:18). [16] And they said to Moses, "surely YHWH our God has shown us his glory and his greatness. And we heard his voice from the midst of the fire. We have seen this day that God speaks with man, yet he still lives. And now, why should we die, for this great fire will consume us. If we hear the voice of YHWH our God any more, then we shall die. For who is here of all flesh who has heard the voice of the living God speaking from the midst of the fire, as we have, and lived. You go near and hear all that YHWH our God may say. And tell us all that YHWH our God says to you, and we will hear and do it (Deut 5:24–27). And let not [God] speak with us, or we will die" (Exod 20:19b).

[17] And [Moses] said to the people, "do not be afraid, for God has come in order to test you, and in order that the fear of him may be before you, that you sin not" (Exod 20:20).

[18] And the people stood at a distance, while Moses approached the fog where God was (Exod 20:21).

And YHWH spoke to [Moses], saying "I have heard the voice of the words of this people which they have spoken to you. They

---

6. *Memar Marqah* 4.10; cited in Louis H. Feldman, *Philo's Portrayal of Moses in the Context of Ancient Judaism* (Notre Dame, IN: Notre Dame University Press, 2007), 306.

7. This translation is taken from Benyamim Tsedaka and Sharon Sullivan, *The Israelite Samaritan Version of the Torah: First English Translation Compared with the Masoretic Version* (Grand Rapids: Eerdmans, 2013). For the reader's sake, I have kept traditional spellings of the names in this text rather than Tsedaka and Sullivan's transliterations (Mooshe, Eloowwem, etc.) and render YHWH in exchange for Tsedaka and Sullivan's "Shehmaa" (translating יהוי).

are right in all that they have spoken. Who will wish that they had such a heart in them that they would fear me, and all the days keep my commandments, that it will be will unto them and unto their children forever (Deut 5:28b–29)? I will raise up for them a prophet like you from among their brethren and will put my words in his mouth. And he shall speak to them all that I will command him. And it shall be that the man who will not hear his words which he will speak in my name, I will require it from him. But the prophet who will dare with malignity to speak a word on my behalf which I have not commanded him to speak, and he speaks on behalf of other gods, that prophet shall die. And if you say in your heart, 'how will it be known the word which YHWH has not spoken?' the prophet speaking on behalf of YHWH, the thing will not happen and will not come—this is the thing which YHWH has not spoken. The prophet has spoken it in malignity. You shall not be afraid of him (Deut 18:18–22). Go say to them, 'return to your tents.' And you stand here by me, and I will speak to you all the commandments, the statutes, and judgments which you shall teach them" (Deut 5:31).

Conflating Exodus and Deuteronomy. Again, the text above is Exodus 20:15–18 in the Samaritan Pentateuch. So, significant chunks of Deuteronomy 5 (the Sinai/Horeb event) and Deuteronomy 18 (the prediction of later prophets like Moses) have been inserted into the Samaritan Exodus text. The effect of this insertion is that even when reading the Exodus version of the Sinai event, one feels the weight of Israel's future—that Israel will always need prophetic voices, divine messengers who call them back to God, back to faithfulness, back to the law of Moses. Exodus makes none of these points; you have to go to Deuteronomy to find them.

The decision to put Exodus and Deuteronomy together in order to describe the Sinai events, as the Samaritan Pentateuch has done, puts this retelling of the Sinai events in some interesting company. The **sectarian** documents from **Qumran** do this frequently, as does Jubilees, as do numerous New Testament authors—including the author of Hebrews.[8] On the other hand, Philo is entirely dependent on Exodus, as are Josephus and 1 Enoch. Pseudo-Philo is Exodus-dominant but does include Deuteronomic elements at times.

Tweaking Moses's Legacy. The reason for this divide, as best I can tell, is

---

8. See, e.g., 4QPaleoExod^m; 4Q158; 4Q175; 4QDeut^n; Jub. 1.1–18; and Matt 17:1–13.

that while both Exodus and Deuteronomy exalt Moses, only Deuteronomy (specifically chapter 18 as a follow-up to chapter 5) indicates that his prophetic mantle will be passed on. Only Deuteronomy frames the Sinai events with the ongoing rebelliousness of Israel and therefore the need for prophets like Moses (even if he remains unsurpassed by any of them) to call Israel, *including its priests and its kings*, to account. In Deuteronomy, the king reads the Torah for himself (17:18–20), the priests read the Torah for the people (31:9–13), but the prophets *are* the Torah—they stand between Israel and its God like Moses did. "I myself will call to account anyone who does not listen to my words that the prophet speaks in my name" (Deut 18:19).

Hebrews 12:18–29

"JESUS THE MEDIATOR OF A NEW COVENANT"

What then of Hebrews 12:18–21? Where does it fit amid the varied versions of the Sinai theophany put to text in the Second Temple era?

> [18] You have not come to a mountain that can be touched and that is burning with fire; to darkness, gloom, and storm; [19] to a trumpet blast or to such a voice speaking words that those who heard it begged that no further word be spoken to them, [20] because they could not bear what was commanded: "If even an animal touches the mountain, it must be stoned to death." [21] The sight was so terrifying that Moses said, "I am trembling with fear."

Hebrews 12:18–29 is fundamentally about the kind of access to God that we can expect, and that is expected of us, as God's new covenant people. A first-century Jewish audience would have known that you do not simply waltz into the throne room; you need a mediator, an advocate, a friend, you might say, who speaks on your behalf and arranges the meet. They would have known from Exodus that the quintessential moment of covenantal human contact with God happened on Mount Sinai, and they would have known from Deuteronomy that God's people had been reenacting that moment ever since. And therein lies the surprise that we find in Hebrews—we do need a mediator, but it is not Moses. We do come to God on a mountain, but it is not Sinai. What brought about these changes, particularly (in this instance) the change in mediator?

Conflating Exodus and Deuteronomy. The description of Sinai in

Hebrews 12 is replete with language from both Exodus and Deuteronomy, as table 19.1 demonstrates (see below).

Table 19.1. Exodus and Deuteronomy in Hebrews 12:18–21

Hebrews 12:18–21	Exodus	Deuteronomy
"come to" (12:18)		4:11; 5:23, 27
"can be touched" (12:18)	19:13	
"burning with fire" (12:18)		4:11; 5:23
"darkness" (12:18)	20:21	4:11; 5:23
"storm" (12:18)		4:11; 5:22
"trumpet" (12:19)	19:13, 16; 20:18	
"voice speaking words" (12:19)		4:12
"begged that no further word . . ." (12:19)		5:25
"stoned to death" (12:20)	19:13	
"I am trembling" (12:21)		9:19

Hebrews stands alongside the Samaritan Pentateuch in its use of both Exodus and Deuteronomy. But its reasons for doing so go beyond a confrontation with the Jerusalem temple establishment, a critical feature of the Samaritan and Essene perspectives (although I leave it to others to determine whether the Jerusalem temple still stood when Hebrews was written). Rather, the combination of pentateuchal narratives in this climactic portion of Hebrews keeps us mindful of the fact that (according to Exodus) Moses was indeed the proper mediator of the Sinai covenant, but also that (according to Deuteronomy) he fell short of the ultimacy often ascribed to him by later Jewish writers. "The sight was so terrifying that Moses said, 'I am trembling with fear'" (Heb 12:21).

Leaving Moses, Following Jesus. Two things are worth mentioning about Hebrews 12:21. The first is that Moses is put in the climactic position: the final thing you need to know about the Sinai theophany is that *the covenant mediator, Moses, was afraid.* So there is a nod to the fact that Moses is somehow set apart from the rest of Israel on the mountain (a point with which every other Jewish text from the first century would have readily agreed), and yet that nod brings into sharper relief the idea that, in the ultimate assize, Moses was scared stiff just like everyone else. The second thing is that this specific citation comes from Deuteronomy 9:19, which isn't technically about the initial Sinai event—it is about the golden calf incident. Putting it in here reminds us that shortly after Moses led Israel into the covenant, the whole thing fell apart. The mediator's job is to keep God and his people *close*, and nothing highlights Moses's failure in that respect as much as Israel's idolatry with the calf.[9]

The next portion of the passage (12:22–24) offers the counterpart to 12:18–21: you *haven't* come there, but you *have* come here. And at the climax of that description (12:24), we again find the covenant mediator. But this mediator isn't shaking in his boots. He is sitting at God's right hand, waving us on in, welcoming us as beloved children. Thus, for Hebrews, unlike the Samaritan and Essene communities, what is needed—indeed, what *has come*—is not a prophet like Moses, but something far better. And when we come to the heavenly Mount Zion (not to Gerizim, not to Jerusalem, not even to Sinai itself), we find there one to whom Moses is hardly worthy to be compared, the mediator of a new covenant, Jesus.

For Further Reading

Additional Ancient Texts

In addition to the Samaritan Pentateuch, one finds representative Moses and Sinai ideologies in Philo's *On the Life of Moses* (esp. 2.66–176) and *On the Decalogue,* Josephus's *Jewish Antiquities* (esp. 3.75–101), Biblical Antiquities 11–12, and 1 Enoch 89. Among the Dead Sea Scrolls, 4Q175 (4QTest), 4Q158 (4QBibPar), and Jubilees are most relevant as far as the use of Exodus and Deuteronomy are concerned.

English Translations and Critical Editions

Tal, Abraham, and Moshe Florentin, eds. *The Pentateuch: The Samaritan Version and the Masoretic Version.* Tel Aviv: Haim Rubin Tel Aviv University Press, 2010.

---

9. In Exodus the golden calf is in some ways the high point of Moses's mediation—he has successfully bargained for their lives. But in Deuteronomy the calf epitomizes Israel's rebellion and Moses's failure to prevent it—"From the day you left Egypt until you arrived here, you have been rebellious against the LORD" (9:7).

Tsedaka, Benyamim, and Sharon Sullivan. *The Israelite Samaritan Version of the Torah: First English Translation Compared with the Masoretic Version.* Grand Rapids: Eerdmans, 2013.

Secondary Literature

Crawford, Sidnie W. "The Pentateuch as Found in the Pre-Samaritan Texts and 4Qreworked Pentateuch." Pages 123–36 in *Changes in Scripture: Rewriting and Interpreting Authoritative Traditions in the Second Temple Period*. Edited by Hanne von Weissenberg, Juha Pakkala, and Marko Marttila. BZAW 419. Berlin: de Gruyter, 2011.

Kibbe, Michael H. *Godly Fear or Ungodly Failure? Hebrews 12 and the Sinai Theophanies*. BZNW 216. Berlin: de Gruyter, 2016.

CHAPTER 20

Philo of Alexandria and Hebrews 13:1–25: Meeting the Forgiving God outside the Camp

GABRIELLA GELARDINI

"Let us, then, go to him outside the camp" (Heb 13:13), states a well-known call of the author of Hebrews to his audience.[1] All well and good, but where is "outside the camp"? The author seems to presume that his audience will know, which is why his silence on the matter seems to leave us—the present readers—in the dark. But as if it were not enough of a riddle already, this exhortation is surrounded by other calls that seem no less puzzling than the first. Who are the "leaders" to be remembered or heeded (13:7, 17, 24)? What are the "strange teachings" by which the hearers are not to be carried away (13:9)? And finally, what is the "altar" the addressees are supposed to have and on which they are to offer not animal sacrifices but "a sacrifice of praise"—and anyway, how does that work (13:10, 15)? In search of possible answers, Hebrews scholars have racked their brains, and some experts have concluded—since neither "outside the camp," "leaders," "teachings," nor "altar" occur in the rest of the work—that chapter 13 is a secondary addition to a homily originally comprising only chapters 1–12.

That this is not the case will become clear in the course of the following discussion. But first it is necessary to find out what chapter 13 actually says and whether it places emphasis on a certain section or word, which is why a structural analysis seems advisable. And in this context, Hebrews experts have noticed that both Hebrews 13:7 and 17 speak of "leaders,"

---
1. I am grateful to Dr. David E. Orton for proofreading this article.

which is why some have recognized here an *inclusio* that separates this part of the passage from what precedes and what follows it. Thus the chapter breaks into three sections: 13:1–6, with a list of five exhortations; followed by 13:7–19, with its enigmatic statements; and 13:20–25, which clearly bears epistolary features and has therefore been recognized by some as a postscript. If we turn our attention to the original Greek text, more profound structures than simply the *inclusio* just mentioned become apparent; in fact, the following loose symmetry, or chiasmus, emerges from the sequence of lexical iterations:[2]

A   13:1–6   God's will
  B   13:7–9   Leaders
    C   13:10   Sacrificial altar
      D   13:11–12   Outside the camp
      D'   13:13–14   Outside the camp
    C'   13:15–16   Sacrifice
  B' 13:17–19   Leaders
A' 13:20–25   God's will

This chiasmus, in turn, reveals that the spatial phrase "outside the camp [or gate]," which occurs three times (13:11, 12, 13), is located in the center of the chapter, where it is accentuated. Our search for answers will therefore begin at this point.

Our study will also be assisted by comparing the passage's use of "outside the camp" with that of a near contemporary Jewish author, **Philo** of Alexandria. He is the most important Hellenistic Jewish thinker of his time with an extensive corpus where we encounter historical, exegetical, philosophical, and theological writings. Philo mentions such a going out of the camp in no fewer than six passages—in *Allegorical Interpretation* 2.54–56 and 3.46–48, *That the Worse Attacks the Better* 160, *On Giants* 54, as well as *On Drunkenness* 100 and 124—and when he does so, he always refers to the same biblical text, namely, Exodus 33:7–11. From the selection just mentioned, I would like to focus on the Philonic passage that promises to be the most useful for our purposes—that is, the one that illuminates not only the spatial center but also the entire thirteenth chapter. That passage is *Allegorical Interpretation* 2.54–56.

---

2. For a detailed discussion of the structure, see Gabriella Gelardini, "Charting 'Outside the Camp' with Edward W. Soja: Critical Spatiality and Hebrews 13," in Gelardini, *Deciphering the Worlds of Hebrews: Collected Essays*, NovTSup 184 (Leiden: Brill, 2021), 168–95.

Philo of Alexandria

"MOSES FIXES HIS TENT OUTSIDE THE CAMP"

Moses's Plea Outside the Camp. Before we can turn to our comparable Philonic text, we need to acquaint ourselves with the biblical reference, Exodus 33:7–11. This text describes how Moses pitched his tent "outside the camp" and that "anyone inquiring of the LORD would go to the tent of meeting outside the camp" (Exod 33:7). The reason why Moses pitched "his" tent outside the camp is well known; it is related to the golden calf (Exod 32) that Aaron had set up inside the camp at the request of the people, defiling it with the idol. The sin weighed heavily and resulted in the destruction of the first tablets of the **covenant**—the ones Moses had received from God after forty days and nights on the mountain—and it was a sign of the breaking of the covenant just solemnly inaugurated between God and his people. For their unfaithfulness and violation of the first as well as the second commandment God intended to eliminate them, but Moses's initial and fervent intercessions were able to prevent this terrible judgment (Exod 32:7–14). Moses continues to advocate for God's continued presence even when God wants to send an angel in his place to lead them into the land (Exod 32:34; 33:2).

What Moses pleads for in the tent outside the camp is the comfort of being led into the land by God, and in an appeal to his favor before God, who speaks with him as with a friend, Moses receives a hearing. As a revelation of God's overwhelmingly merciful character, Moses received the assurance he was seeking and consequently the second tablets of the covenant as an expression of God's grace, forgiveness, and covenant renewal—a renewal, which, of course, includes the renewal of the land promise (Exod 34).

Exodus 32–34 thus forms a narrative unit, from which Philo quotes in numerous other places besides the aforementioned passages.[3] The weight of this compelling story of sin and forgiveness, however, is evident not only in Philo, for already in the Torah (e.g., Deut 9–10, with Deut 9:19 being quoted in Heb 12:21) and likewise in the other parts of the **Tanakh** (e.g., Jer 31:31–34 quoted in Heb 8:8–12), numerous receptions of this narrative are found. They are also found in the New Testament (besides Hebrews, e.g., in Acts 7:39–43) and even more frequently in other genres of Jewish literature—especially rabbinic but also liturgical writings.[4]

---

3. See "Scripture Index," in *Philo*, trans. F. H. Colson and index. J. W. Earp, vol. 10, LCL 379 (Cambridge, MA: Harvard University Press, 1962), 189–268, esp. 231–32.

4. For references, see Devorah Schoenfeld, "'A Good Argument to Penitents': Sin and Forgiveness in Midrashic Interpretations of the Golden Calf," in *Golden Calf Traditions in Early*

Moses's Plea as a High-Priestly Sacrifice. Let us now turn to our comparator text. It is found in one of Philo's exegetical writings, in a treatise belonging to the large commentary, interpreting Genesis only, with the title *Allegorical Interpretation of Genesis II, III.* The title at the same time indicates the primary method. Allegorical interpretation is not only meant to bridge the gap between biblical and Greek perspectives. Philo also has in mind the Homeric exegesis of the Stoics, who, with the help of allegory, aimed both to justify the ancient poems from the reproach of godlessness and to give them a new, mysterious charm by establishing an "underlying meaning" recognizable only by the "consecrated." Shouldn't the same proof be possible for the Bible? Shouldn't it show a different face to the "wise" from the one it shows to the dull masses on whom Philo looked down with contempt? If not, then Philo could hardly have viewed the Torah as the book of paramount importance that deserves a place alongside and even above the literature of the Greeks.

Within the treatise, our text is found in the second book, which interprets Genesis 2:25 and speaks of the nakedness of Adam and Eve. It is the last verse before the story of the fall, which begins in Genesis 3:1, and in which—as is well known—the first human couple become aware of their nakedness and thus encounter shame rooted in sin for the first time. Here Philo establishes a very interesting connection, which has been repeatedly taken up in later midrashim (e.g., Pesiqta de Rab Kahana 15), between the first sin of the first humans in Eden and that of the first people of God at Sinai.

And this is how our comparator text in *Allegorical Interpretation* 2.54–56 puts it:

> [54] Now there are three ways in which a soul is made naked. One is when it continues without change and is barren of all vices, and has divested itself of all the passions and flung them away. For this reason "Moses fixes his tent outside the camp, a long way from the camp, and it was called the tent of testimony" [Exod 33:7]. [55] What this means is this. The soul that loves God, having disrobed itself of the body and the objects dear to the body and fled abroad far away from these, gains a fixed and assured settlement in the perfect ordinances of virtue. Wherefor witness is also borne to it by God that it loves things that are noble: "for," says he, "it was called the

Judaism, Christianity, and Islam, ed. E. F. Mason and E. F. Lupieri, TBN 23 (Leiden: Brill, 2019), 176–93.

tent of witness." He leaves unmentioned who it is that calls it so, in order that the soul may be stirred up to consider who it is that bears witness to virtue-loving minds. [56] This is why the high priest shall not enter the Holy of Holies in his robe [Lev 16], but laying aside the garment of opinions and impressions of the soul, and leaving it behind for those that love outward things and value semblance above reality, shall enter naked with no coloured borders or sound of bells, to pour as a libation the blood of the soul and to offer as incense the whole mind to God our Saviour and Benefactor. (Colson and Whitaker, LCL)

In the quoted text, Philo elaborates on what he means by nakedness. The first hero of virtue he discusses is Moses, and his argumentation proceeds in three steps. He begins by explaining that a naked one is someone who is "barren of all vices" from the beginning and continues to remain just that. In other words, Philo understands Moses as a sinless person, one like the first humans before the fall. This is also the reason, in Philo's interpretation, why Moses had to leave the defiled camp and set up "his" tent—as in the LXX—outside of it. In this unprotected place, Philo continues, the virtuous one was not left alone or in uncertainty but received "testimony" of God's favor, as is evident in the tent being referred to—again following the LXX—as the "tent of testimony." Like Moses, Philo states in conclusion, when they enter the holy of holies, which as we know they do only on Yom Kippur, the high priests are to, like him, selflessly intercede for the people by offering "the blood of their soul" as "libation" and "their whole mind" as incense to God.

We note that Philo interprets Moses as sinless, which is why with his tent he had to leave the defiled camp. What Moses does on the outside— the vicarious plea for God's forgiveness and assistance in the ascent to the promised land—Philo not only interprets as high priestly but additionally as having a sacrificial quality for the people. Because God speaks to Moses there on the outside, in the tent, from the pillar of cloud, Philo interprets this space as the holy of holies. And because, finally, God promises Moses reconciliation on this day, it is a great day of reconciliation, a Yom Kippur *avant la lettre* (before the letter), so to speak. Thus, a preceding (oral) tradition is found that connects Exodus 32–34 with Leviticus 16, and which the author of Hebrews seems to share with Philo, one that—as has been stated—found reception in numerous later midrashim as well as in synagogue liturgies.

Hebrews 13:1–25

"Jesus also suffered outside the city gate"

Our author seems to have adopted all the hermeneutical conclusions that Philo draws in relation to Moses as he applies them to Jesus. Already in Hebrews 3:1–6 he states that he is interpreting Jesus's work of mediation in analogy to that of Moses. But our author is not Philo, and his hermeneutical method is not allegorical interpretation, nor is he under any duty to portray the Bible as a work superior to Greek literature. Unlike Philo, then, our author never quotes from Greek literature, but exclusively from the Tanakh. Our author's concern is thus a classical one, namely, to interpret the present on the basis of the past and by means of Scripture. Or, in other words, to interpret events at the assumed location of our addressees, in Rome, with the help of the events in Jerusalem and Sinai, which matches the function of a synagogue homily very well.

Bodies of Sacrificial Animals Burned Outside the Camp. The first mention of a going out in the passage that interests us is connected with Sinai. Hebrews 13:11 says, "The high priest carries the blood of animals into the Most Holy Place as a sin offering, but the bodies are burned outside the camp." Explicitly mentioned are the high priest carrying the sacrificial blood of animals into the holy of holies, as well as the bodies of these animals, which were burned outside the camp according to the instruction in Leviticus 16:27. Since the high priest did this only once a year, on Yom Kippur, that special day is implied. The word "camp" furthermore implies Sinai, where the laws on Yom Kippur were issued (Lev 16).[5]

Jesus, Too, Suffered outside the City Gate. In the second mention of a going out, our author connects Jesus—as Philo did Moses—with the high priest. This is a particular perception of Jesus that is to be found in various places in Hebrews and is not known from any other New Testament writing. Moreover, he connects Jesus with Yom Kippur and interprets his "suffering," too, as a sacrifice, specifying that it is the sacrifice for the people (elaborated in Heb 9:11–10:18).[6] Unlike for Aaron, a sacrifice for Jesus himself is not deemed necessary since the author views Jesus—like Philo did Moses—as "sinless" (Heb 7:26). Thus, Hebrews 13:12 states,

---

5. See also Exod 30:10; Lev 23:26–32; Num 29:7–11. The arrival at Sinai is mentioned in Exodus 19:1–2, and the departure from there in Numbers 10:11–13.

6. For a detailed discussion on Jesus's sacrifice and Yom Kippur, see Gabriella Gelardini, "The Inauguration of Yom Kippur according to the LXX and Its Cessation or Perpetuation according to the Book of Hebrews: A Systematic Comparison," in Gelardini, *Deciphering the Worlds of Hebrews: Collected Essays*, NovTSup 184 (Leiden: Brill, 2021), 229–58.

"And so Jesus also suffered outside the city gate to make the people holy through his own blood." As at Sinai, also in Jerusalem on Yom Kippur the sacrificial animals for the people were burned not outside the camp but outside the "city gate," to the east of it, which in the case of Jerusalem was the Mount of Olives. On Yom Kippur, however, it was not the high priest who burned the sacrificial animals outside, but an assistant (Lev 16:28). Moreover, the animals burned outside were dead, but our verse here does not speak of Jesus's death, but rather of his "suffering." Since there is only one passage in the entire Torah that speaks of a leader going outside the camp, Exodus 33:7–11, it must be concluded that our author was comparing Jesus to Moses not only in Hebrews 3 but also here.[7] He seems, in fact, to compare his intercessory struggle in the tent outside with Jesus's struggle at Golgotha, that place where Jesus was sent to his fate as an atoning sacrifice for the people.

Let Us Go Outside the Camp. The last mention of going out in our passage refers to the addressees' mentioned location. Against the background of our narrative matrix, it is now clear which "leaders" are not to be followed and by what "foreign teachings" the addressees are not to be carried away. For it had been Aaron (criticized in Heb 7) who had made the idol and had proclaimed a feast in its honor, which included the eating of idol meat (Exod 32:5–6). Rather, the addressees are admonished to follow Moses, and after his example Jesus, who served the living God and not an idol.[8] It is Jesus, like Moses before him, who answered for us following our great sin of apostasy from God (Heb 3:12). On the outside, however, there is no physical altar, only a metaphorical one, on which both Moses and Jesus gave their utmost for the people and obtained the reward of forgiveness. With their intercession they also won a covenant renewal (the theme of Hebrews 8), and with it the renewal of the promised land, and with it, furthermore, nothing less than a future. So when Hebrews 13:13 says, "Let us, then, go to him outside the camp, bearing the disgrace he bore," the author is not thinking of a feast of joy in honor of the idol in the camp, but rather of repentance and, as in the narrative matrix in Exodus 33:10, of a "sacrifice of praise" to God (Heb 13:15) in response to God's ending his aversion, manifested in his gracious appearance in the tent outside the camp.

---

7. There are numerous good reasons to assume that Hebrews is based not only on Exodus 33:7–11 but on the entire narrative of Exodus 32–34, which is why chapter 13 must then be considered an integral part of the whole text rather than a secondary appendix.

8. In Hebrews, therefore, it is the brothers Aaron and Moses who are being compared, not Judaism and Christianity.

FOR FURTHER READING

Additional Ancient Texts

The reading of the primary text Exodus 32–34 (retold also in Deut 9–10) is worthwhile not only in its Hebrew and Greek versions but also in its partly extended Aramaic version (Targumim Neofiti, Onqelos, and Pseudo-Jonathan to Exod 32–34). Enlightening are also the other passages of Philo mentioned above (*Allegorical Interpretation* 3.46–48; *That the Worse Attacks the Better* 160; *On Giants* 54; and *On Drunkeness* 100, 124), as well as **Josephus**, who in his retelling of the exodus, prominently omitted the episode of the golden calf (*Ant.* 3.75–101). Other Jewish treatments include Liber antiquitatum biblicarum 12 and 1 Enoch 89.28–35, as well as Acts 7:38–43; Romans 1:18–32; 1 Corinthians 10:1–22; and 2 Corinthians 3:4–18 in the New Testament.

English Translations and Critical Editions

Philo. Translated by F. H. Colson and G. H. Whitaker. Vol. 1. LCL 226. Cambridge, MA: Harvard University Press, 1929.

Secondary Literature

Gelardini, Gabriella. *Deciphering the Worlds of Hebrews: Collected Essays*. NovTSup 184. Leiden: Brill, 2021.

Schoenfeld, Devorah. "'A Good Argument to Penitents': Sin and Forgiveness in Midrashic Interpretations of the Golden Calf." Pages 176–93 in *Golden Calf Traditions in Early Judaism, Christianity, and Islam*. Edited by Eric F. Mason and Edmondo F. Lupieri. TBN 23. Leiden: Brill, 2019.

Glossary[1]

Ancient Near East, ANE: The phrase describes the peoples who lived in Egypt, Palestine, Syria, Mesopotamia, Persia, and Arabia from the beginning of recorded history to the conquest of Alexander the Great, though some also informally use this term to refer all the way up to the first century AD.

Antiochus IV Epiphanes (ca. 215–164 BC): A ruler of the Seleucid Kingdom, the Hellenistic state in Syria partitioned from Alexander the Great's vast empire. Antiochus provoked the Maccabean conflict by trying to Hellenize the Jewish people.

Apocalypse, apocalyptic, apocalyptic tradition, apocalypticism: An apocalypse is literally a "revelation" of previously hidden things. These terms are most associated with the revelation of God and of heavenly realities through visions and dreams, and the revelation of divine actions to establish God's (future) rule among his covenant people and the whole world. Thus, there is often focus on spatial (heaven/earth) and temporal (present/future) dualisms.

Apocrypha, apocryphal (also known as the **deuterocanonical** books): A collection of Jewish texts written after the Old Testament period and which make up a majority of the texts constituting the Septuagint. These were considered authoritative by patristic Christians and were therefore accepted by Roman Catholic and Orthodox Christians as canonical but are rejected by Protestants as Scripture. In nonacademic settings, *apocryphal* is often used as a description of stories that sound true but are not.

Canonical: Texts are considered canonical when they are included in a collection of texts considered to be inspired and authoritative Scripture. The Old Testament and New Testament are indisputably part of the Christian canon, whereas different Christian traditions dispute the inclusion of the Apocrypha. See *Apocrypha*.

---

1. Some definitions are adapted from Mark L. Strauss, *Four Portraits, One Jesus: A Survey of Jesus and the Gospels* (Grand Rapids: Zondervan, 2007).

Christology, christological: This term generally refers to the person and work of Jesus. More specifically, the term relates to Jesus's role as the Christ. *Christ* (*christos*) is Greek for "anointed one," and it often serves as the direct translation of the Hebrew term *messiah*. See *Messiah*.

Covenant, covenantal: An agreement between two parties that places obligations on each party. Important covenants in the Bible include the Abrahamic covenant (Gen 15, 17), the Mosaic covenant (Exodus; Leviticus; Deuteronomy), the Davidic covenant (2 Sam 7), and the new covenant (Jer 31; Ezek 34–37).

Dead Sea Scrolls: An ancient library discovered in caves near the Dead Sea in 1947 and likely associated with the first-century Jewish community at Qumran. The scrolls include copies of biblical and other Jewish literature as well as sectarian texts arising from the Qumran community. See *sectarian*.

Deuterocanonical: See *Apocrypha*.

Eschatology, eschatological: Literally "the study of the end times." The term indicates any event or idea that is associated with the final days. In Jewish and Pauline studies, though, the term *eschatology* does not refer simply or only to the end times, but to God's action to restore his rule through key agents or events.

Hasmoneans, Hasmonean period (167–63 BC): The Jewish family who ruled a semiautonomous and later fully autonomous kingdom as the Jews secured independence from the Seleucids. As a result of infighting among the family, the Jews lost their independence to the Romans in 63 BC. See *Maccabean Revolt*; *Seleucids*.

Hellenism, Hellenistic, Hellenization: The spread and influence of Greek language and culture in the ancient world, particularly after the military conquest of Alexander the Great (ca. 333 BC).

Josephus (AD 37–ca. 100): Once a Jewish Pharisee and military leader, Josephus was taken captive during the Jerusalem War against Rome and eventually made a Roman citizen and dependent of Emperor Vespasian. His four extant works are very important for our understanding of the history and culture of Second Temple Judaism: a history of the Jewish people (*Jewish Antiquities*), an account of the Jerusalem War (*Jewish War*), a work in defense of Judaism and the Jewish way of life (*Against Apion*), and an autobiography (*The Life*).

LXX: The abbreviation for the Septuagint. See *Septuagint*.

Maccabean Revolt (or crisis/conflict): The Jewish rebellion against Seleucid rule in 175–164 BC. The conflict is titled after "the Maccabees" (Hebrew for "hammer"), which was a name given to Judas and his brothers who led Israel during this period.

Messiah: A transliteration of a Hebrew word meaning "anointed one" and which is translated into Greek as "Christ." There is no single Jewish view about the messiah, though all views envision this person as God's agent who will deliver his people.

Pharisees: One of the Jewish sects mentioned by Josephus and throughout the Gospels. They were widely known for their skill in interpreting the law.

Philo (ca. 20 BC–AD 50): A diaspora Jew influenced by Platonism from Alexandria, Egypt. He authored numerous philosophical treatises and exegetical studies on the Pentateuch. See *Platonism*.

Platonism, Platonic philosophy: Plato is a famous Greek philosopher who lived in Athens (ca. 428 BC–347 BC). He wrote a number of philosophical treatises on ethics, physics, creation, logic, and rhetoric, among other things. Various forms of Platonism draw in differing ways from Plato's thought, but a primary aspect was a dualism based on a distinction between the realm of conceptual realities (immaterial and unchangeable) and the realm of concrete realities (material and changeable).

Pseudepigrapha, pseudepigraphic: Literally "falsely ascribed writings." A pseudepigraphic text is a text written under the name of another, often centuries earlier, person. The Pseudepigrapha specifically refers to Jewish pseudepigraphic texts not included in the Apocrypha, but since this was a common practice for Second Temple Jews, the term has generally become a catch-all for all Jewish texts not included in another specific category, such as the Apocrypha or Dead Sea Scrolls, or authored by specific writers, like Josephus and Philo.

Qumran: A site located near the Dead Sea and close to the caves in which the Dead Sea Scrolls were found. The common view is that the community who lived there during the Second Temple period were Essenes and responsible for producing the Dead Sea Scrolls.

Second Temple period, Second Temple Judaism, Second Temple Jewish (ca. 516 BC–AD 70): The period in Jewish history roughly from the return from exile (about 516 BC) until the destruction of the temple by the Romans in AD 70. Other phrases used for all or part of this time period are Early Judaism, Middle Judaism, and the intertestamental period.

Sectarian: That which pertains to a particular religious group, notably the texts composed by and for the Dead Sea Scroll community. See *Dead Sea Scrolls*.

179

Seleucids, Seleucid Kingdom (312–115 BC): A kingdom in the region of Syria that was formed after Alexander the Great's kingdom was subdivided after his death. Judea was eventually ruled by the Seleucids who attempted to force the Jews to assimilate to Hellenism. See *Hellenism; Maccabean Revolt*.

Septuagint (LXX): A collection of authoritative Jewish texts in Greek that includes the Greek translation of the Hebrew Bible as well as other Jewish writings. The abbreviation LXX is the Roman numeral for seventy and is based on the tradition that seventy (or seventy-two) men translated the Hebrew Pentateuch into Greek.

Testament: A "testament" is a literary genre in which an author records a person's last words of advice and instruction to his children. This genre was popular in the Second Temple period, the most well-known being the Testaments of the Twelve Patriarchs.

Theodicy: A defense or explanation of how God is just, even though evil exists, especially with regard to the righteous who suffer unjustly at the hands of the wicked.

Zealots, zeal: Jews during the Second Temple period who sought freedom through military means to free Judea from foreign domination. They were not only looking for political independence but also for Torah purity, which was not attainable with a pagan presence in the land.

Contributors

Ben C. Blackwell (PhD, University of Durham) is professor of early Christianity at Houston Theological Seminary.

Félix H. Cortez (PhD, Andrews University) is associate professor of New Testament literature at Andrews University.

Angela Costley (PhD, St. Patrick's College, Maynooth) is lecturer in New Testament Greek and wisdom literature at St. Mary's College, Oscott.

Susan Docherty (PhD, University of Manchester) is professor of New Testament and early Judaism at Newman University.

Bryan R. Dyer (PhD, McMaster Divinity College) is senior acquisitions editor, New Testament, at Baker Publishing Group.

Matthew C. Easter (PhD, University of Otago) is associate professor of Bible and director of Christian studies at Missouri Baptist University.

Gabriella Gelardini (PhD, University of Basel and Harvard University; Habil., University of Basel) is professor of Christianity, religion, worldview, and ethics at Nord University.

Radu Gheorghita (PhD, University of Cambridge) is professor of biblical studies at Midwestern Baptist Theological Seminary.

John K. Goodrich (PhD, University of Durham) is professor of Bible at Moody Bible Institute, and adjunct professor at Compass Bible Institute, Aliso Viejo, California.

Dana M. Harris (PhD, Trinity Evangelical Divinity School) is associate professor of New Testament at Trinity Evangelical Divinity School.

Dominick S. Hernández (PhD, Bar-Ilan University) is associate professor of Old Testament and Semitic languages at Talbot School of Theology, Biola University.

Michael Kibbe (PhD, Wheaton College) is associate professor of Bible at Great Northern University.

Eric F. Mason (PhD, University of Notre Dame) is professor and Julius R. Mantey Chair of Biblical Studies at Judson University.

Jason Maston (PhD, University of Durham) is associate professor of theology at Houston Christian University.

David M. Moffitt (PhD, Duke University) is reader in New Testament at the University of St. Andrews.

Zoe O'Neill (PhD, Queen's University Belfast) is adjunct faculty at Union Theological College.

Amy L. B. Peeler (PhD, Princeton Theological Seminary) is associate professor of New Testament at Wheaton University.

Madison N. Pierce (PhD, University of Durham) is associate professor of New Testament at Western Theological Seminary.

Ben Ribbens (PhD, Wheaton College) is associate professor of theology at Trinity Christian College.

Ken Schenck (PhD, University of Durham) is vice president for University Partnerships at CampusEdu.

Bryan Whitfield (PhD, Emory University) is professor of religion at Mercer University.

Passage Index

Subject Index

*t indicates a table

covenant
Aaronic, 64
Abrahamic (aka "the divine oath").
See chapter 8 (77–83); 35, 103, 178
in Biblical Antiquities, 146–49
in the Community Rule, 71–73
Damascus, 94, 103–4
defined, 178
God bound by (in 4 Ezra), 35
God bound by (in Hebrews), 36–37,
with the forefathers (Damascus),
102–3
Mosaic / first / old / Sinai, 14, 15,
16, 63, 85, 103–4, 114, 119, 124, 129,
136, 166–67, 171, 178
new. *See* new covenant
renewed (land of Damascus), 103–4
two covenants contrasted, 104–5
creation and resurrection hope,
141–42, 143–43
Cyrus of Persia, 14

Damascus Document, xiv, 19
and Hebrews 7. *See chapter 10*
(92–100)
and Hebrews 8. *See chapter 11*
(101–8)
Day of Atonement, xiv, 92–93, 113, 119,
121, 127, 132–37
Dead Sea Scrolls, xiv, 8–10, 17, 19, 70,
86, 94, 102, 161, 178, 179
death
faith in the face of 138–40, 143
in Hebrews 11, heroes and, 138–39
hope of resurrection in the face of,
141
and persecution, 140
deliberate sin(ning)
and atonement. *See chapter 15*
(131–37)
Christ's sacrifice and, 135–36
the Day of Atonement and, 134
no sacrifice for sin is left for, 134–35
repentance and, 133
demons, 41, 44

destroyer, the, 42–44, 139
devil
the destroyer as the, 43
Jesus's defeat of the, 40, 43–44
Passover and the defeat of the *See*
chapter 3 (39–45)
See also Satan
deuterocanonical books (aka deu-
terocanonicals). *See* **Apocrypha**
discipline
communal vs. individual, 158
of God, the paternal. *See chapter 18*
(153–60)
from the Messiah (Pss Sol), 155–56
for one's good (Pss Sol), 155
punitive vs. educative (Heb), 157
for the righteous (versus
destruction) (Pss Sol), 154–55
divine oath to Abraham. *See chapter 8*
(77–83)
in Hebrews 6, 80–81
Documents of Jewish Sectaries, Vol.
1: Fragment of a Zadokite Work
(Schechter), 94

early Jewish literary genres, 17–19
Egyptians, 41–42
elder angel, 25
11QMelchizedek, xiv, 8, 19
and Hebrews 7. *See chapter 9* (84–91)
Epicureans, 24
Epicurus, 24–25
eschatological judgment, 7, 71
"Esseno-Christians," 8

faith
creation, and resurrection hope. *See*
chapter 16 (138–45)
in the face of death, 138–40, 143
of Israel's early leaders, 150–51
Moses as an exemplar of 150
famine, 138, 158
firstborn
and the image of God, the. *See*
chapter 1 (23–31)

Author Index